Beasts of the Deep

Beasts of the Deep

Sea Creatures and Popular Culture

Edited by Jon Hackett and Seán Harrington

British Library Cataloguing in Publication Data

Beasts of the Deep: Sea Creatures and Popular Culture

A catalogue entry for this book is available from the British Library

ISBN: 9780 86196 733 9 (Paperback); 9780 86196 939 5 (Ebook)

Published by
John Libbey Publishing Ltd, 205 Crescent Road, East Barnet, Herts EN4 8SB,
United Kingdom
e-mail: john.libbey@orange.fr; web site: www.johnlibbey.com

Distributed worldwide by **Indiana University Press**,
Herman B Wells Library – 350, 1320 E. 10th St., Bloomington, IN 47405, USA.
www.iupress.indiana.edu

Printed and bound in the United States of America.

Contents

Acknowledgements

The editors would like to acknowledge 'Grow Fins', Words and Music by Don Van Vliet © 1971 and reproduced by permission of EMI Music Publishing Limited, London W1F 9LD.

We would like to thank our colleagues at St Mary's University, Twickenham, without whom neither the original conference nor this volume would have been possible. First, our academic colleagues who have contributed some of the wonderfully diverse chapters in the pages that follow. One of these, Lee Brooks, has kindly provided the striking cover to this volume too. Second, our administrative and technical support staff, particularly Susanne Gilbert and Fallon Parker, whose contributions to our conference schedules have been imaginative and invaluable.

We also wish to thank Rupert Norfolk, our talented and dedicated illustrator, who provided us with the wonderful images for this collection.

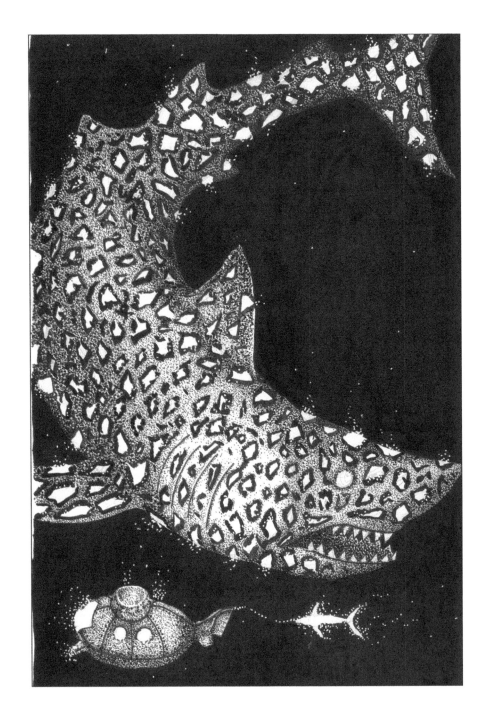

Introduction

Beasts of the Deep

D iscussing recent scholarly trends, Asa Mittman observes that 'in the space of a few years, the study of monsters has moved from the absolute periphery – perhaps its logical starting point – to a much more central position' in academia (2012: 1). *Beasts of the Deep: Sea Creatures and Popular Culture* aims to focus attention within this field of enquiry to the sea and its beastly inhabitants, in the widest sense. Most of the chapters in this volume emerge from the proceedings of a conference on 4 June 2016 at St Mary's University, Twickenham. As with the conference in 2016, this volume presents an eclectic and insightful collection of research findings, from a number of disciplines and interpretive frameworks.

There are a number of recent academic works directly addressing monstrosity, both monographs (such as Halberstam, 1995; Kearney, 2003; Asma, 2009; and Wright, 2013) and edited collections (such as Cohen, 1997; Mittman & Dendle, 1997; Levina & Bui, 2013; and Hunt, Lockyer & Williamson, 2013; these lists are not intended to be exhaustive). However, academic books specifically addressing the sea in relation to monstrosity in popular culture are lacking, to the editors' knowledge. This collection seeks to address this deficiency, while broadening analysis to as diverse a range of media as possible. This introduction will mostly outline the research focus of the individual chapters. However, it will be pertinent before this to highlight some of the main themes that emerge across the chapters – and that were encouraged in the original call for papers for our conference.

First, many of the chapters, perhaps especially in the section on 'Folklore and Weird Tales', address the *mythical resonance* of the sea and its creatures. That is, no matter how questionable the appeal to essential qualities or meanings, nonetheless the sea is often used to signify timelessness or sublimity, the archaic and the prehistoric. Many representations in myth, literature and more recent film and television draw on this cultural resonance – and authors in the first section of this volume in particular consider how to conceptualise this aspect of marine representations, from a number of perspectives.

Equally, appeals to the archaic and eternal can be vague and ineffable without reference to concrete *historical context* of the production and reception of media and cultural texts. Each of the authors in this volume has contextualised the texts and practices under consideration here in relation to the wider social, cultural, industrial and political contexts in which they are inserted and from which they have emerged. The section on 'Depths of Desire' locates texts on desiring and the sea in relation both to cultural traditions as well as the wider social and gendered contexts of reception. 'Aquatic Spaces and Practices' extends analysis to cultural geography, news media, fandom and tourism contexts and provides perhaps the most diverse range of research frameworks in the volume as a whole.

One of the main concerns for the editors (and conference convenors) was to focus discussion on the *medium specificity* of texts that represent the sea. Of course, it has been noted recently that media convergence challenges simple notions that particular media have formal elements that can be analysed in isolation from other media (see Lister, Dovey, Giddings, Grant & Kelly, 2003: 384). This proviso granted, we wish to ask nonetheless: how do film, television or literature (to take just three) 'do' the sea and its creatures? What are the particular challenges associated with representing the marine environment and sea creatures that derive from the formal aspects of media in any given era? Such questions are a constant concern in the final section, 'Screening Sea Creatures', but they are implicit in many of the other chapters that have appeared earlier in the volume.

This collection does not aim for an exhaustive analysis of monstrosity as a concept, so much as to open up the cultural analysis of the sea and sea creatures through a diverse set of case studies. Many analyses of monstrosity derive the term from the Latin, *monstrare*, 'to show', following the analyses of Michel Foucault (see discussion in Baldick, 1987: 10), among others. On this definition, monsters serve as symptoms, portents or warnings. If so, monsters – including those of the sea (or indeed the sea as monster) – call for further analysis in order to elucidate the cultural work they are called on to perform.

The sea and its creatures represent a number of overlapping functions in the chapters that follow. First, they offer an evident mythical resource on which to draw, either to explore myths directly or to draw on their connotations in order to fashion new representations of sea creatures. Second, the sea and the depths can be used as a figure for the unrepresentable, the sublime or the ineffable. Taken together, these first two functions are particularly evident in the first section of this book, 'Folklore and Weird Tales'. More obviously, perhaps, the sea and its creatures provide numerous opportunities for antagonists, given the importance of hero narratives to popular culture.

Just as importantly, the sea and its creatures provide tropes for representing various social or cultural concerns. In this volume, the essays in the second section, 'Depths of Desire', highlight the versatility of such imagery for figuring desire, specifically in gendered terms, in diverse media. The essay by Carole Murphy in the third section, 'Aquatic Spaces and Practices', discusses the media's negative construction of refugees through analysis of discourses that draw on aquatic imagery. More benignly, the sea and its beasts can also be the basis for various practices that use them as a starting point for subcultural or fan activities. The third section of this book also covers these usages.

Finally, we might say that the sea and its beasts provide an opportunity to showcase various media technologies or embody the logic of what Erich Herhuth (2017) calls 'product essentialism'. That is, successful representation of the aquatic realm offers cultural industries, from digital (or analogue) cinema, to theme parks and digital games, an opportunity to foreground their ability to demonstrate verisimilitude through spectacle. Furthermore, this allows for the promotion of prominent media brands and products as intimately tied to these bravura spectacles via discourses of creativity. The essays in the last section, 'Screening Sea Creatures', as well as Lee Brooks' essay in the third section respond to this affordance of aquatic imagery.

Part one of our collection examines the 'Folklore and Weird Tales' of the deep sea. These first papers provide a thorough analysis of the deep sea as a context that provides reflections of the human psyche – its unconscious guilts, anxieties and fascination. The tumultuous reactions that accompany our experience of the uncanny apparitions that emerge from the depths of fiction, and into our nightmares.

Alexander Hay begins this discussion with his paper on the 'sea draugr' of Norse sagas. The draugr is a mythological zombie, the dead who return from the seas and barrows in which their bodies lay, to remind the living of their failings and forgotten guilts. The draugr is argued to have an archetypical function in these stories, as is evidenced in the narratives discussed by Hay. Each of the stories analysed involve a token or object returning from the sea, be it drowned and forgotten sea-farers or, as Hay suggests, the body of Alan Kurdi, returning from the depths to remind us of the disavowed horrors of the refugee crisis in the Mediterranean.

This chapter is followed by Seán Harrington's analysis of the 'oceanic horrors' of H.P. Lovecraft, contextualised within a Lacanian psychoanalytic discussion of thalassophobia – intense fear of the deep sea. This is the first of several chapters that discuss the work of Lovecraft, for whom the sea was the hiding-place and habitation of some of his darkest horrors. Here the concept of the 'gap' between known and unknown is discussed in tandem with a structural account of Lacan's formulation of the Real – that which is beyond signification and key to unlocking the structure of Lovecraft's oceanic horrors.

Vivan Joseph's chapter 'From Depths of Terror to Depths of Wonder: The

Sublime in Lovecraft's *Call of Cthulhu* and Cameron's *The Abyss'* offers up an alternative analysis of the essential value of Lovecraft's weird fiction – providing a philosophic discussion of the value of the 'sublime' and how it operates in both Lovecraft's *The Call of Cthulhu* (1928) and James Cameron's *The Abyss* (1989). Joseph addresses the simultaneous appeal and trepidation one experiences when reading Lovecraft's work – as the reader is positioned in a curiously gratifying space from which to enjoy the core horror of these beasts from the darkest depths.

Part two of this collection, titled 'Depths of Desire', features further elaboration of the discussions on the sea as context. This time providing a accounts of the ways in which creatures of the sea facilitate the dark desires of fiction, fantasy and music. A range of media is addressed within these analyses, which when examined together provide an overview of the curious ability of the sea to provide a venue for forbidden and feared desires.

Marco Carbone's paper titled 'Beauty and the Octopus: Close encounters with the other-than-human' provides a discussion of the evolution of and contemporary fascination with Octopuses within an erotic context. Focusing on current examples from popular science, fiction and visual cultures, the paper individuates the cephalopod as the most iconic creatures for the visual trope of *tentacle erotica* – an emerging stream of fantasy, animation and pornographic material, characterised by representations of intercourse between humans and monsters, animals, and fantastic creatures. This discussion puts tentacle erotica on the couch, engaging in a psychoanalytic analysis of the appeal and structure of this very particular aquatic content. Given the recent theatrical releases and critical acclaim of films such as *The Handmaiden* (Park Chan-wook, 2016), *The Untamed* (Amat Escalante, 2016) and *The Shape of Water* (Guillermo del Toro, 2017), analogous themes continue to pervade contemporary popular culture.

Laura Ettenfield's paper 'The Octopussy: Exploring representations of female sexuality in Victor Hugo's *The Toilers of the Sea* (1866) and *The Laughing Man (1868)'* provides an in-depth textual analysis of Hugo's nautical fictions, providing us with a detailed account of Hugo's obsession with the octopus as a coded representation of the fear of female sexuality. Her analysis addresses the textual themes that connect the form of the octopus to female sexuality, bringing to light Hugo's, and in turn society's fear of independent and sexually liberated nineteenth century woman. Fears directly tied to contemporary masculine anxieties of responsive female desire, and reflective of Hugo's own hypocritical notions of supremacy and sexuality, having been renowned for his debauchery and adultery.

Richard Mills examines Psychedelic Deep Blues in Jimi Hendrix's, 1983 *A Merman I Should Turn to be* (1968), Tim Buckley's, *Song of the Siren* (1968) and Captain Beefheart's, *Grow Fins* (1972), as texts which foreground male fears concerning the unresolved tension between male and female binaries. Each of the artists are male musicians in the rock/folk/blues/jazz tradition of late-1960s music-business culture, and as such their lyrics are often crude sexist stereotypes. However, the imagery and characterisation of mermaids and sirens in these songs can be argued to be complex actualisations of sexual politics. This paper suggests that these texts represent a Lacanian fear of woman, and that the narrative of each song, is a desire to return to the womb combined with a loss of male ego.

The chapters in 'Aquatic Spaces and Practices' extend the analysis of the previous chapters with discussions of fandom and participatory cultures, news media and theme parks. In this respect, this section is particularly original in applying perhaps unexpected research perspectives to the concerns of this collection. Far from being mere contingent eddies, these chapters plunge to the depths of the volume's concerns.

Brigid Cherry analyses the 'affective investments' of fans of horror, science fiction and fantasy through discussion of a range of patterns of taste and fan practices. Sea creatures have the ability to become 'fan totems' that facilitate desire and a becoming-animal for those consuming them. Practices such as prop building, textile crafting and cosplay allow imaginative play with marine creatures, both real and fictional. Cherry's article brings out the complexity of Bolter and Grusin's (1999) notion of the remediation of media texts – and their insistence that it is not just 'new' media that are involved in this; those involved in the fan practices discussed in her chapter are involved in art and craft practices that are then disseminated online; each of these processes is a remediation of existing media texts.

Maria Mellins continues the attention to fandom with a chapter on the emerging global mermaid community. At the time of writing this introduction, the *BBC News* website has just covered the UK Miss Mermaid contest on its homepage; this chapter provides context and analysis of the participatory culture from which such events emerge. Mellins draws from her own research into this community, locating prominent figures in terms of Sarah Thornton's (1997) conceptualisation of 'subcultural capital'. Mellins provides case studies of prominent community members, showing how mermaids are able to utilise their subcultural capital for various ends, both entrepreneurship and advocacy. The gendered nature of this fandom is also considered, along with the sometimes liberating potential involved in donning a silicone tail in relation to body image and pleasure.

Lee Brooks turns his attention to the place of the sea and sea creatures in Disney theme parks and cruises. He provides a detailed account of the development of these parks as well as the attractions that mediate the sea specifically. Links are made to the film and television representations so well known by the public that mediate this environment too. The full extent of Disney's involvement with the aquatic realm is underscored by the fact that its fleet of 750 ships constitutes the 'world's fifth largest navy'. In addition, Brooks considers the parks and ships in relation to Baudrillard's (1988) arguments on hyperreality and simulation, with the observation that

Disney's artificial marine environment is for this chapter's author more satisfyingly authentic than the real thing.

The final chapter in this section, by Carole Murphy, considers the sinister connotations of the sea in media discourses on refugees. Drawing on her research for the Centre for the Study of Modern Slavery at St Mary's University, Murphy considers the genealogy of modern xenophobic and racist discourses on refugees and their link with Enoch Powell's notorious 'Rivers of Blood' speech of 1968. Here, aquatic spaces take on a much darker significance than in the foregoing chapters. The analysis of UK print media in 2015 reveals the depiction of refugees as a 'mass of invaders' in reporting that focuses on numbers and on borders. Occasional articles written with humanitarian aims are often drowned by articles that seek to set the agenda in more negative terms, with various implications for politics and the public sphere.

The final section, 'Screening Sea Creatures' returns the analysis to fictional representations in screen media. Film provides the focus for three of the chapters; digital games is also covered in the chapter by Michael Fuchs. Analysis in these chapters considers the industrial contexts of media production as well as narrative and spectatorial pleasures involved in the consumption of aquatic media texts.

Fuchs' chapter opens the section, with a discussion of the *Jaws Unleashed* video game in which the player is encouraged to control a great white shark. The game is contextualised in relation to the famous film franchise; aspects of narrative, design and gameplay are discussed as well as how these contribute to the experience of the player controlling the shark avatar. In particular, Fuchs considers the implications of encouraging the player to identify with an apparently 'unanthropomorphisable' creature as well as the posthuman or becoming-animal potentials opened up in the various scenarios in the game. Crucially, ecological implications are discussed in relation to narrative aspects of the game.

Mark Fryers' chapter is the first on film in this section, providing a thorough survey of animated representations of the sea and its creatures, with reference to various national cinemas and eras in cinema's history. Fryers' main case studies are *The Little Mermaid* (Ron Clements & John Musker, 1989), *Ponyo* (Hayao Miyazaki, 2008), *Song of the Sea* (Tomm Moore, 2014) and *Moana* (Ron Clements & John Musker, 2016), but the analysis delves back to the animation pioneer Winsor McCay's (1918) *The Sinking of the Lusitania*. Close textual analysis of the films locates them in relation to various national cinemas and mythical traditions, as well as exploring the environmental implications of the film narratives.

Damian O'Byrne's chapter is a fascinating analysis of *Jurassic World* and the significance of its aquatic dinosaur, the *Mosasaurus*. The viewing experience of the film and its ancillary media are discussed in relation to the 'immediacy' discussed by Bolter and Grusin (1999). A narrative analysis is framed in the wider context of the film's industrial production contexts and a bold thesis is advanced regarding the significance of the *Mosasaurus*'s victory over the fictional park's new hybrid dinosaur, *Indominus rex*. In a sly instance of industrial self-reflexivity, the outcome of this battle is seen to have significance for Hollywood in the age of the contemporary blockbuster.

Finally, Ian Hunter and Kieran Foster write an intriguing chapter on the one that got away – Hammer Films' proposed film on the Loch Ness Monster that in fact never commenced production. Their chapter reflects a recent interest in film studies on what Peter Krämer (2015) has called a 'shadow history' of the film industry, that is, analysis of the (non-)production histories of films that were never made. The authors' research draws on unpublished archival materials that reveal a fascinating and fraught pre-production context from one of Britain's most important film studios in its then decline. It is possible to wonder wistfully 'what if?', even if Hunter and Foster conclude that the film would likely have been 'a British nautical disaster to rival *Raise the Titanic*', had it ever been completed.

As will be evident from this introduction, the authors in this book have ventured far wider than a cursory consideration of the sea and sea creatures in popular culture would allow. The discussions of representations in literature and screen media are pleasingly concrete in their contextualisation and close textual analyses; these are supplemented by chapters from a diverse array of disciplines perhaps not always associated with the sea and its monsters.

The strength of this collection is its eclecticism, revealing a conviction shared by the editors and implicit in the range of contributions received that popular culture's engagement with the sea and its creatures may be studied from numerous theoretical frameworks and via diverse media, spaces and practices. Together, the chapters in this volume bear witness both to the 'timeless' appeal and resonance of the sea and its creatures; as well as to the particular forms and concrete social, industrial and cultural contexts in which they are mediated.

References

The Abyss (1989), [DVD] USA: 20th Century Fox.

Asma, S.T. (2009), *On Monsters: An Unnatural History of Our Worst Fears*, Oxford & New York. Oxford University Press.

Baldick, C. (1987), *In Frankenstein's Shadow: Myth, Monstrosity, and Nineteenth-century Writing*, Oxford: Clarendon

Baudrillard, J. (1988), *Selected Writings*, Stanford: Stanford University Press.

Bolter, J.D. & Grusin, R. (1999), *Remediation: Understanding New Media*, Cambridge: MIT Press.

Buckley, T. (1970), 'Song to the Siren', *Starsailor*, Straight Records, Track [Album]

Captain Beefheart (1972), 'Grow Fins', *The Spotlight Kid*, Reprise, Track [Album]

Cohen, J.J. (ed.) (1996), *Monster Theory: Reading Culture*, Minneapolis: University of Minnesota Press.

Halberstam, J. (1995), *Skin Shows: Gothic Horror and the Technology of Monsters*, Durham: Duke University Press.

Hendrix, J (1968), '1983... A Merman I Should Turn to Be', *Electric Ladyland*, Reprise, Track [Album]

Herhuth, E. (2017), *Pixar and the Aesthetic Imagination: Animation, Storytelling, and Digital Culture*, Oakland: University of California Press

Hugo, V. (1866), *Les travailleurs de la mer,* Paris/Bruxelles/Leipzig:Librairieinternationale Lacroix.

Hugo, V. (1866), *The Toilers of the Sea*. Translated from the French by an unnamed translator. London: Walter Scott Limited.

Hugo, V. (1868; 1900), *The Laughing Man*. Translated from the French by an unnamed translator. London & Glasgow: Collins' Clear-Type Press.

Hunt, L., Lockyer, S. & Williamson, M. (2013), *Screening the Undead: Vampires and Zombies in Film and Television*, London. I.B. Tauris.

Kearney, R. (2003), *Strangers, Gods and Monsters*, Abingdon & New York: Routledge

Krämer, P. (2015), 'Adaptation as Exploration: Stanley Kubrick, Literature, and *A.I. Artificial Intelligence*', *Adaptation* 8 (3), pp.372–82.

Levina, M. & Bui, D.-M.T. (2013), *Monster Culture in the 21st Century*, New York & London: Bloomsbury Academic.

Lister, M., Dovey, J., Giddings, S., Grant, I. & Kelly, K. (2003), *New Media: A Critical Introduction*, London & New York: Routledge

Lovecraft, H.P. (1928), 'The Call of Cthulhu' in *H.P. Lovecraft: The Complete Cthulhu Mythos Tales*, New York: Barnes and Noble pp.36–61

Mittman, A.S. (2012), 'Introduction: The Impact of Monsters and Monster Studies'. In A.S. Mittman & P.J. Dendle (eds), *The Ashgate Research Companion to Monsters and the Monstrous*, Farnham: Ashgate.

Serck, L. (2017), 'Mermaids gather to compete for UK title', BBC News [online], ttp://www.bbc.co.uk/news/uk-england-40675250 (accessed 30 July 2017).

Thornton, S. (1997), 'The Social Logic of Subcultural Capital'. In K. Gelder, & S. Thornton (eds), *The Subcultures Reader*, London & New York: Routledge, pp.200–209.

Wright, A. (2013), *Monstrosity: The Human Monster in Visual Culture*, London. I.B. Tauris.

Part 1

Folklore and Weird Tales

Chapter 1

"From Beneath the Waves": Sea-*Draugr* and the Popular Conscience

Alexander Hay

The sea looms large in human psychology, both as a source of guilt and its metaphor. As Joseph Conrad noted, the sea has never been "friendly to man" (Conrad 1907), nor has it shown generosity towards him or time for any of his professed values. Fittingly, Conrad's *Pincher Martin* had its protagonist undergo a purgatorial experience as he drowns in the sea, his 'survival' an extended penance where his guilt and sins are scourged (Sinclair 1982, pp.175–177).

For Coleridge's ancient mariner, meanwhile, the sea is a place of unending dread and a guilty conscience that cannot be absolved. As Miall has observed, the sea was the stage upon which Coleridge explored his own sense of guilt, haunted by the death of his father and a looming sense of some unfathomable judgement for sins committed (Miall 1984, pp.639–640).

Just as significantly, the *Rime of the Ancient Mariner* (1908) features walking corpses, in the form of the reanimated crewmates of the mariner, brought back to life once he admits his sins, who then steer his ship back to land. The Mariner himself is now the property of Life-in-Death, a sinister female figure that condemns him to a living death of his own, doomed to tell his story forever more. As the chapter will argue, this juxtaposition of reanimated corpses, guilt and the sea has become a recurring motif in popular culture, a means whereby guilt is confronted though not always resolved.

Walking corpses and the restless dead have, of course, been prominent in recent decades as metaphors and means of satire. As representations of mindless conformity and relentless social conflict, zombies are of course one such example. Though recently neutered in potency by over-exposure and their relegation to the rank of 'macguffin' for soap opera and sadistic, faintly right wing survival fantasies, as most notably depicted in *The Walking Dead* comic book and its attendant spin-off media.

Vengeful aquatic spirits are a common theme in horror films, as are tortured souls in need of salvation: in *The Devil's Backbone* (2001), we have a juxtaposition of both, as is the case with *Ringu* (1998), though both involve a well as both crime scene and root of the ensuing horror, rather than the sea per se.

As this paper will discuss, however, the *Sea-Draugr* not only combines these but also demonstrates a recurring reckoning with guilt and its consequences. This has become more subliminal over time, to the extent that we have *Sea-Draugr* in function if not form, where there is no reanimated corpse per se, but there is a substitution that serves the same role. In other cases, the presence of *Sea-Draugr* swings towards the other direction, where these creatures are *Sea-Draugr* not only in function but in all but name. They have even begun to manifest themselves in our news media and press coverage, where depictions of disasters and tragedies at sea have strange parallels to the drowned dead and their role as both conscience and nemesis.

Sea-Draugr and other revenants

What, however, is a *Sea-Draugr?* The archetype that will now be discussed is what can be best described as the *Draugr*, or reanimated corpse, an invariably malignant and dangerous reanimated corpse that figures large in Scandinavian mythology. They are sentient, calculating, cannibalistic objects of fear (Chadwick June 1946a, p.50). *Draugr* spread diseases and grow long talons. They inhabit their barrows, often full of treasure, and violently resist any tomb robbers. Those slain by a *Draugr* are sometimes bound to their killer as enslaved ghosts (Jakobsson 2009, p.310). Unlike their mainland counterparts, Icelandic *Draugr* are free-roaming, able to roam far from their barrows and pose a threat to any human they encounter, though a certain mischievousness means they may sometimes grant a gift rather than a violent death onto their victims (Chadwick 1946a, pp.54–55). They are fearsome foes, often requiring a ritualistic means of exorcism to be fully quelled. This ranges from being decapitated with their own sword, to being wrestled into submission, to being staked through the heart, and incineration – their ashes scattered, significantly, into the sea (Andrews 1913, p.48, Keyworth 2006, p.244, Chadwick 1946a, p.55).

While primarily land-based *Draugr* come in another variety, however, namely that of a drowned seafarer. A particularly vivid example of this is given in *Eyrbyggja saga* (Morris and Magnusson 1892), where a seafarer named Thorod Scat-Catcher and his men drown in mysterious circumstances. Their ship and its catch of fish are found but with none of its crew. Yet at their burial feast the drowned crew appear dripping with water, and take up their seats. At first they are welcomed but when they continue to appear in the subsequent evenings, now joined by another group of undead, they cause the mortal men to flee in horror, and subsequently cause the outbreak of an un-named sickness.

In response to this, the living organise a *Thing*, or court, and proceed to pass judgement on each of the *Draugr* who each say, in mitigation, that they had simply remained for as long as they could, before heading off into the night. Thorod himself states, rather caustically, that since he and his men are no longer welcome, they will go somewhere else instead. The dead no longer return and the sickness passes.

Unlike typical *Draugr*, these drowned men are not directly malign, though their presence causes, unintentionally, much trouble for the living. Instead, they seem sympathetic and willingly depart when told to go (One doubts a normal *Draugr* would be so accommodating, somehow). One interpretation of this story is as a metaphor for remembrance – of lost friends and acquaintances whose ongoing memory causes distress. The only way to be rid of them is to objectify them and their memory, in this case through a legal process. By passing sentence, the *Thing* drives the *Sea-Draugr* away, but their dignified response to this, and their own (not entirely unjustified) parting words suggest this is not in itself an answer. There is a comedic quality to the scenario, but also a melancholic one. Thorod and his peers seem to say "you can't forget us, even if you try." Here the real antagonist is the urge to forget those who have passed, to trivialise bereavement through omission. Perhaps it is fitting then that one way to drive off the undead in the Icelandic sagas is to verbally abuse and scold them – the troubling memories of the dead swept away by a wilful desecration of their memory.

Another alternative to dealing with *Sea-Draugr* is demonstrated in *Laxdæla saga* (Press 1880); here one protagonist, Gudrun, loses her husband and crew to drowning. On her way to church one evening she sees her husband, resurrected, along with his crew, but refuses to speak to them. Instead she goes into church "as long as it seemed good to her", only to find that her returned husband and crew had disappeared. Prior to this, she had repelled another ghost by insulting him. Gudrun's response to the affair is to embrace Christianity even further, digging up the remains and effects of an evil wizard and eventually becoming a nun and hermit. Despite this, she "lived in such sorrow and grief" and when pressed by her son as to which of her dead husbands she loved the most, she replies, enigmatically: "to him I was worst whom I loved best." Again, the notion of guilt, loss and mourning are subsumed by a dismissal, even a purging of the dead, and immersal in faith and the rejection of a troubling pagan past. Yet, as the saga observes, even this does not grant Gudrun peace. Jakobsson (2011, p.30) refers to the actions of these undead as being in the grip of 'spectral selfishness', though this underestimates a desperate need to relieve oneself of grief and the post hoc rationalisations that requires.

Another trait of *Sea-Draugr*, as this paper will discuss later, is how their idea can spread, adapt and yet retain their essential meaning. This has lead to the more recent Norwegian myth of the *Draug*, which, as the name suggests, reflects a cross-pollination within Scandinavian cultures (Jordahl 1975, p.12). *Draug*, according to the Folklore of North Eastern Norway, are the reanimated remains of drowned fishermen, often headless or with heads replaced by seaweed. They are invariably omens of impending disaster, or agencies of it, and in one particular legend have been said to rise from the depths en-masse to wage war against land-dwelling ghosts or perhaps *Draugs*, who are closer in form and function to their traditional Icelandic equivalents. Interestingly, in this folktale, the land ghosts or *Draugr* prevail, having emerged from a Christian churchyard, a heavily symbolic clash between an orderly, ritualised death, in the form of a Christian burial, and the ambivalent horror of being lost at sea, and so unable to be disposed of in a decent fashion. Again, this can be read as an attempt to address deep-seated fears and anxieties. For coastal communities, losing sons, fathers, brothers and husbands at sea was an all too regular occurrence. The story ends with the caveat that the *Sea-Draugr* never return, which appears to be wishful thinking. After all, the story does not say they have been destroyed, but merely driven back. Mourning, guilt and lives ended before their proper resolution can be pushed aside, but they cannot be completely dismissed.

Another *Draug* narrative features a family pursued in a boat by another, this time piloted by a *Draug*. All attempts to outrun the other boat fail, and the entire family is washed away bar one child who manages to cling on until rescued (Jordahl, p.15). Interestingly, the boy later marries the family's servant girl and never goes to sea again, a poignant juxtaposition of survivor's guilt and the urge to move away from grief by avoidance and forgetfulness. The boy, let us not forget, has created a new family and a new life, but only by avoiding the source of the original trauma – the place where the *Draug* lurk – does he managed to elude his bereavement.

In many ways, of course, the traditional *Draugr* and their surrounding mythology are not that far removed from the *Sea-Draugr* either. The archetypical *Draugr* is huge, bloated and either pale or black (Keyworth 2006, p.244). In other words, they more closely resemble the distended corpses of the drowned than the withered, rotted or skeletonised contents of barrows. Perhaps this was due to the nature of death in Iceland where corpses were buried as soon as feasible, but where, like Norway, an altogether more grisly sight could be found washed up on a beach at any time.

This is not the only connection with the sea that land-based *Draugr* demonstrate. Many barrows and pre-Christian burial sites were either on the Icelandic coast or close by (Vesteinsson 2011, p.42). Beaches were the scenes of executions, such as hangings (Chadwick 1946b, p. 126). Even some of the means of disposing of *Draugr* had a maritime element, with the ashes of a slain (or rather, re-slain) *Draugr* being thrown into the sea as a final act of exorcism (Ellis Davidson 1968, p.38). Water was also seen as a place where valuable objects could be obtained, whether it be a mighty sword from the stomach of a fish (Andrews 1913, p. 627), or gifts awarded for saving a troll's child from drowning (Simpson 1966, p.5).

However, how did the *Sea-Draugr* continue its journey, or perhaps rampage, into modern popular culture? Certainly, the Icelandic aspect of the myth continued into the early modern period, with reports of *Draugr* being made as late as the 17th century (Keyworth 2006, p.246). The Old English poem *Beowulf* (Hall 1892) suggests one route. The cannibalistic monster, Grendel, resembles a *Draugr* in terms of his predatory behaviour, cunning and physical monstrosity. Aspects of the *Sea-Draugr* meanwhile, can be seen in the titular hero's diving down to the bottom of the lake to finally vanquish the monster and his mother. Similarly, the pathos and surprisingly sympathetic aspect of the mother echoes aspects of themes already discussed – of regret, mourning and pain:

> "Known unto earth-folk, that still an avenger
> Outlived the loathed one, long since the sorrow
> Caused by the struggle; the mother of Grendel,
> Devil-shaped woman, her woe ever minded,
> Who was held to inhabit the horrible waters," (Hall 1892)

With both mother and son disposed of, Beowulf later dies in battle fighting against a dragon threatening his kingdom. He is buried in a barrow, perhaps significantly, overlooking the sea. Though his soul may be at rest, the poem nonetheless laments his loss:

> "Thus made their mourning the men of Geatland,
> For their hero's passing his hearth-companions:
> Quoth that of all the kings of earth,
> Of men he was mildest and most beloved,
> To his kin the kindest, keenest for praise." (Ibid)

Parallels can therefore be made between *Beowulf* and *Sea-Draugr* narratives. Nonetheless, there is one challenge to this reading; the poem may have been composed as early as the 7th Century (Clark 2009, pp.678–679), and written down in manuscript form in the 10th or early 11th Century AD (Vandersall 1972, p.10). By contrast, Iceland was only permanently settled for the first time in the late 9th Century (Byock et al 2005, p. 198), and the Icelandic sagas recorded in the 13th Century onwards (Ólason and Tómasson 2006, p.125). How, then, can it be said that *Beowulf* spread the idea of the *Sea-Draugr*? Both should instead be seen as stemming from an original myth and set of cultural motifs that were expressed in one form in Iceland and another in Old English. Indeed, it is the similarities that are most interesting here; the spread of a series of sinister maritime and personal traumas with their roots in a shared Scandinavian experience. As Kiessling (1968, p.201) has argued, Grendel's description as a *Maere*, or night monster, has shared roots with the Icelandic *Mara*, or night demon, and the Old English *Mare*, or latterly, *Nightmare*.

One other route of transmission was through Scotland. In *Grettirsaga*, witch fire is described as burning above the barrow of a powerful *Draugr*: This was a sign of a supernatural, and malign presence. In Scottish folklore, mean-

15

while, strange lights at sea were seen as harbingers of a death by drowning, with the lights often also signifying where a drowned body could be found floating (Maclagan 1897, p. 211). At other times, the lights not only foretold a death but were accompanied by a physical haunting:

> Further, the whole family, father, mother, and several sons and daughters, respectable and reliable persons, assert that during that season, for a good while before the drowning accident, they over and over again heard rapping at the door, not one, but all of them; and when they went to the door, no one was to be seen (Maclagan, p.216).

Again, a death by drowning is accompanied by a dread and a supernatural horror that seems to represent a deeper sense of grief and foreboding. Another example of Scottish folklore echoing *Sea-Draugr* motifs is the folk song, 'The Wife of Usher's Well'. First collected in 1802, where the titular wife's three sons die after she had "sent them over the sea", and who return like the *Sea-Draugr* of *Eyrbyggja saga*, after she vows neither the wind nor the flood will stop until her sons return "in earthly flesh and blood." This happens one night, and the three sons appear at their mother's house. Sadly, for the Wife, this is for one night only, and her sons leave once more the following morning, departing with an apology, and some flirting with "the bonny lass" who tends their mother's fire. As in *Eyrbyggja saga*, the returning dead have died at sea and gather around a fire. There are, of course, differences – the sons leave reluctantly after only one night and it is plain that their mother would rather they stayed, unlike the still-living Icelanders and their gate-crashing *Sea-Draugr*. Nonetheless, the themes are the same – loss, guilt, heartbreak, mourning and an inability to let the dead go. Similarly, the means are similar – the dead walk, though they are not malign, and they must all be laid to rest or at least sent on despite the regrets they feel. In both examples, the process of grieving is demonstrated as neither without end nor, ultimately, relief. The main difference is that the three sons leave on a bittersweet note, while the *Sea-Draugr* leave with sour humour.

When did the *Sea-Draugr* archetype enter the modern popular conscience, however? As the examples of Coleridge or Edgar Allen Poe's *Manuscript Found In A Bottle* (1833), with its crew of ancient, wizened sailors "with unquiet and tremulous step" heading towards their doom, he was not alone in exploring these themes and archetypes. In short stories such as *Oh, Whistle, And I'll Come To You, My Lad* (1904) and *A Warning To The Curious* (1925), with their evil spirits able to take physical form, tomb robbing and their coastal settings, MR James also demonstrated a possible influence.

However, as the next section will discuss modern *Sea-Draugr* are far more overt. Their aquatic nature is as pronounced as the personal tragedy they embody.

Modern *Sea-Draugr* in all but name

As said earlier, modern *Sea-Draugr* come in two forms. Firstly, there are the ones that closely resemble the classic archetype in terms of how they function, their role in the plot of a story and their physicality. While they may deviate from the original *Sea-Draugr* template in some ways, there are clear parallels between them and their antecedents. What they all share in common, with some exceptions, are the following features: they are walking corpses or can manifest in such a way; they show intelligence, signs of personality and malicious intent; and thirdly they are symbolic representations of repressed guilt or justice for unjust acts. Finally, while they can be driven off or contained, they remain as either a threat or an ongoing blot on the conscience of their mortal counterparts.

One clear example of this is John Carpenter's 1980 film, *The Fog*. Here a coastal community, about to celebrate its centenary, is assailed by the dead spirits of lepers who were murdered on board their ship. The wealth plundered from the wreck is then used to found the town which is now under attack. Like *Draugr* and *Sea-Draugr*, they are a corporeal menace and are capable of violently killing their victims through brute force, in a fashion that would not be out of place in an Icelandic saga. While they materialise from the titular fog and can, it is implied, dematerialise back into it at will, there are precedents for this in *Draugr* mythology. For example, in *Laxdaela saga* one *Draugr* evades his human opponent by merging into the earth, while it is also implied that other *Draugr* can move through the stones of their barrows via a kind of elemental intangibility. Another trait the vengeful spirits share with *Draugr* is their ability to reanimate the corpses of their victims or spread their curse onto them, albeit temporarily in the case of the lepers (Jakobsson 2009. p.310). Finally, the lepers can be driven off like *Sea-Draugr* by either Christian rituals or acts. In *The Fog*, the lepers vanish after seizing a cross in a church made from the stolen gold. In *Laxdæla saga*, as we have seen, Gudrun's Christianity wards off the *Sea-Draugr* her husband has become, while the previously mentioned clash between the Norwegian *Draug* and the Christian ghosts is another case in point. Ironically, the last victim of the lepers is the priest of the church, himself a descendant of the original murderers, who is claimed after the threat has apparently been vanquished. A local disc-jockey, having held off the lepers, meanwhile broadcasts a warning that the fog remains a threat. Here the implied peril of the *Sea-Draugr* is made explicit – your guilt and shame will come back to haunt you, regardless of how hard you try to avoid it.

Another example is George A. Romero's 2005 instalment of his zombie series *Land of the Dead*. The film continues to develop the concept of zombies reacquiring some degree of intellect, selfhood and morality, as first introduced in the series' previous film *Day of the Dead* (1985). *Land of the Dead* has a sapient (awakened?) zombie called Big Daddy who unites an army of fellow zombies, some more mindless than others, to take a bloody revenge on the human enclave that had attacked their town. Where the similarities between these zombies and *Sea-Draugr* become clear is in one major scene, where Big Daddy leads his army into the river which blocks their passage, across its bed and then, in a scene that could be described as a perfect depiction of *Sea-Draugr* rising from the depths, emerging en masse at the other side. While this scene involves a large, deep river (to be precise, the Ohio River) rather than the sea, the scene nonetheless has a maritime flavour in that the night-time setting of the scene and the surrounding darkness remove all context from the water. This could be a river near you, or an estuary, or a beach. The zombies then proceed to wreak bloody vengeance on the humans, not entirely wiping them out but certainly destroying their corrupt ruling elite. Scores settled, Big Daddy and his zombies return home, being spared by the protagonists who realise they have more in common than they may have otherwise admitted.

This has all the typical aspects of a *Sea-Draugr* narrative – the zombies represent not only a repressed underclass but also guilt and repressed mourning. One cannot, after all, mourn a dead body when it is trying to eat you, nor in a world with few survivors can one easily set aside the horror that has befallen the world, and the shame of surviving where others have not. Of course, there are many innocent victims in the zombie assault too; like all good *Sea-Draugr* stories, the undead creatures emerging from the depths bring about as much harm as catharsis until they are finally sent on their way.

Another example comes in the form of a computer game. Red Hook's *Darkest Dungeon* (2016). In this dark fantasy RPG, you lead a band of dysfunctional and damaged, or morally dubious, adventurers in an attempt to restore the lands of your ancestor and undo the harm his arcane experiments have left behind. The ghost of the ancestor provides both narration and a Greek chorus of sorts as you heal the family estate and do your best to preserve the mental and physical health of your adventurers. In that sense alone – facing up to previous sins and traumas – the game has resonance, though it slowly emerges that the ancestor is a monstrous psychopath in his own right and the emissary of the ultimate evil that lurks beneath the surface of the ruined family manor.

Most significant however is one of the levels in the game – The Cove. This aquatically themed dungeon not only has all manner of 'pelagic nightmares' – based on Lovecraft's Deep Ones – and other oceanic monsters to fight, but, specifically, its own *Sea-Draugr*. These come in two varieties – the first of these is the 'Drowned Thrall', a bloated carcass that shows all the signs of having been in the water for a long time, but also a considerable resemblance to both *Draugr* and *Sea-Draugr*. In addition to causing both physical harm and mental trauma to the player's adventurers through its 'Gargling Grab', the Drowned Thrall also has another attack. Igniting the putrid gases that have built up in its swollen body, the thing explodes, causing massive damage. Interestingly, this attack is referred to as 'The Revenge' – the implication being that this was once a sailor, abandoned and drowned and now returned, seeking vengeance on the landlubbers that left him to rot.

The other version of *Sea-Draugr* in the game comes in the form of 'The Sodden Crew'. This is a ship's crew, once hired by the ancestor to discreetly deliver some of his more dubious artefacts and occult material, but who fell out of his favour after demanding more money for their continued silence. The ancestor instead placed a hex on their anchor, dragging their ship down to the depths and drowning them. Reanimated either by the injustice of their betrayal or a side effect of the curse, or a combination of both, they return, vengeful, semi-decayed and very much in the form of *Sea-Draugr* as one of the Cove's boss monsters. Even their murderer cannot help but note that they are "poor devils, chained and drowning, for eternity..." and that they "are cursed to float forever, deep in the swirling blackness, far beyond the light's reach."

Again, we have an example of *Sea-Draugr* who represent loss, guilt and an ability to escape the past. Given the utter immorality of the ancestor, it falls onto the player to either drive them back below the water or free them from their curse once and for all. They reflect the pessimism and dark humour that underpins the game – one attack they can inflict on the adventurers is 'Drink with the Dead' where one undead sailor swigs grog while driving – but also provide an excellent example of modern day *Sea-Draugr*, proxies for guilt and inescapable memory in equal measure. The Cove itself is an ideal stage for this to play out on; its classical-style ruins hint at a bleak past, barely remembered, while obstacles come in the form of shipwrecks, and boons in the form of ship figureheads, lucky only in the sense that they didn't sink down with the rest of their ships. Once again, the seashore is portrayed as a place where death, memorials to death and tragedy are all washed up. It also demonstrates how the *Sea-Draugr* has continued its progress from Scandinavian myth into new regions of popular culture.

Finally, there must be a mention of Lucio Fulci's *Zombie Flesh Eaters* (1979). While the zombies in this film are neither sentient nor driven by any other purpose other than to devour the living, they do nonetheless reflect the *Sea-Draugr* in two significant ways. Firstly, there is the infamous shark scene, where an underwater zombie fights a shark for the right to devour a nubile topless scuba diver. While sleazy and absurd in equal measure, it does explore one aspect of the *Sea-Draugr* myth that is otherwise overlooked; how these undead sea dwellers interact with their home environment. While the sagas and Norwegian folklore have *Sea-Draugr* and *Draugs* emerging from the sea, they do not ever address what role these creatures play in those deep waters. In that sense, while the *Sea-Draugr* are examples of maritime horror, in that sense alone they seem cut off or isolated even from the sea itself, though Norwegian *Draug* folklore does at least describe some of them having heads made out of seaweed (Jordahl, p.10) or adopting the form of a malignant seal (Jordahl, p.12). For *Sea-Draugr*, the sea is something to come from and to return to, but not to actually be a part of.

There is also a maritime subtext. The film's first act sees an apparently abandoned ship drift into New York, which brings with it a zombie, who attack and infects a 'Patient Zero' who then spreads it throughout the city while the protagonists search for its origins on a remote island. The zombie itself, played by a bald, bulky actor, resembles a particularly bloated *Draugr*. When shot, it falls overboard, echoing the disposal of some *Draugr* in Icelandic sagas. The final act, meanwhile, inverts the *Sea-Draugr* archetype altogether. The last two survivors find themselves trapped on another ship, their former-ally-turned-zombie trying to break out and eat them. They are adrift and unable to return home; New York has been overrun by the undead, and so in a curious way these survivors have become a kind of living *Sea-Draugr*, adrift from their previous lives and unable to find closure.

Finally, *Zombie Flesh Eaters* also addresses issues of guilt and regret. The island's resident doctor is a tortured man, who is forced to keep killing, or re-killing, all the corpses that reanimate. This blatant metaphor for trying and failing to evade grief is later followed by one of the film's set-pieces, where the rotten corpses of long-dead conquistadors emerge from their graves and attack the protagonists. Here the horrors of Empire and imperial conquest literally come back to haunt the (American) characters, the sea-borne colonisation of the Americas, with all its attendant cruelties and violence, refusing to be forgotten.

Modern *Sea-Draugr* in function, not form

Sea-Draugr also appear in another form. This is an altogether more subtle definition as many of the examples in this section are not walking corpses, or even (un)dead in some cases. However, what they all share in common is that they serve the same purpose as a *Sea-Draugr* – to represent guilt, loss and regret, to do so in a fashion that haunts the subject and in a fashion that is, in one way or another, unnerving. These are *Sea-Draugr* taken to their logical conclusion, where all vestiges of the original myth are shed, leaving behind only those universal themes and motifs at its heart.

This allows for a far greater diversity of realisation than the other type of modern *Sea-Draugr*. One example of this is James Cameron's *Titanic* (1997), not in itself a ghost story until its very last scene where the now-ancient survivor of that disaster, Rose, is reunited with her true love, Jack, and all the other passengers who died on that fateful night in 1912. Whether this is a dream or Rose's death and subsequent ascent into the afterlife is left to the audience to decide, but it is significant to note that this vision of the afterlife is still contained within the Titanic itself. Neither Rose, nor Jack, nor the other passengers seem able to escape or transcend the disaster. While this vision of the afterlife is certainly a happy one, where the noxious class divisions and conflicts on-board before the disaster are set aside, and a divine light seems to stream in through the skylights, all on-board are still caught in a sort of faintly melancholy, bittersweet stasis – albeit one that is implied to he heavenly. This discordance is made explicit in the original script for the film, which concludes with the following direction:

> THE WRECK OF TITANIC looms like a ghost out of the dark. It is lit by a kind of moonlight, a light of the mind... WE GO INSIDE, and the echoing sound of distant waltz music is heard. The rust fades away from the walls of the dark corridor and it is transformed... WE EMERGE onto the grand staircase, lit by glowing chandeliers.... At the bottom a man stands with his back to us... he turns and it is Jack. Smiling he holds his hand out towards us. IN A SIDE ANGLE Rose goes into his arms, a girl of 17. The passengers, officers and crew of the RMS Titanic smile and applaud in the utter silence of the abyss. (Cameron 1996)

While the ending features a kind of living death, or afterlife, that is quite the opposite from the gloomy vision of the traditional *Sea-Draugr*, it does not retreat from the disaster of the Titanic, which continues to haunt the popular imagination, nor the horror of hundreds of lives lost at sea. The inhabitants of the Titanic are trapped there in death as they were in the last moments of life. Once the love story and melodrama of the film is stripped away, it quite deliberately directs us to the terrible reality of death at sea, injustice, and of unresolved tragedy.

The Titanic, of course, continues to loom in the public conscience as various film and television adaptations demonstrate. Another example of its conflation with *Sea-Draugr* is in *Ghostbusters II* (1989), where the ship itself re-floats and docks in its intended New York, disgorging sinister streams of ghostly passengers from its rusted hulk. Here the Titanic itself becomes a *Sea-Draugr* of sorts; a traumatic memory that continues to re-surface, the humorous undertone of the scene undermined by its menace and the on-going cultural response to its tragedy.

Two other notable examples of this archetype demonstrate its versatility. The 1972 *Doctor Who* serial, *The Sea Devils*, by Malcolm Hulke, does not, of course feature *Sea-Draugr*, but it does feature sinister sea creatures who emerge from the depths in a famous scene that echoes the rising dead from other examples in this paper. The story itself is a sequel of sorts to Hulke's *The Silurians* (1970), and shares its themes of clashes between species – an ancient civilisation confronting with the one that has replaced it and the essential tragedy of this conflict. What gives it relevance in this case is the maritime nature of the story – the Sea Devils are aquatic relatives of their Silurian cousins and their intention to awaken the other sleeping colonies of their kind and re-conquer the world. The essential conflict of the story is summarised in the fifth episode by the leader of the creatures: "This is our planet. My people ruled the Earth when man was only an ape." The Doctor attempts a treaty between humanity and the Sea Devils, but this fails and, as in *The Silurians*, (1970) the conflict ends in the destruction of the ancients by humanity.

Here, the essential *Sea-Draugr* theme is again played out. That is, tragedy, conflict, horror, an uncertain resolution – in that it is stated that there are other Sea Devils still in stasis – and a lingering sense of regret. The Sea Devils, as former rulers of the world, haunt humanity in the fashion of vengeful spirits or undead monsters. They could easily be substituted with *Sea-Draugr* and the story would require little change.

The other example is the 2009 film, *Triangle*. Here, a woman, Jess, is pursued through a ghost ship by a shadowy killer who butchers her friends. The twist is later revealed; the protagonist is caught in a perpetual time loop where the same events, or variations thereof, continue to repeat themselves. She discovers that she is in fact the killer, from a previous cycle, and so sets about trying to escape from it, up to and including having another version of herself killed. Further complicating matters is the fact that the protagonist also realises, by seeing another version of herself abusing her son, that she is in fact more monstrous than she has realised. She kills the version of herself who has been cruel to her son, before commencing on yet another loop. It is not clear whether she is able to break the cycle, as she continues to find evidence of many previous loops, but she continues, regardless.

Where is the *Sea-Draugr* here, however? It is, in fact, Jess herself. Her constant repetition of prior events and traumas represents the burden of a guilty conscience, her acts of self-murder subliminal gestures of self-loathing and disassociation from the reality of the scenario. In that sense, Jess is in fact a unique form of *Sea-Draugr*, trapped in a state between life and death – her reality subverted by the sea and her actions driven by guilt, remorse and shame. Like the *Sea-Draugr*, she is both alive and dead, albeit in a fashion quite different from more 'typical' examples, and like them, there is no certain resolution for her. Here the *Sea-Draugr* reaches its next destination, where the line between unliving aquatic monster and human is blurred. Anyone can become a *Sea-Draugr*, although, as *Triangle* suggests, perhaps that was not as great a change as we may have first imagined.

The *Sea-Draugr* in the news

Where will the *Sea-Draugr* go next? It has, in fact, already colonised the great longform narrative of our times – namely news media. An example of this is the fate that befell German sailor Manfred Fritz Bajorat. In February 2016, his mummified remains were found on his half-sunken yacht off the coast of the Philippines (Sample 2016). Inside, witnesses saw a ghastly sight – Bajorat, dead, yet mummified in the dry air of the boat's interior. His features, facial and head hair and even his facial features and fingerprints, while all showing the signs of desiccation, were nonetheless remarkably preserved. As the eerie photography of the dead man demonstrates, the scene was strangely poignant, in that the dead sailor seemed to be sleeping, horrific, in that the condition of the man's remains were still dreadful to behold, and haunting in that he had died alone, having lost his ex-wife several years before.

The coverage of the death consistently featured the shot of his corpse, regardless of whether it was a 'quality' or 'popular' news outlet. Most used the word 'mummy' to describe the remains, though this seems inappropriate, given where the man died and where his remains were found. Could Bajorat be seen as a kind of real life *Sea-Draugr*? He was of course no walking corpse, but the melancholy and macabre circumstances echo the unquiet dead of the Icelandic sagas, who will not be ignored or simply forgotten.

Another recent, and notorious example was the tragic death by drowning of the three-year-old Syrian refugee, AylanKurdi. The iconic image of his small body gently being picked up off a Turkish shore by a policeman, who seems to cradle him in his hands, made an immediate impact on the on-going debate regarding migration in the wake of the Syrian war (Homans 2015). Kurdi's death caused a reappraisal of public attitudes across the world (BBC 2015) with many, but not all, UK media outlets softening their previous anti-refugee rhetoric (Greenslade 2015). In terms of symbolic impact, Kurdi certainly fulfilled the function of a *Sea-Draugr* in the sense that he invoked conflicted feelings of guilt, bereavement, horror and a pricking of the conscience, but he also became a symbol of fear, as the cartoon by *Charlie Hebdo* which implied that he could have become a rapist or criminal if he had made it to Europe demonstrates (Meade 2015). Certainly, his death has not changed much in the way of the refugees' plight – since his death, more than 300 children have subsequently drowned when their boats capsized, and with little of the same coverage (Stanton 2016), while anti-refugee rethoric has continued to harden (Conolly 2016). Yet the image of Kurdi's body nonetheless has an undeniable poignancy – it is an accusation and a challenge that threatens our preconceptions and sense of certainty. In that sense, of course, this tragedy has much in common with *Sea-Draugr* narratives.

Similar dynamics lay behind other images of washed up human bodies. Images of the thousands of corpses washed up in the wake of the 2011 Japanese tsunami share the same combination of pathos, horror and a sense of an accusation being made to the viewer (Guttenfelder 2011). The wreckage of destroyed villages and towns, and beached ships and boats, have similar significance. As Caple and Bednarek have argued, (2016, pp.443–444) photojournalism covering the disaster has an element of artifice involved; images that fit into existing preconceptions and enable 'superlativeness' in terms of news writing and visual aesthetics are the ones that are featured, as demonstrated, for example, by a series of photographs of a 'ghost ship', shaken free of its moorings by the Tsunami and left to float aimlessly. (Rosen 2012) In this sense, it is safe to say that these images were chosen because they fit into existing narratives, including that of the *Sea-Draugr*.

Conclusion

In this sense, the *Sea-Draugr* has become a widespread, even international archetype as a result of widespread dissemination and its compelling nature. It would seem a guilty conscience is a fertile place for the imagination and the *Sea-Draugr* also allows us to express a strange, often adversarial relationship with the sea, as well as our own tragedies and sense of civic, social and personal responsibility.

Yet the main strength of the *Sea-Draugr* is this – it is able to travel and spread into a broader public consciousness, though not necessarily as obviously as might be expected. The archetype is also able to evolve and develop over time, to undertake shifts and alterations in tone. Like the Ancient Mariner's tale, it would seem that the *Sea-Draugr* has become a story we must continue to re-tell.

References

Andrews, A.L., 1913. Studies in the FornaldarsǫgurNorðrlanda *Modern Philology* 10(4) 601–630.

BBC Trending. 2015. *Alan Kurdi: Has one picture shifted our view of refugees?* [viewed 29 March 2017] Available from: http://www.bbc.co.uk/news/blogs-trending-34142804.

Byock, J., Walker, P., Erlandson, J., Holck, P., Zori, D., Guðmundsson, M., and Tveskov, M. 2005. A Viking-Age Valley In Iceland: The Mosfell Archaeological Project. *Medieval Archaeology* 49, 195–218.

Cameron, J. 1996. *Titanic* [Screenplay] [viewed 29 March 2017]. Available from: http://www. pages.drexel.edu/~ina22/splaylib/Screenplay-Titanic.pdf.

Caple, H. and Bednarek, M. 2016. Rethinking news values: What a discursive approach can tell us about the construction of news discourse and news photography. *Journalism* 17(4), 435–455.

Chadwick, N.K., 1946a. Norse Ghosts (A Study in the Draugr and the Haugbúi). *Folklore*, 57(2), 50–65.

Chadwick, N.K., 1946b. Norse Ghosts II. *Folklore* 57(3), 50–65.

Clark, G., 2009. The Date of Beowulf and the Arundel Psalter Gloss. *Modern Philology* 106(4), 678–679.

Coleridge, S.T., 1908. *Coleridge's Ancient Mariner And Select Poems* [viewed 23 July 2017]. Available from: http://www.gutenberg.org/cache/epub/11101/pg11101-images.html.

Connolly, K. 2016. *German anti-refugee party targets 'political earthquake' in elections* [viewed 29 March 2017]. Available from: https://www.theguardian.com/world/2016/mar/11/german-anti-refugee-party-afd-political-earthquake-state-elections.

Conrad, J. 1907. *The Mirror Of The Sea – Memories And Impressions* [viewed 23 July 2017]. Available from: http://www.gutenberg.org/files/1058/1058-h/1058-h.htm.

Ellis Davidson, H.R., 1968. *The Road to Hel: A Study of the Conception of the Dead in Old Norse Literature.* New York: Greenwood Press.

Greenslade, R. 2015. *Images of drowned boy made only a fleeting change to refugee reporting* [viewed 29 March 2017]. Available from: https://www.theguardian.com/media/greenslade/2015/nov/09/images-of-drowned-boy-made-only-a-fleeting-change-to-refugee-reporting.

Guttenfelder, D. 2011. *Japan-based Associated Press photographer David Guttenfelder documents the aftermath of the earthquake and tsunami that devastated the north-east of the country* [viewed 29 March 2017]. Available from: https://www.theguardian.com/artanddesign/gallery/2011/mar/31/photojournalist-david-guttenfelder.

Hall, L.H. *trans.* 1892. *Beowulf – An Anglo-Saxon Epic Poem* [viewed 29 March 2017]. Available from: https://www.gutenberg.org/files/16328/16328-h/16328-h.htm.

Homans, C. 2015. *The Boy on the Beach* [viewed 29 March 2017]. Available from: https://www.nytimes.com/2015/09/03/magazine/the-boy-on-the-beach.html.

Jacobs, W.W. 1911. *Over The Side* [viewed 29 March 2017]. Available from: http://www.gutenberg.org/cache/epub/11186/pg11186.txt.

Jakobsson, A. 2009. The Fearless Vampire Killers: A Note about the Icelandic Draugr and Demonic Contamination in Grettis Saga. *Folklore* 120(3), 307–316.

Jakobsson, A. 2011. Vampires and watchmen: categorizing the mediaeval Icelandic undead. *The Journal of English and Germanic Philology* 110(3), 281–300.

Jordahl, O. 1975. Folkloristic Influences upon Rølvaag's Youth. *Western Folklore* 34(1), 1–15.

Keyworth, G.D., 2006. Was the Vampire of the Eighteenth Century a Unique Type of Undead-Corpse? *Folklore* 117(3), 241–260.

Kiessling, N.K. 1968. Grendel: A New Aspect. *Modern Philology* 65(3), 191–201.

Maclagan, R.C. 1897. Ghost Lights of the West Highlands. *Folklore* 8(3), 203–256.

Meade, A. 2015. *Charlie Hebdo cartoon depicting drowned child Alan Kurdi sparks racism debate* [viewed 29 March 2017]. Available from: https://www.theguardian.com/media/2016/jan/14/charlie-hebdo-car-toon-depicting-drowned-child-alan-kurdi-sparks-racism-debate.

Miall, D.S., 1984. Guilt and Death: The Predicament of The Ancient Mariner. *Studies in English Literature*, 1500–1900, 24(4), 633–653.

Morris, W. and Magnusson, E. *trans*. 1892. *Eyrbyggja* ('The Saga of the Ere-Dwellers') [viewed 29 March 2017]. Available from: http://www.sagadb.org/eyrbyggja_saga.en.

Morris, W. and Magnusson, E. *trans*. 1900. *Grettir's Saga* [viewed 29 March 2017]. Available from: http://sagadb.org/grettis_saga.en.

Press, M.A.C. *trans*. 1880. *The Laxdale Saga* [viewed 29 March 2017]. Available from: http://sagadb.org/laxdaela_saga.en.

Rosen, Y. 2012. *U.S. Coast Guard scuttles Japanese tsunami ship* [viewed 29 March 2017]. Available from: http://uk.reuters.com/article/us-usa-tsunami-ship-idUSBRE8341D820120406.

Sample, I. 2016. *How long was 'mummified' German sailor adrift?* [viewed 29 March 2017. Available from: https://www.theguardian.com/science/2016/mar/01/how-long-was-mummified-german-sailor-adrift.

Simpson, J., 1966. Otherworld Adventures in an Icelandic Saga. *Folklore* 77(1), 1–20.

Sinclair, A., 1982. William Golding's The Sea, The Sea. *Twentieth Century Literature*, 28(2), 171–180.

Stanton, J. 2016. *'I will never understand how or why I have carried the dead body of a three-year-old boy': Rescuers reveal THREE HUNDRED infants have drowned trying to get to Europe since Aylan Kurdi six months ago* [viewed 29 March 2017]. Available from: http://www.dailymail.co.uk/news/article-3444475/I-never-under-stand-carried-dead-body-three-year-old-boy-Rescuers-reveal-THREE-infants-drowned-trying-Europe-Aylan-Kurdi-six-months-ago.html.

Vandersall, A.L., 1972. The Date and Provenance of the Franks Casket. *Gesta* 11(2), (1972), 9–26.

Vésteinn, Ó., and Tómasson, S. 2006. The Middle Ages. In: D.L. NEIJMAN, ed. *A History of Icelandic Literature*. Lincoln: University of Nebraska Press, pp.1–173.

Vesteinsson, O. 2011. A note on the regional distribution of pagan burials in Iceland. *ArchaeologiaIslandica* 9 (2011), 41–49.

Chapter 2

The Depths of our Experience: Thalassophobia and the Oceanic Horror

Seán J. Harrington

'The most merciful thing in the world, I think, is the inability of the human mind to correlate all its contents. We live on a placid island of ignorance in the midst of black seas of infinity, and it was not meant that we should voyage far.'
(H.P. Lovecraft, *The Call of Cthulhu*, 1928: 1)

The deep sea offers us an oppressive and foreboding context – a space unexplored, unknowable and overwhelming. In the farthest reaches of this abyss there is only darkness; light can barely penetrate past 200 metres and beyond these depths the sea is populated by monstrous creatures of the real, the fictional and the 'possible'. The sea offers a fleeting experience of an absolutely unknowable realm – less than 5% of the Earth's waters have been explored and only a handful of humans have travelled beyond the 'hadal zone' of 20,000 feet into the deep (Than, 2012). The open sea has been subject to our fascination since the earliest attempts at sea faring, and has since been repeatedly visited through our scientific explorations and our imaginative speculations.

These two discourses of science and speculation are confronted with profound gaps and voids when approaching the Real of the deep sea. The deep sea is a place and context that offers disturbing reflections on the precarious nature of the boundaries of knowledge, and more specifically as I shall argue, knowledge of the self. In Lacanian terms, the 'self' or ego is the image we acquire in the tenuous attempts at identification with a specular image – the reflection in the mirror. It will be argued that the gap between the concept of self/ego and the Real is analogous to the confrontation of scientific knowledge with the seemingly unknowable reality of the abyssal, uncharted ocean. These dichotomies represent an experience of boundary; the psychical safety of the self is met with fear and anxiety in the revelation that there is something more beyond the limits of human experience. This fear of boundaries is central to our understanding of thalassophobia, a phobic response to the sea and deep, open water. It will be proposed that these gaps between the known and the unknown generate an anxiety related to the experience of profound depth in the sea. Yet these gaps offer our speculative engagement a never ending fount of fantasy horrors. This structure will be addressed in terms of the mirror stage, the Lacanian Real, and what Freud (1930) references as an 'oceanic feeling'. The particular horror discussed in this paper can perhaps be best referred to as an *oceanic horror*.

The structure of this oceanic horror will become all the clearer through an exploration of media that plays on the innate anxiety of transgression of boundaries and the experience of limitlessness. Discussed within this chapter are the fictional cosmic horrors of Howard Philips Lovecraft, and the pseudo-scientific explorations of The History Channel's *MonsterQuest*. Lovecraft and *MonsterQuest* might seem like unnatural bedfellows, the former being a purveyor of weird fiction with the later offering highly sensationalised pseudo-documentaries about the existence of monsters, yet both offer up confrontations with the horror of oceanic depth and darkness, the space occupied by the greatest and most fearful of sea monsters.

A story of the sea...

Let me begin my discussion by relaying a genuine story of the deep, an authentic big-fish-story. In the places I grew up, I was always close to the sea. My father was an avid fisherman and there were many occasions that we embarked on adventures to go fishing on the open sea. Each of these expeditions I found utterly fascinating; for me the most simultaneously exciting and disquieting part of deep-sea fishing was (and still is) looking overboard into the deep – my distorted reflection on the choppy surface and the unknowable depths lurking behind it. The simultaneous excitement and anxiety that I experienced when looking overboard was amplified when coupled with the rare and often unexpected event in which we caught something on our lines.

On one such occasion my fishing line went taught and I began to reel it in, while tensely watching the point in the sea where my line met the choppy water. Looking past my distorted reflection on the surface, all I could see was the deep and dark blue of the ocean below me and I knew something below, something deeper than light could penetrate, was attached to my line and slowly rising to the surface. Eventually a white shape started to appear, a glimmer at first and then larger and clearer as it drew closer to the boat. This thing was fiercely resisting my attempt to bring it to the surface, this unwilling token from the deep, dark depths, darting about below the face of the tumultuous sea... In good Lovecraftian fashion, all I can tell you is that when it eventually emerged this Thing was an eldritch and primitive form that defied all description – or truth be told, I could describe it, but that would take all the fun out of my story and the point from my little anecdote. For now, let me simply say that my own epic struggle with this beastly haddock of the deep reminds me of Nietzsche's portentous lines from *Beyond Good and Evil*:

> He who fights with monsters should look to it that he himself does not become a monster. And when you gaze long into an abyss the abyss also gazes into you. (Nietzsche, 1886, pp. 102)

The first part of this woefully overused quotation speaks to our fears of tackling an unpleasant and fearsome apparition – the monstrous, and shall be left till later in our discussion when I have presented some creatures of the deep. For now I would like to talk about this second line – the very special gaze we extend to the depths of the sea and the two unsettling points of reflection from which our gaze is returned.

Reflections and the surface of the sea

As we gaze into the abyss of the deep sea, what is it what we see? A mirrored surface and the depths behind it. The reflective nature of the sea is the frequent subject of fictions and folk-tales. Indeed, many old Irish sea stories are structured by an equivalency existing between sea and land. Fine examples of these stories can be found in Lady Augusta Gregory's 1920 collection *Visions and Beliefs in the West of Ireland*, many of which begin with the axiom:'It's said there's everything in the sea the same as on the land' (Gregory, 1920). The sea reflects objects and creatures; whether they be people or animals, the sea has its equivalent. The line above, from 'Account of A Man on the Height near Dun Conor', continues with ominous tales of 'sea-horses'. This story, and others like it, depict the sea as an uncannily similar space to land yet threatening in its differences:

> This boy here saw a horse one time out in the sea, a grey one, swimming about. And there were three men from the north island caught a horse in their nets one night when they were fishing for mackerel, but they let it go; it would have broke the boat to bits if they had brought it in, and anyhow they thought it was best to leave it. One year at Kinvara, the people were missing their oats that was eaten in the fields, and they watched one night and it was five or six of the sea-horses they saw eating the oats, but they could not take them, they made off to the sea. (Gregory, 1920)

These sea horses are the apparitions that mirror horses as they appear on land, but they are ultimately unsettling, ambivalent creatures from another, darker world. The horses do not come to graze, they come to steal oats and even, according to other stories, to steal women before returning to the sea. When we look to the sea for reflection, what returns to us is a distorted and threatening facsimile.

The mirrored surface of the ocean is rarely still enough for us to see the reflection of our faces, yet the deep sea has a reflective quality that we find even more dubious than the reversed image we find in mirrors. In Lacan's

(1949) conception of the *mirror stage*, he suggests there is a key developmental moment in our psychical life in which we constitute a sense of self based on our first experience of a mirror. This mirror can be a literal reflective surface, or the experience of the social sphere responding to our presence (the figurative mirror of the other's gaze). He suggests that the mirror (literal or figurative) poses a conundrum – we see an image that we take to be the self: our delimited sense of being. This reflection seems coherent and boundaried, a form that provides a semblance of a whole – that helps to consolidate an egoistic subject, who prior to this moment experiences a fragmentary state of consciousness – unsure of where the Other begins and the body of the subject ends. We see in our reflection that the hands and legs that float in front of our vision are parts to a whole; we see the eyes that we look through, planted in our face which expresses our emotions through smiles, grimaces etc.

The conundrum of course, is that it is a mistake to take this delimited and boundaried form as our self in its corporeal entirety – it is simply an image. Yet the importance we invest in this image sets the up a looming crisis for the subject. In support of this, Lacan (1949) also notes that while both young chimps and human babies can recognize their reflection in a mirror, it is only the human baby that takes this image to be their own body. The subject is never really free of this confusion – the experience of regarding an imaginary representation, of the self as the self, will cause tension throughout our lifespan (Lacan, 1948), as the tendency to over-invest images with significance becomes a fundamental attribute of the subject's gaze.

This is what leads Lacan (1954) to refer to the 'recognition' in front of the self as our '*méconnaissance*', which can be translated as 'misunderstanding', 'failed knowledge' or perhaps even 'mis-knowledge'. We are more than what is contained in this image of the corpus; the motions and depths of the psyche are poorly captured in an image and yet this mirage is captivating, and it is on the basis of this image that the Ego is formed.

In Lacan's (1949) formulation of the mirror stage the Ego represents a token or object which takes on the significance of 'who-we-think-we-are'. Yet as the Ego is founded on the basis of a fundamental '*méconnaissance*' it has an alienating potential – we are not an image on a reflective surface; we are also the profound depth underneath. The symbolic dimension of the Ego stems from the need for this image to be validated within the social sphere – the image allows for a representation of the self to be located within a symbolic relation to the Other. The function of the image and ego is predicated on a fantasy and therefore belongs to the imaginary register as much as the symbolic. Lacan (1954) also suggests that like consciousness itself, the Ego functions to cover the unconscious depths of the psyche. Our Ego thus has a protective capacity that allows the subject to mediate the primal drives of the Id, but as it is founded on a misrecognition it is also the basis for a problematic and tenuous structuring of the psyche.

To sum up – the mirror stage initially marks the subject's entry into an imaginary relation with the body and a symbolic relation to the Other. The creation of an image that the subject takes to be their own body lays the groundwork for these relations by enabling the possibility of an Ego, a point from which an 'I' can exist. The image we have reflected back to us is a false representation – a *méconnaissance*. The person in the mirror is not us but a distorted image we take to be a stand-in for the self. What lies behind this image is the depths of the unconscious, all that which is repressed and unacceptable to the conscious mind. This is the point of tension with the image, as if we are waiting and watching for something else to 'break the surface' – exposing the Real: that which appears between the cracks of our conscious experience.

The problematic relation to the specular image is neatly represented by the reflection we experience on the surface of the sea. We see a reflection of the world above that is obviously disrupted by the motions and currents of the deep sea. The gaps that appear in this image betray the depths below: a realm that is outside our knowledge and perhaps even beyond our wildest fantasies. The unknowable depths of the the sea pose a problem for the consciousness; they reflect our fear of what is beyond the limits of our comprehension, as the experience of depth reflects something else – the Real. The Real of the deep sea disrupts our imaginary attempts to delimit our experience, to fit our reality into a boundaried fantasy – such as we try to do in our relation to the mirror image, shimmering on the surface of the sea. These depths reflect the Real of Lacan's late work, that which is beyond the limits of signification and fantasy. It is that which defies our attempts at representation; it is the realm beyond boundaries of the social order; it is jouissance and chaos.

The Real, depth and oceanic horror

The Real within psychoanalysis is an ever changing construct and indeed across the work of Lacan the Real took on a range of significance. In his later work the Real becomes a register opposed to the symbolic and the imaginary orders (Lacan, 1974–1975). He postulated that the Real is that which cannot be signified or approached through imaginary or symbolic engagement. The Real presents us with a great hole in our subjectivity, a gap – that our investment in the specular image tries to cover up. Nonetheless, the Real is experienced all the same – and is experienced unconsciously as the core of trauma (Lacan, 1954–1955). Trauma in turn is a gap in signification, it is a profound source of anxiety.

While the Real as we have described it is a threatening immensity, it also holds a fascination and attraction for the subject. The Real is the domain of jouissance – the gratification that rests beyond the pleasure principle, the end-goal of Freud's (1920) death drive – our drive towards self-destruction and subjective obliteration. As Lacan summarizes in his 1938 paper *Family Formations*:

> the nostalgias of humanity: the metaphysical mirage of universal harmony; the mystical abyss of affective fusion; the social utopia of totalitarian dependency – all derived from the longings for a paradise lost before birth and from the most obscure aspirations for death. (Lacan, 1938)

The 'nostalgia' referred to is this tendency in within the subject that wishes to undo their own subjectivity, to return to a point of fragmented immediacy. For Lacan (1972–1973) it is this drive that motivates us to love, and in turn to obliterate the symbolic distance between the self and the Other. It is the death drive that thus underlies our fascination with both death, depth and, as Freud argued – religious experience. These are the contexts of jouissance – the experience of limitlessness that overwhelms and destroys our subjectivity (Lacan, 1966: 694)

In *Civilisation and its Discontents*, Freud (1927) discusses the energic value he describes as an 'Oceanic Feeling', which is brought on by moments of religious transcendence. Interestingly, Freud argues that this particular 'feeling' is beyond scientific enquiry and contra to the Reality Principle. It is a bliss that is afforded an ego that seeks to go beyond the bounds of the Pleasure Principle – the domain to which Lacan (1966) situates jouissance and the free-fall of signification as represented by the traumatic potential of the Real. Perhaps this polarity of experience, between traumatic torment and religious bliss, explain the curious draw of the phobic object for the phobic subject – why the acrophobic person feels that they will jump off a high building when staring over the edge, or why the thalassophobe keeps imagining what lies beneath the surface of the ocean which they claim to be afraid of. It is my argument that the conceptual transparency between the Real and this Oceanic Feeling, is perhaps better captured by the term *oceanic horror* – the terror that comes from the discord between the reflective surface and the depths beneath, that draws our gaze into dark places from which we may never return.

Emergence, the Thing from the deep

Having discussed the two points of reflection that return our gaze into the sea, and termed the experience 'oceanic horror', we must now turn our attention to the next part of our story and the first half of Nietzsche's quotation: monstrosity – the Thing that returns from the depths.

Hopefully the more memorable element of my 'big fish story' is that moment of emergence, a creature rising to the surface that encapsulates the deep's 'unknowable' nature. In my earlier discussion I made mention of the 'Thing', referring to Lacan's (1959: 51) discussions of Freud's *das Ding*. The Thing in this instance is a token of the Real, it is an object of trauma, an uncanny creature rising from the depths of the unconscious – too Real to be signified. Thus the 'emergence' of the Thing from the depths, is perhaps better described as a 'resurgence' – implying that what is traveling to the surface has already been here before, just lurking outside of conscious experience. The Thing from the deep frightens us as an uncanny token of our unconscious – a reflection of the traumatic and oppressive experience of the Real. The Thing literally 'breaks the surface' and disrupts our tenuous image on the surface of the sea. It threatens to overwhelm and destroy our fragile Ego. This experience of that which is beyond our limits is precisely a moment of confrontation with the Thing. The emergence that threatens our subjectivity is precisely that which features in 'the money shot' of stories structured by the aforementioned oceanic horror – the moment that the impossible creature of the deep breaks the surface and reflects back to us the limits of our subjectivity.

Beyond Lovecraft, visualising the oceanic horror

The gaps I have mentioned, between the Real and Symbolic/Imaginary realms, have previously been addressed in the philosophic discussions of speculative realism – specifically within the work of Graham Harman (2012). Harman describes Lovecraft's work as an exercise in 'weird realism'. Realism being weird as 'reality' is beyond empirical attempts to reduce or measure it. In a sense he is simply reaffirming the the Real is beyond signification. Harman proposes that it is this failure of scientific discourse that haunted the work of H.P. Lovecraft. The gaps between the known and unknown are the central points of the Lovecraftian story, indeed it is these gaps that Lovecraft situates his darkest apparitions and horrors.

The turbulent imagination of Lovecraft filled fictitious seas with monsters, aliens and old gods; eldritch apparitions beyond our comprehension and frequently defying all description. Lovecraft's use of the 'indescribable' within his stories is what gives them their most unsettling and memorable moments. Into these carefully crafted aesthetic gaps we project our own archaic horror – the primordial fear of envelopment by the existential void of the Real. The aesthetic gaps within these stories can be related to their failure to materialise as effective visual media, where previously 'indescribable' elements of his stories are continually realised and exhibited – through kitsch practical effects (*From Beyond* (1986), *The Unnamable* (1988) and unsuccessful, dis-enchanting CGI (*Dagon* (2001)). Conversely, some renderings of Lovecraft's work have paid homage to the mystery beyond description, such as Daniel Gildark's *Cthulhu* (2007). The work of HP Lovecraft is all about the disruptive 'truths' that threaten and break our sense of 'reality'. His work is about the gaps in and depths of our experience, and more to the point the things that emerge from these depths that threaten to break our world apart.

HP Lovecraft was born into proud anglophilic family in Providence RI in 1890, portrayed by biographers as a figure out of place, asexual, alien and from another time (Houellebecq, 1988 and Roland, 2014). His works have had a profound influence on American science fiction and horror, with such notables as Stephen King, H.R. Giger and Guillermo del Toro, all claiming his influence. Despite his far-reaching influence Lovecraft would die in relative obscurity and with little critical success in his lifetime. Perhaps what Lovecraft is best known for today, is his distinct literary style and his complex fictional mythos.

Lovecraft has an easily identifiable use of language – he was a man who liked his obscure adjectives; his creatures and places would frequently be described as 'gibbous', 'eldritch' or 'cosmic'. Of particular interest to us is his tendency to overuse description, yet the central horror of his stories would always be left as gaps; the creatures, old gods and aliens would make their appearance, but would often be left as indescribable and defying all description. A classic example of this is his 1928 story *The Call of Cthulhu*, in which he spends a great deal of time discussing the dark, godlike creature Cthulhu, yet when the first of his characters lays eyes on Cthulhu itself, all he can say is that: 'The Thing cannot be described – there is no language for such abysms of shrieking and immemorial lunacy, such eldritch contradictions of all matter, force, and cosmic order' (Lovecraft, 1928).

The Lovecraftian horror is fundamentally 'unknowable', there is a core to his characters that is beyond signification, something traumatic and Real. His creatures are from other realms that are frequently decided as 'deep' or dark. His monstrosities come from the depths of time, deep space, deep holes in the ground or from the deep sea. They are from a space beyond human comprehension and experience and the revelation of their existence turns their discoverers mad (*At the Mountains of Madness* (1931), *The Lurking Fear* (1932)) or leaves them dead or in danger (*The Shadow over Innsmouth* (1936), *The Call of Cthulhu* (1928) and *Dagon* (1919)).

The structure of the Lovecraftian text is dependent on the oceanic horror that we have postulated and theorised. The conflict within his stories is predicated on a Thing rising from the depths of the unknown; this Thing is threatening due to its origins beyond human experience and its centrally indescribable nature. The Lovecraftian horror is dependent on *resurgence*. This structure is perhaps best exemplified through a brief telling of Lovecraft's first published short story, and arguably the 'ur-text' to the numerous tales that would follow: *Dagon* (1919).

Dagon is written in the first person; we are told that it is the account of a sailor who is in mortal danger, having survived a dark ordeal. The sailor had been serving on a ship sunk by the German navy in WWI, he escapes from the Germans in a small boat and tries to navigate his way home. While he traverses the sea he comes across an island, the surface of which is desolate and devoid of life, though it is covered in dead and decaying sea-life. The appearance of the island leads him to believe that the land mass was brought to the surface by an underwater volcanic eruption; it is the deep ocean-floor, brought to the surface to be exposed to daylight for the first time. He decides to explore the island and sets off towards a high mound, in the middle of which there is a gully so deep that it still holds water. At the edge of this lapping water there is a stone idol, carved by what he assumes were non-human hands. As he marvels and wonders at the otherworldly creatures evidenced by this obelisk, he is startled:

> Then suddenly I saw it. With only a slight churning to mark its rise to the surface, the thing slid into view above the dark waters. Vast, Polyphemus-like, and loathsome, it darted like a stupendous monster of nightmares to the monolith, about which it flung its gigantic scaly arms, the while it bowed its hideous head and gave vent to certain measured sounds. I think I went mad then. (Lovecraft, 1919, pp. 4)

The sailor flees the scene, confessing he does not fully remember his journey back to his boat, or indeed his journey back home after being found by the crew of a passing ship. The fleeting moment of contact with the Thing from the deep sea has left him traumatised and mad and no one will believe his stories. He attempts to communicate what he saw to an academic, a representative of scientific discourse and indeed 'knowledge', yet he is unable to render what he has seen into words the professor will understand or believe. The story ends with our narrator about to leap out his window to his death, convinced that the monstrous entities of the deep have returned and are at his door.

As mentioned, the death or doom of the narrator is a common trope of Lovecraft's stories – which frequently end in madness, suicide and approaching danger. The penultimate horror is faced, yet is ultimately indescribable. The only witness is broken and doomed by the experience, which exposes the traumatic space beyond experience, a trauma from which they can never recover. The death of the narrator is essentially the obliteration of the story's subjective voice. This death is a direct consequence of the collision with the Thing – the apparition of the Real made flesh, framed through floral description and a wealth of adjectives. This is perhaps why adaptations of Lovecraft's work have struggled to recreate the 'oceanic horror' that structures his texts – as it is dependent on a core unknown. The oceanic horror of the Lovecraftian monster might be framed in floral description, but at its core it is a traumatising void that destroys the narrator.

The Thing confounds our fantasies, it is outside of the imaginary and *beyond the image*. Perhaps the attempt to capture this Thing in visual media (i.e. film) is doomed to fail, by virtue of this core piece of the Real. While the creature on screen might hold a horrific appearance, it will never hold the terror for us that it did when it was beyond sight, lurking off screen and in the darkness of possibility. Our disenchantment with terror is only furthered when this creature is imagined into being through clunky CGI, poor animatronics or even poorer latex costumes. The oceanic horror must be experienced as a gap or absence, its central being must be kept off screen; it is this which puts the Lovecraftian text somewhat at odds with screen media, which has as its prerogative the need to show and make things *seen*. It is in the rendering into the visual field that leaves films such as *The Unnnamable* (1988), *From Beyond* (1986), *H.P. Lovecraft's Necronomicon* (1994) or *Dagon* (2001) so devoid of the unsettling horror that makes the Lovecraftian story so memorable. Each of these films can offer up an assortment of satisfying practical effects, with beastly creatures formed by latex, animatronics and puppetry, but they all suffer from the same urge to show too much. There is no absence which breaks and unsettles our narrators and protagonists, and it is precisely the lack of the believability of these 'traumatic experiences' that disrupts our suspension of disbelief in the filmic space. Among the adaptations and films inspired by Lovecraft, only one that I have come across touches on the unique uncanny value of the oceanic horror.

Daniel Gildark's 2007 film *Cthulhu* is an odd adaptation of Lovecraft's *The Shadow over Innsmouth* (1936). It takes the same basic story structure as the original text though it places it in a contemporary setting on the eve of some unknown apocalypse. The protagonist is a young academic, Russ, who is returning to his home town for his mother's funeral. His father is the head of a cult that worships Cthulhu, an entity whose home is in the deep sea. Russ is reunited with Mike, the love interest of his youth, and together they embark on a dark and confusing journey of discovery to uncover a sacrificial plot to conjure Cthulhu and bring up from the depths a new future for humankind. Over the course of the film Russ becomes increasingly haunted and troubled by his dreams, the supernatural happens around him and his rape by several members of the cult seeking to attain his genetic material. The film ends with a broken Russ on the sea shore amongst his father's cult, standing in front of Mike with a sacrificial blade in hand. His father asks him to sacrifice Mike and the film ends, we are unsure what happens – if Russ has been indoctrinated into his father's cult, or if he decides to strike his father and save Mike.

Cthulhu is structured by gaps and absence, framed in stark tantalising images that set the tone for horrors from beyond the filmic space. Cthulhu is never seen, but he is referred to. We see his agents in the form of monstrous fish-people as Russ negotiates the subterranean network of tunnels below the town, using only a camera's flash for a source of light. These creatures are only experienced for brief fractions of a second as the camera's flash goes off, before being called back into the pitch blackness of the tunnels. Upon Russ's escape from this place, he can convince no one of their existence.

Perhaps the most striking scene of the film is the protagonist's lucid dream of a sacrificial offering. Russ finds himself standing on a stormy beach, wearing ceremonial dark clothing similar to his father's. He confidently strides across the beach exposing to the viewer a great wooden cube. Limbs come out of the gaps in the box and we see that it is full of people, an offering to something in the tumultuous sea. Again, the Cthulhu is not seen, he is out of view and out of the filmic space – he is experienced as a foreboding absence that will bring about some form of cataclysm. In the film's final scene with Russ and the cult on the sea shore, the camera approaches over the sea towards the long strands of the town's beaches and we see masses of people coming out of the sea, harbingers of the deep. While *Cthulhu* might seem disappointing for those that want to see the monstrosity lurking below the waves, the film manages to capture the core of Lovecraft's oceanic horrors – fear of that which lies below, in the great unknown that is beyond our experience.

MonsterQuest

The moments that we get a sense of the dark forces looming below the waves in *Cthulhu* present us with an experience of lack – in this case the horror is alluded to continually, exposing the limits of our experience of the filmic space, and in turn a limit of our knowledge as viewers. It is interesting then that one of the rare occasions that this particular sense of oceanic horror is captured in visual media is in a fleeting moment of the History Channel's *MonsterQuest*.

MonsterQuest was marketed as a series of sensationalist documentaries claiming to be searching for the existence of monsters. Each episode across their four seasons would take as its subject a different cryptid and go about searching for evidence in support of the existence of the creature in question.

At its base, the series represents a flirtation with realms of possibility. We never see any compelling evidence for the creatures, and often we the audience come away even less convinced of the existence of monsters than before we began watching. Each episode follows a simple format; a portentous narrator provides the structure and narrative we follow in pursing the beast in question, while we are also provided with information from a host of 'experts' and 'witnesses' who all weigh in their opinions and experience. The experts come from a range of background; some are actual scientists and academics, others are rangers, divers and occasionally cryptozoologists – people that claim an expert understanding of cryptids.

In the episode titled 'Black Demon Shark' we are taken to the Sea of Cortez off the coast of California, where we are told there have been rumours of a large aggressive shark that possibly reaches lengths of 60ft. We are told by the narrator that this is made possible by the bountiful prey available and the sea's great depths – reaching over 12,000 feet in some places. Our narrator continually reminds us that anything could potentially be in these waters. *MonsterQuest* is perpetually flirting with the realms of possibility as it goes over pieces of evidence that could point to the existence of the creature under discussion, only to leave as many open questions as possible for the viewer. They will take the story of a fisherman whose boat was nearly turned over by what he claimed to be the giant tail of a shark, only to offer up other possible explanations – that the tail could belong to a whale shark – then to return to open the question again: what is it? Could it be the mysterious shark for which there is no evidence? Or was it the more likely explanation – one of the many known creatures that frequent the area. The episode is arrayed with experts (technicians, biologists), 'witnesses' (sea stories, second hand accounts) and the narrator (boldly speculating where many have speculated before). For this episode the mysteries of the deep sea are left just at that; the mystery of the black demon shark opens questions but answers none. In a sense they are flirting with a horror that never truly crystallises beyond the half-remembered stories of fishermen.

The episodes typically end as they begin, the surface of the water undisturbed by their ineffectual inquiries. At their most menacing, *MonsterQuest* simply exposes us to a realm of light-entertainment. In most episodes of *MonsterQuest* the Thing fails to materialise; there is no point where the Real interrupts or disrupts our fantasmatic engagement with the stories being tirelessly reproduced in their compelling, but ultimately unconvincing fashion. *MonsterQuest* is often a disappointing reaffirmation of the reality we know. The banality of reality offers a point of narrative closure at the end of every episode, as experts remain unconvinced, and witnesses are ultimately discredited. All except for one episode of course – which gives us the tiniest of glimpses into a bizarre, uncanny and threatening realm – that of the deep, deep sea.

'Giant Squid Found'

Titled 'Giant Squid Found' (2007) *MonsterQuest* assembles its curious team of experts (in this case divers, technicians and biologists), 'witnesses' (sea stories, second hand accounts) and the narrator (boldly speculating). They are in search of a giant squid, once again taking them to the Sea of Cortez off the coast of California. The Sea of Cortez is apparently the perfect possible hiding place for a squid of giant proportions, with depths of up to 12,000 feet in places.

The *MonsterQuest* diver-team consult biologists and audio-visual technicians to formulate a plan for capturing images of a giant squid. As larger squid tend to cannibalise smaller specimens, the team decide to attach a camera to a tethered Humboldt Squid and set it loose into the sea. The smaller squid reaches 1000ft into the black depths below into the boat, but the team cannot see the recordings until the squid is brought back aboard. Much to our surprise they capture 'the money shot' – startling images of what is possibly a squid of giant proportions.

We catch a glimpse of a creature, a monstrous beast of the deep; having sent the footage to a range of experts they set about analysing how big the creature could be and what species it belongs to. Dr Roger Hanlon (a marine biologist) simply says 'it's big!'. The inventor of the camera meanwhile, is quite willing to speculate and estimates that the suckers on the tentacles would be the size of coffee cups. Their final expert – Peter Schmidtz (a video forensics expert from Motion Engineering) attempts to judge the squid's size taking into account the camera's light/recording performance in salt water and points on the squid's anatomy. He estimates that based on distance between beak and eye, the squid could potentially be 108 feet in length with arms over a foot and a half in diameter... Quite a monster indeed! This scene provides the proverbial 'money shot'; it gives us the resurgence of the horrific Real of the deep sea. The creature that we have this passing glimmer of, that 'might' exist in truly monstrous form, is the crystallisation we seek, the traumatic and monstrous form of the deep sea made flesh.

This moment of confrontation with something beyond the realms of known science is utterly compelling, particularly in a setting that should reaffirm our cynicism in regarding what is below the surface of the sea. From the depths we see an apparition come forth, a Thing from the deep that disrupts the shaky foundations of our science and subjectivity. Scientists, as they appear in *MonsterQuest*, tend to reassure us that our subjectivity is boundaried, that monsters and giant sea beasts do not exist. Here we have a moment where the gap between the known and unknown is exposed, a great and threatening creature that is experienced as a void in our experience, a great chasm beneath our superficial engagement and identification with the surface, that reflects back to us the safety of the imaginary and symbolic foundations of ourselves and our subjectivity. We are exposed to the Real of the deep sea – the great unknown – an experience beyond limits of scientific discourse and empirically established knowledge as shaky representatives of the symbolic order. It represents the unknown fathoms of the sea, the space beyond our perceptions, framed in the nonsensical preamble of weird science and weirder speculation. It is in fact speculation made flesh, the centre of which is a great hole or mystery – a gap that exposes the tenuous limits of our knowledge and the depths of our experience, a truly oceanic horror indeed.

References

Cthulhu (2007) [Film] Dir. Gildark, D., USA: Regent Releasing.

Dagon (2001) [Film] Dir. Gordon, S., USA: Lionsgate International.

Freud, S. (1920) *Beyond the Pleasure Principle*, DuFresne, T. (Ed.) Richter, G. (Trans.) London and Peterborough ON: Broadview Press.

Freud, S. (1923) 'The Ego and the Id' In *On Metapsychology*, Richards, A. (Ed.) Strachey, J. (Trans.) London: Penguin Books, pp.339–401.

Freud, S. (1930) *Civilisation and its Discontents*, McLintock, D. (Trans.) London: Penguin Books.

From Beyond (1986) [Film] Dir. Gordon, S., USA: Empire Pictures.

Gregory, A. (1920) *Visions and Beliefs in the West of Ireland* (Online) Source: http://www.sacred-texts.com/neu/celt/vbwi/vbwi02.htm [Accessed: 21:12:2016].

Harman, G. (2012) *Weird Realism: Lovecraft and Philosophy*, London: Zero Books.

Houellebecq, M. (1988) *H. P. Lovecraft: Against the World, Against Life*, London: Orion Publishing.

Lacan, J. (1938) *Family Complexes in the Formation of the Individual*, Gallagher, C. (Trans.) (Online) Source: http://www.lacaninireland.com/web/?page_id=123 [Accessed: 23:01:2017].

Lacan, J. (1948) 'Aggressivity in Psychoanalysis' in Lacan, J. (1989) *Ecrits: A Selection*, Sheridan, A. (Trans.) New York: W. W. Norton, pp. 9–32.

Lacan, J. (1949) 'The Mirror Stage as formative of the function of the *I* as revealed in psychoanalytic experience' in Lacan, J. (1989) *Ecrits: A Selection*, Sheridan, A. (Trans.) New York: W. W. Norton, pp. 1–8.

Lacan, J. (1954) 'On Narcissism' In *The Seminar of Jacques Lacan Book 1: Freud's Papers on Technique*, Miller, J. A. (Ed.) Forrester, J. (Trans.) London and New York: W. W. Norton and Company, pp.107–117.

Lacan, J. (1954–1955) *The Seminar of Jacques Lacan, Book II: The Ego in Freud's Theory and in the Technique of Psychoanalysis (ed. J-A Miller)*, N.Y.: Norton, 1988.

Lacan, J. (1954) *The Seminar of Jacques Lacan Book 1: Freud's Papers on Technique*, Miller, J. A. (Ed.) Forrester, J. (Trans.) London and New York: W. W. Norton and Company.

Lacan, J. (1957) *Le Seminaire Livre IV: La relation d'objet*, Paris: Éditions Du Seuil.

Lacan, J. (1959) 'Das Ding' In *The Ethics of Psychoanalysis*, Miller, J. A. (Ed.) Porter, D. (Trans.), pp.51–69.

Lacan, J. (1966) 'The Subversion of the Subject and the Dialectic of Desire in the Freudian Unconscious' In *Écrits*, Fink, B. (Trans.) London and New York: W. W. Norton and Company, pp.671–702.

Lacan, J. (1972–1973) *The Seminar of Jacques Lacan Book XX: On Feminine Sexuality, The Limits of Love and Knowledge* Miller, J. A. (Ed.) Fink, B. (Trans.) London and New York: W. W. Norton and Company.

Lacan, J. (1973) *The Four Fundamental Concepts of Psychoanalysis*, Miller, J. A. (Ed.) Sheridan, A. (Trans.) London and New York: Karnac Books.

Lacan, J. (1974–1975). *Le séminaire. Book 22: R.S.I*, Gallagher, C. (Trans.) (Online) Source: http://www.lacaninireland.com/web/wp-content/uploads/2010/06/RSI-Complete-With-Diagrams.pdf [Accessed: 23:04:17].

Lovecraft, H.P. (1919) 'Dagon' in *H.P. Lovecraft: The Complete Cthulhu Mythos Tales*, New York: Barnes and Noble, pp.1–5.

Lovecraft, H.P. (1928) 'The Call of Cthulhu' in *H.P. Lovecraft: The Complete Cthulhu Mythos Tales*, New York: Barnes and Noble, pp.36–61.

Lovecraft, H.P. (1931) 'At the Mountains of Madness' in *H.P. Lovecraft: The Complete Cthulhu Mythos Tales*, New York: Barnes and Noble, pp.258–344.

Lovecraft, H.P. (1932) *The Lurking Fear* (Online) Source: http://www.hplovecraft.com/writings/texts/fiction/lf.aspxD [Accessed: 22:01:2017].

Lovecraft, H.P. (1936) 'The Shadow over Innsmouth' in *H.P. Lovecraft: The Complete Cthulhu Mythos Tales*, New York: Barnes and Noble, pp.345–398.

'Black Demon Shark (2007) [DVD] *MonsterQuest* in *Monsterquest: Season 1*, USA: The History Channel.

'Giant Squid Found' (2007) [DVD] *MonsterQuest* in *Monsterquest: Season 1*, USA: The History Channel.

Nietzsche, F. (1886) *Beyond Good and Evil*, Hollingdale, R.J. (Trans.), London: Penguin Books.

Roland, P. (2014) *The Curious Case of H.P. Lovecraft*, London: Plexus.

Than, K.2012 'James Cameron Completes Record-Breaking Mariana Trench Dive' in National Geographic:http://news.nationalgeographic.com/news/2012/03/120325-james-cameron-mariana-trench-challenger-deepest-returns-science-sub/.

The Unnamable (1988) [Film] Dir. Ouellette, J.P., Italy: Vidmark Entertainment.

Chapter 3

From Depths of Terror to Depths of Wonder: The Sublime in Lovecraft's *Call of Cthulhu* and Cameron's *The Abyss*

Vivan Joseph

The sea can arouse a great variety of thoughts and feelings. Some people are inspired by the challenge of a sea-voyage, while others are made uneasy by the thought of having vast watery gulfs beneath them; though the play of light on water can be captivating, stormy seas will, for many, be terrifying. As air-breathing creatures, most of our experiences of the sea are likely to be liminal – we splash around its shores, and get little sense of what an aquatic existence might be like, floating on its surface. Life on this planet may have originated around deep-sea vents, but for us those abyssal places are inimical and alien. Because the deep parts of our seas and oceans have proved to be much more difficult to explore than remote areas of land, they have remained a reservoir of possibilities. Stories that set out to stretch our imagination by pushing at the boundary between the known and unknown have speculated about their hidden depths, and the creatures that might inhabit them.

Of course, the way we encounter the sea will influence our thoughts and feelings about it. Reading about the sea, or seeing visual depictions of it in films, will be a less immediate experience, but however we encounter it, the nature of our relationship with the sea forces us to acknowledge both its splendour and its dangers. An aesthetic concept that effectively captures this uncomfortable combination of qualities is the *sublime*. There might very well be a case to be made for thinking that a genuinely aesthetic appreciation of the sea, including depictions of it in the visual arts and literature, *requires* something like the sublime. My aim in what follows will be less ambitious. I will be arguing that we need the sublime in order to properly understand the role the sea plays in two particular works: H.P. Lovecraft's short story *The Call of Cthulhu*, and James Cameron's film *The Abyss*. Admittedly, to talk of *the* concept of the sublime may be a little misleading, given the variety of accounts of both the nature and the objects of the sublime over its "broad and deep history" (Brady 2013, p.1). Nevertheless, for at least part of that history, there is something the different theories have in common, as Robert Doran argues in his monograph on the sublime:

> ... what unites the key theories of sublimity, such as they were understood and articulated during the early modern period (1674–1790), is a common structure – the paradoxical experience of being at once *overwhelmed* and *exalted* – and a common concern: the preservation of a notion of transcendence in the face of the secularization of modern culture. (Doran, 2015 p.4)

In both Lovecraft's *The Call of Cthulhu* and Cameron's *The Abyss* the sea is used to combine spectacle and danger, awe and terror, as we would expect with experiences of the sublime. But, as I hope to show, the sublime plays a further role. In both the story and film – albeit in different ways – the sublimity of the sea becomes, in effect, a remedy for what Max Weber (1946, p.155) called the "disenchantment of the world". In picking out a certain kind of experience, the kind of experience of being both "overwhelmed and exalted", the sublime identifies a way of achieving what Robert Doran calls "secular transcendence", and with it the prospect of going, as the Roman author Longinus eloquently puts it, "beyond the limits that confine us" (Longinus 1995, p.277).

In the next section, I give a very brief and selective history of the sublime, from its Greek roots to its eighteenth century incarnation with Edmund Burke and Joseph Addison. In the following section, I examine the role of the sea in Lovecraft's *The Call of Cthulhu*, and consider an objection from Vivian Ralickas to the identification of Lovecraft's 'cosmic horror' with Burke's sublime. In the section after that, I turn to Cameron's *The Abyss*, focussing on three key parts of the film to bring out the sublime qualities of the sea, and to conclude I look at how the sublimity of the sea in the story and film might provide an antidote to Weber's "disenchantment of the world."

The Sublime

The aesthetic idea of the sublime has its roots in an incomplete Greek text, 'Peri Hypsous' (translated as 'On Sublimity'), from the first or third century AD, attributed to 'Longinus'.[*] The little that has been surmised about the author is derived from the text, which is a treatise on rhetoric.[**] For our purposes, one of the most relevant of the rhetorical techniques for producing sublimity that Longinus identifies is *visualization*, when the author uses her

---

[*]   Malcolm Heath (2012) has argued, against others, that the 'Longinus' in question is Cassius Longinus, a rhetorician and scholar from the third century AD.

[**]   See Doran (2015, pp.33–39) on the question of whether 'hypsos' (sublimity) as used by Longinus had a subjective and aesthetic dimension.

descriptive powers to excite the audience's imagination and make her imagery vivid (Longinus 1995, pp.215–217). 'Peri Hypsous' became widely known in Europe during the seventeenth and eighteenth centuries after its translation into French by the poet and critic Nicolas Boileau, in 1674. Doran, in his monograph, notes that Boileau occupies "a singular position" in the history of the sublime because he was "at once the midwife, champion and popularizer of this concept" (Doran 2015, p.97).

A decade and a half later, the English writer and critic John Dennis started the shift from the primarily rationally based sublime of Longinus towards a more emotional conception, describing walking in the Alps as "a delightful Horror", and "a terrible Joy" (quoted in Doran 2015, p. 125). In the early eighteenth century, the essayist Joseph Addison, in one of his pieces for the Spectator, singled out the sea as a source of such emotions:

> ... of all objects that I have ever seen, there is none which affects my imagination so much as the sea, or ocean. I cannot see the heavings of this prodigious bulk of waters, even in a calm, without a very pleasing astonishment; but when it is worked up in a tempest, so that the horizon on every side is nothing but foaming billows and floating mountains, it is impossible to describe the agreeable horror that rises from such a prospect. A troubled ocean, to a man who sails upon it, is, I think, the biggest object he can see in motion, and consequently gives his imagination one of the highest kinds of pleasure that can arise from greatness. (Addison, 1845, p.244).

Addison's "agreeable horror" is nearly identical to Dennis' "delightful horror", and their combination of almost contradictory constituents, together with the emphasis on natural objects of great size, became firmly associated with the sublime.

One of the best known eighteenth century writers on the sublime is Edmund Burke, with his 1757 'A Philosophical Enquiry into the Origin of our Ideas of the Sublime and Beautiful'. Like Dennis, Burke believed the most intense emotions most deeply affect us, and also that pain and terror produce the "strongest emotions which the mind is capable of feeling". That, in combination with the Longinian thesis that "inspired emotion" is a mark of the sublime, with sublime objects producing feelings of awe and astonishment (see Doran 2015, pp.72–74, pp.145–146), gives us an indication of why Burke identifies *terror* as the primary source of the sublime:

> Whatever is fitted in any sort to excite the ideas of pain, and danger, that is to say, whatever is in any sort terrible, or is conversant about terrible objects, or operates in a manner analogous to terror, is a source of the *sublime*; that is, it is productive of the strongest emotion which the mind is capable of feeling. I say the strongest emotion, because I am satisfied the ideas of pain are much more powerful than those which enter on the part of pleasure. (Burke, 1990, p.36)

The identification of terror as a mark of the sublime is, however, a little puzzling. Burke is equating the sublime with whatever is the source of "the strongest emotion the mind is capable of feeling" and identifying terror as that emotion, but to be in pain or be terrified of something does not seem to be a very desirable sort of experience to have. Yet, Addison's "agreeable horror" is supposed to produce "one of the highest kinds of pleasure", so the immediate question Burke must answer is how pain and terror can be at least desirable, if not also agreeable in some sense.

Burke provides an answer by qualifying the connection between danger and the sublime:

> When danger or pain press too nearly, they are incapable of giving any delight, and are simply terrible; but at certain distances, and with certain modifications, they may be, and they are delightful, as we every day experience. (Burke 1990, pp.36–37)

What Burke means by 'delight' here is something a little unusual – he means "the sensation which accompanies the removal of pain or danger" (Burke 1990, p.34). Delight, Burke maintains, is a relative pleasure and therefore different in kind from pleasure *simpliciter*. On Burke's binary division of the passions, there are those that are concerned with *self-preservation*, including the passions associated with pain and danger, and those that are concerned with *society*, which include the various forms of pleasure. The removal or distancing of pain is not, according to Burke, the same as pleasure, but it is – or certainly can be – agreeable: if pain or terror "are so modified as not to be actually noxious," "they are capable of producing delight; not pleasure, but a sort of delightful horror" (Burke 1990, p.123). Sources of the sublime in nature, Burke tells us, produce a kind of astonishment accompanied by "some degree of horror," where the mind is "entirely filled with its object" (Burke 1990, p.53). So great natural objects such as seas and oceans that can cause us to feel fear can, when the danger they pose is removed, avoided, or in some other way 'at a distance', be sources of the sublime. This not only accords well with what Addison meant by "agreeable horror," it also provides an explanation for *why* the horror is agreeable, in terms of self-preservation.[*]

On the picture of the sublime that is emerging, when we are confronted by great natural phenomena like mountains or oceans, they captivate us, replacing the predictable with new possibilities. As Burke's version of the sublime emphasises, what makes these possibilities thrilling is the presence of danger, setting our pulses racing and making us feel alive. Now, as an explanation of why we feel as we do in the presence of mountains and oceans it makes sense, but as an explanation of our encounters with the sea in literature and film, it seems to need some further argument. Since neither reading about the sea or watching a film that is set underwater involves any

---

[*] Burke's answer to the question of how horror can be 'agreeable' or 'delightful' was prefigured by Dennis – see Doran (2015, p.134).

actual danger to us as readers or audience, we need to know whether they can evoke the kind of emotions Burke's account requires.

The obstacle that appears to be in the way of attributing sublimity to fictions is, I suggest, an instance of a more general problem, sometimes called the 'paradox of fiction' (e.g. Gaut, 2003; first identified in Radford and Weston, 1975). The supposed paradox is generated when the readers or audience of a fictional work – which they know to be fictional – react in an apparently normal emotional way to some event in the fiction. The question is how rational people can respond with genuine emotions to something they know to be fictional. Listeners might, conceivably, be taken in by a fictional radio broadcast masquerading as news, and as a result become terrified that the Earth is being invaded by aliens, but – according to the worry motivating the paradox of fiction – this should not happen to a knowing audience. Yet there is little doubt that people *can* have emotion-like responses of *some* kind to fictions: readers and film audiences might cry at a sad ending, or be 'on the edge of their seats' through a thriller. But can these be *genuine* emotional responses? And if not, can we apply Addison's and Burke's accounts of the sublime to fictions?

While some responses to the paradox of fiction (e.g. Walton, 1978; 1990) have concluded that we cannot have genuine emotional responses to fictions, others (e.g. Carroll, 1990; Gaut, 1999; Feagin, 2011) have argued that we can. Noel Carroll has argued that believing something is true need not be a prerequisite for having a genuine emotional response to it; simply entertaining it as a thought might be sufficient (Carroll, 1990). Berys Gaut has highlighted the importance of identifying with characters in fictions (Gaut, 1999)), and Susan Feagin has made a case for the importance of mental simulation in creating empathy with fictional characters (Feagin, 2011)). No-one, however, wants to deny that people's responses to fictions can be intense and very like emotions, despite their full knowledge that what they are reading or watching is fictional. The further question, therefore, of how best to characterise the response – whether as an emotion, or as some other kind of qualitatively similar reaction – does not need to be answered to apply accounts of the sublime like Addison's and Burke's to fictions. All that is required is that the experience is emotion-like, and sufficiently intense.

It is also quite clear that Burke himself means to include poetry and art as sources of the sublime. In the passage from Burke quoted earlier, where he links the sublime with terror, it is *ideas* of pain and danger, and not *actual* pain or danger that he is interested in.* Most revealingly, what Burke has to say about sympathy sets out the way he thinks fictions can elicit emotions. Sympathy, Burke tells us, is a means by which we "enter into the concerns

---

* Compare what Burke says towards the end of the first part of the Enquiry, in the Recapitulation: "The passions which belong to self-preservation, turn on pain and danger; they are simply painful when their causes immediately affect us; they are delightful when we have an idea of pain and danger, without being actually in such circumstances..." Burke (1990, p.47).

of others", and "are moved as they are moved" (Burke 1990, p.41). Sympathy is also the means by which "poetry, painting, and other affecting arts, transfuse their passions from one breast to another" (ibid.). Combining these two points, he tells us "It is a common observation, that objects which in the reality would shock, are in tragical, and such like representations, the source of a very high species of pleasure" (ibid.). Finally, as we have already seen, Burke's theory explicitly requires the danger that causes the experience of the sublime to be 'at a distance', and one way of fulfilling that requirement is for the danger to be fictional and not real. Having established that Burke's version of the sublime is clearly applicable to fictions, we now need to see how well suited it is to the marine horror of *The Call of Cthulhu*.

The Call of Cthulhu

As those familiar with Lovecraft's work will know, though *The Call of Cthulhu* was first published in the magazine *Weird Tales* in 1927, the mythos it is part of continues to be added to and written about today. For those not so familiar with the story, I begin with an overview.

Purporting to be "found among the papers of the late Francis Wayland Thurston, of Boston" (Lovecraft, 1927, in Jones, 2008, p.201), the first-person narrative combines the immediacy of an epistolary with the apparent verisimilitude of a false document. The narrator, Francis Thurston, becomes involved while going through the papers and possessions of his recently-deceased great-uncle, George Angell, who had been a professor in Rhode Island. The piecing together of evidence that forms much of the content of the narrative is precipitated by the professor's death, in the winter of 1926.

Among the professor's possessions Thurston finds newspaper cuttings and reports of a large number of unusual events, many involving psychological disturbances, all concentrated on the spring of 1925, yet located in quite different parts of the world. Thurston also finds the professor's notes of a New Orleans inspector's encounter many years earlier, in 1908, with a secret cult that had been conducting horrifying ceremonies deep in the Louisiana swamps. Among the notes is a description of an idol the police had seized during their raid, a grotesque tentacle-headed creature with wings. The description is strikingly similar to a young artist's impression of a creature that appeared in his nightmares while he was ill, in the spring of 1925. The professor, Thurston realises, had been conducting an investigation.

Prompted by growing curiosity mixed with scepticism, Thurston starts his own investigation into the strange events, and eventually comes across an old copy of an Australian newspaper from April 1925, with a picture of an identical tentacle-headed idol. The accompanying article describes the voyage of the ship Emma from New Zealand, as recounted by the sole surviving crew member, a Norwegian named Gustaf Johansen. After being sent off course in a storm, the Emma came across another ship heavily armed and with an "evil looking crew" of Pacific Islanders (ibid., p.218), who promptly attacked. Soon after killing their attackers, they came across a small island that did not appear on their maps. Johansen, described in the article as of excellent character, claimed most of his crewmates died on the island, though he provided almost no details. He himself was found, the sole survivor, delirious and clutching the idol.

Thurston realises that something truly momentous occurred around the end of March 1925, and determines to fit the final pieces of the jigsaw together. His journey takes him, by sea, from America to New Zealand, then to Australia, and finally to Norway. In Oslo, he discovers Johansen died soon after returning, in potentially suspect circumstances. Johansen's widow allows Thurston to take away the sailor's personal account – which she has not read – of his fateful voyage on the Emma, and it is with his story that the most obvious link between the sea and Burkean sublimity emerges. Just before summarising Johansen's narrative, Thurston warns us "I cannot attempt to transcribe it verbatim in all its cloudiness and redundance, but I will tell its gist enough to show why the sound of the water against the vessel's sides became so unendurable to me that I stopped my ears with cotton" (ibid., p.221). This single sentence transforms the way we think about the sea in *The Call of Cthulhu* as powerfully as Spielberg's direction in *Jaws*, but for a different reason: the sea becomes, in Thurston's mind, *contaminated* by what it conceals. In his reaction we also read an intense emotion at one step removed, like seeing someone scream in fear before we see what has caused them to scream.

The ancient citadel Johansen and his crewmates discover in the middle of the ocean is described as a "fantasy of prismatic distortion" (ibid., p.223), suggestive of the refraction of light by water. The remaining sailors are unfortunate enough to encounter the "gelatinous green immensity", the "mountain" (ibid.) that is Cthulhu, in whose image the idols were fashioned. Some of the sailors go mad at the sight, and others are killed by Cthulhu, but Johansen and one other make it back to the boat. Cthulhu pursues them, and they narrowly make their escape, though only Johansen remains sane and survives.

Drawing together all the pieces of evidence, Thurston learns that millennia before the appearance of mankind, Cthulhu "and his hordes" "seeped down from the dark stars" (ibid., p.222) to the Earth, and that Cthulhu's city R'lyeh remains sunken in the middle of the South Pacific Ocean until "the stars are right" (ibid., p.214) and they are liberated by their followers. Once liberated, Cthulhu and the Great Old Ones will help mankind become "free and wild and beyond good and evil, with laws and morals thrown aside and all men shouting and killing and revelling in joy," and "all the Earth would flame with a holocaust of ecstasy and freedom" (ibid.) Fortunately for Thurston (and the majority of the rest of the human race), Cthulhu and the Great Old Ones are not liberated *on this occasion*, perhaps as a result of the killing of the "evil looking crew" of the Alert, and their city R'lyeh sinks back to its abyssal purgatory. Having learnt all this, we can shudder with Thurston as he writes "When I think of the *extent* of all that may be brooding down there I almost wish to kill myself forthwith" (ibid., p.222). The sea is revealed as both containing and concealing the most horrifying of creatures, whose release spells the end of the order, morality and life we know and value.

It is tempting to identify the utter terror that Johansen and his crewmates experience at the sight of Cthulhu as an experience of the sublime in Burke's sense, and this is made more tempting by the description of Cthulhu as "immense" and like a "mountain", recalling the attribution of sublimity to objects of great size. However, Vivian Ralickas (2007) has argued quite persuasively *against* making this identification. Though her argument is more wide-ranging, for our purposes it comes down to this. As we have seen, for Burke terror can be a mark of the sublime only if the terror is "at certain distances." In *The Call of Cthulhu*, however, for all the main characters the terror is either fatal, or a prelude to their demise. Though Johansen survives his encounter with Cthulhu, he dies under odd circumstances. "[A] bundle of papers falling from an attic window had knocked him down. Two Lascar sailors at once helped him to his feet, but before the ambulance could reach him he was dead" (Lovecraft, 1927, in Jones, 2008, p.221). The Professor, the narrator's great-uncle, "had been stricken whilst returning from the Newport boat; falling suddenly, as witnesses said, after having been jostled by a nautical-looking Negro…" (ibid., p.203). And even Thurston, the narrator, fears for himself. "I do not think my life will be long. As my uncle went, as poor Johansen went, so I shall go. I know too much, and the cult still lives" (ibid., p.225).

Now, one could try and press the point that the narrator survives long enough to write his account which, as the story is presented, is found after his death. But rather than pursue that line, I want to argue that the sublime operates at a different level here. It is significant that the story as a whole is presented as a 'found document', and that the link is clearly made between *knowing too much* and the possibility of being murdered by the *still active cult*. The feeling of terror the story aims to create is not merely based on our sympathy as readers with the fate of its main characters; the story also aims to make us concerned about *our own safety*. All of *The Call of Cthulhu* is structured around the piecing together of evidence, and part of what comes to light from this exercise is that *everybody else* who has managed to piece together the same evidence has died in suspicious circumstances. Simply by finishing the story, the reader has placed him- or herself in the very same danger!

Of course at one level, as readers, we know the story is fictional. Yet there remains, nevertheless, the quite thrilling possibility that, like Thurston, we have *discovered* something concealed from the masses, even though this discovery places us in danger. In imagining we are reading Thurston's account, we must also imagine ourselves in danger, a danger we can distance ourselves from only by recalling that the story is fictional. The most intense fear the story is capable of eliciting is not what we feel in sympathy with characters like Johansen, but rather fear for our own safety when we imagine what we are reading is Thurston's account. The distance Burke insists is necessary for something fearful to be sublime is achieved by recalling the story is fictional. Alongside the appeal of uncovering the 'truth', I suggest there is also a shift in the sublime qualities of the sea, from Addison's description of an *object* we see that excites the imagination with an "agreeable horror" at its "prodigious bulk of waters" to a *place* which can contain Burke's "terrible objects" that are themselves the source of intense fear. It is no longer just the sea which is a source of fear; in *The Call of Cthulhu* we discover the greatest sources of fear lie concealed in its depths.

More, perhaps, could be said about the kind of effect the story might have had on its readers when first published, but I want to end this section on Lovecraft by mentioning something any reader of *The Call of Cthulhu* cannot ignore: the racism that permeates the whole story. The biographer and Lovecraft fan S.T. Joshi has tackled this issue in the wider context of Lovecraft's life and work (Joshi, 2001), but I want to note, just in connection with *The Call of Cthulhu*, two things. First, without exception *all* the (human) villains are non-white. And second, the characters who, we must suppose, are responsible for the death of Johansen ("Lascar sailors") and the Professor ("a nautical-looking Negro") are not only not white, they are also, from Lovecraft's point of view, *foreigners*. We might wonder, therefore, whether there is some sort of identification between the threat of personal, cultural and moral destruction posed by Cthulhu, deep under the sea, and similar though lesser dangers from ethnically distinct immigrants, coming over the sea.

In the next section I turn to the slightly different kind of marine sublime found in James Cameron's film *The Abyss*. The sea in the film plays a much more central role than it does in Lovecraft's story, and as we descend below the water's surface, the shift from the sea being an object of fear and awe, to its becoming a place within which events that are frightening and awe-inspiring take place, is even more pronounced. From being a source of what Addison called "agreeable horror," the sea turns into a source of "pleasing astonishment", but common to both *The Call of Cthulhu* and *The Abyss* is a portrayal of the sea as an unknown place, and, therefore, a place of the unknown.

The Abyss

For our purposes, *The Abyss* can be usefully thought of as having three main plot strands: the rekindling of a relationship, a series of disasters that have to be overcome, and a discovery. I will not have much to say about the first strand, since it is mostly in events belonging to the other two strands that the sea plays a relevant role. I will focus in particular on three parts of the film – the fluid-breathing rat, the pseudopod, and the NTI ship – to try and show how the role the sea plays in the film relies on aspects of its sublimity.

The film begins with a nuclear powered US Navy submarine, the USS Montana, crashing into part of the Cayman Trough, a deep sea trench in the Caribbean Sea not far from Cuba. The submarine's crash is the result of it losing power just as its crew detect a very fast moving underwater object in its vicinity. The site of the crash is close to an experimental underwater drilling platform, 'Deepcore'; since a hurricane is expected, the Navy does not have enough time to deploy its own rescue craft, so commandeers Deepcore and its crew. The crew's foreman, Virgil 'Bud' Brigman (played by Ed Harris) is reluctantly convinced to assist a Navy SEAL (i.e. special forces) team that is sent down to supervise the operation. Lindsey Brigman (played by Mary Elizabeth Mastrantonio), Bud's estranged wife and Deepcore's designer, also insists on joining the operation. It is clear from the outset that there are tensions between the SEALs and Deepcore's civilian crew, and between Bud and Lindsey.

The Fluid-Breathing Rat: While the Deepcore crew and SEALs prepare for the excursion to the Montana's location, two of the crew notice a SEAL preparing some unfamiliar equipment, which turns out to be a fluid-breathing system, for "really deep" dives. As the SEAL is quizzed, it becomes clear that the system involves *breathing in liquid*, an "oxygenated fluorocarbon emulsion". One of the Deepcore crew, Alan 'Hippy' Carnes (played by Todd Graff) is sceptical, so the SEAL grabs Hippy's pet rat from his shoulder, and immerses it in a glass trough of pink fluid, holding it under using a wire mesh. We see the rat panic, and struggle, before finally relaxing, and *breathing the fluid*, its chest visibly moving in and out.[*]

While there may have been other ways to achieve the same sort of effect, the scene was in fact filmed using an oxygenated perfluorocarbon, and the rat was *actually breathing using the fluid*, which (at least for short periods of time) can provide sufficient oxygen, and absorb enough carbon dioxide, to make respiration possible. Oxygenated perfluorocarbons have a range of potential medical uses, including providing respiratory support for pre-term infants and adults with acute respiratory problems that could be exacerbated by the use of conventional mechanical ventilation (Shaffer, Wolfson and Greenspan, 1999).

Lieutenant Coffey, the SEAL team leader (played by Michael Biehn), who has a neurological condition caused by the deep-sea environment's atmospheric pressure becomes increasingly unstable. Believing they are about to be attacked by the Russians, he arms a nuclear warhead salvaged from the

[*]   The scene is cut from U.K. DVDs.

wrecked Montana. Though he tries to hide what he is doing from Deepcore's crew, they become aware of it.

The Pseudopod: Unobserved by anyone, a column of water rises out of Deepcore's moon pool. Our point of view switches to that of whatever is controlling or contained in the water; as the 'pseudopod' of water, almost like a giant snake, moves around the surviving parts of Deepcore, our view of the surroundings from inside the water is distorted by refraction. Lindsey wakes up, sees the pseudopod, and – at first terrified – wakes Bud and the other Deepcore crew, and our point of view switches back. The pod focusses on Lindsey, mimicking her face and expressions, and it becomes clear it means no harm.

The NTI ('Non-Terrestrial Intelligence') Ship: The final sequence I want to pick out takes place near the end of the film, after Coffey's attempt to blow up the NTIs using the warhead. Though Coffey dies, Bud has to use the experimental liquid-breathing apparatus to descend – into the abyss – to disarm the warhead. He succeeds, but does not have enough oxygen to return. As he prepares to die, an NTI appears and guides him to an enormous violet-lit structure. He is led through tunnels and passageways lit like airport runways, and deposited in a chamber from which the water *retreats*, a vertical wall of water moving away from him.

More could be said about the making of the film, the threat of nuclear destruction the film highlights, and Cameron's continued interest in deep sea exploration, but space is limited. Though the film is not without its faults, one of the most striking things about it is that nearly all of it was actually filmed underwater, some of it in the enormous containment tank of an unfinished and abandoned nuclear power plant. Water is either actually present, or driving the plot, in almost the whole film, creating parallels between the making of the film and the fiction it portrays. One of the dangers actors and crew faced is also one of the greatest dangers the sea poses – suffocation. In the first and third parts of the film I have picked out, the danger of suffocation threatens and then recedes in a very Burkean way: the rat initially panics before realising it can breathe the fluid, and Bud is saved from suffocation by the intervention of the NTIs. The pseudopod sequence is an interesting reversal, where instead of the characters entering the water, the water reaches out to meet them, but in all three sequences the danger is 'at a distance' in just the way Burke requires it to be as a source of the sublime.

I return to the NTI ship sequence briefly in the next and final section, where I want to suggest that the sea provides a way for Lovecraft and Cameron to create what Doran calls a "secular transcendence," and in doing so offers a way of "re-enchanting the world."

Re-enchantment

In his lecture *Science as a Vocation*, Max Weber says, of the "intellectualist rationalization created by science and scientifically oriented technology," that

> it means that principally there are no mysterious incalculable forces that come into play, but rather that one can, in principle, master all things by calculation. This means that the world is disenchanted. One need no longer have recourse to magical means in order to master or implore the spirits... (Weber 1948, p.139)

And a little later he says, of the natural sciences, that they are "apt to make the belief that there is such a thing as the 'meaning' of the universe die out at its very roots" (ibid., p.142).

Scientific discoveries may very well have their own kind of sublime qualities, but the sublime that emerges from danger and the unknown must retreat before the mapped, familiar and controlled modern world. The belief in 'meaning' that Weber thinks is undermined by science necessarily requires the human subject to be central, since the meaning in question is *for* human subjects. In a disenchanted world, the significance of the sublime, of feelings of being "at once overwhelmed and exalted" as Doran puts it, is lost: the natural sciences can assign no special value to such feelings, since they cannot favour humans and human feelings above any other part of nature. This appears to pose a dilemma for my analysis of both *The Call of Cthulhu* and *The Abyss*. Either we view the story and film as at odds with a scientific, materialist view of the world, or we abandon the sublime as a useful concept for understanding them.

Ralickas makes a similar observation as part of her argument against construing Lovecraft's 'cosmic horror' as a kind of Burkean sublime, and some of Lovecraft's materialist views, expressed in his essay *The Defence Reopens!* seem to support her. He asks "what right have we to invent a notion of purpose in the utter absence of evidence? Of course our savage forefathers could not conceive of a cosmos without a purpose any more than they could conceive of one without an anthropomorphic deity, but what place have their legends in 1921?" (Lovecraft 1921, in Joshi 1985, p.17.)

Yet though Lovecraft vigorously defends his mechanistic materialism in essays, there are clearly tensions. Near the end of *The Defence Remains Open!*, he says "Materialism is not the tragedy – at least, not the utter tragedy – that idealists picture" (ibid., pp.30–31). And, at the very end of that essay, almost plaintively, "Surely we can think of life as having something of beauty..." (ibid., p.31). There are also clear indications in *The Call of Cthulhu* that humanity *does* have a central role to play – Cthulhu and the Great Old Ones are dependent on human worshippers to liberate them, and much if not all of their malice is also directed at humans. Lovecraft's monsters are certainly far from *indifferent* to humans.

In his examination of the role the fictional worlds of Lovecraft and others have played, Michael Saler (2012) has argued that the vogue for fantastic imaginary worlds… is best explained in terms of a larger cultural project of the West: that of re-enchanting an allegedly dis-enchanted world. Fantastic virtual worlds of the imagination emerged at the turn of the century not to replicate the everyday… but to complement it – to secure the marvels that a disenchanted modernity seemed to undermine, while remaining true to the tenets intellectuals ascribed to modernity at the time, such as rationality and secularism. (Saler 2012, p.7)

Saler's "disenchanted enchantment" that "delights without deluding" (ibid., pp.12–13) shares some key qualities with Doran's "secular transcendence," in particular the emphasis on rationality and secularism, rather than magic and the supernatural. And it is in service of this objective, to create a space for things that might cause feelings of being overwhelmed and exalted yet are also consistent with a scientific secularism, that the sea plays a vital role. In *The Call of Cthulhu*, the unexplored and uncharted deeps of the sea both confine and conceal the nemesis of mankind, allowing us as readers to entertain the sublime possibility that our reading of the story actually involves *us* in it, by placing us in danger of being pursued by Cthulhu's cult, without forcing us to suspend our commitment to a scientific and secular materialism.

In *The Abyss*, the sea changes from the Deepcore crew's place of work to a threatening environment, and then, most powerfully in the NTI ship sequence described earlier, to a sanctuary for enchantment. Once again, it is the unexplored and uncharted depths of the sea that (quite literally) form a space in which the sublime can exist consistently with the secular materialism that the film's director and his intended audience accept. We, as that audience, can feel Bud's loss of control, his sense of being overwhelmed in the face of his physical frailties and the great technological prowess of the NTIs. But we can also feel exalted by the revelation of possibilities that the unexplored seas and oceans offer; perhaps the last part of our planet that affords us "something commensurate to our capacity for wonder," to borrow F. Scott Fitzgerald's memorable phrase from the end of *The Great Gatsby* (1925). Addison's "agreeable horror," Burke's "terror," and Doran's "transcendence" are varieties of that feeling of being intensely alive that both nature and works of art can produce. For the moment, there is still space for a secular sublime to shelter in the deepest parts of our seas and oceans which, as unknown places, can be a refuge for the unknown.[*]

References

Addison, J., 1845. *The Works of Joseph Addison Volume II*. New York: Harper.

Brady, E., 2013. *The Sublime in Modern Philosophy: Aesthetics, Ethics, and Nature*. New York: Cambridge University Press.

[*] Thanks to all the participants of the Beasts of the Deep conference at St. Mary's, in particular Pete Fossey and the editors of this volume, Seán and Jon. A special thanks to Liz Barry for very helpful comments on a draft.

Burke, E., 1759. *A Philosophical Enquiry into the Origin of our Ideas of the Sublime and Beautiful*. Edited by A. Phillips, 1990. New York: Oxford University Press.

Carroll, N., 1990. *The Philosophy of Horror*. New York: Routledge.

Costelloe, T. M. ed., 2012. *The Sublime from Antiquity to the Present*. New York: Cambridge University Press.

Doran, R., 2015. *The Theory of the Sublime from Longinus to Kant*. Cambridge: Cambridge University Press.

Feagin, S.L., 2011. Empathizing as Simulating. In: A. Coplan and P. Goldie, eds. 2011. *Empathy: Philosophical and Psychological Perspectives*. New York: Oxford University Press. pp.149–161.

Gaut, B., 1999. Identification and Emotion in Narrative Film. In: C. Plantinga and G.M. Smith, eds. 1999. *Passionate Views: Thinking About Film and Emotion*. Baltimore: Johns Hopkins University Press. pp.200–216.

Gaut, B., 2003. Reasons, Emotions, and Fictions. In: M. Kieran and D. M. Lopes, eds. 2003. *Imagination, Philosophy, and the Arts*. London: Routledge. pp.14–34.

Heath, M., 2012. Longinus and the Ancient Sublime. In: T. M. Costelloe, ed. 2012. *The Sublime from Antiquity to the Present*. New York: Cambridge University Press. pp.11–23.

Joshi, S. T., 2001. *A Dreamer and a Visionary: H. P. Lovecraft in his Time*. Liverpool: Liverpool University Press.

Longinus, The Sublime. Translated by W. H. Fyfe; Revised by Donald Russell, 1995. In: G. P. Goold, ed. 1995. *Aristotle: Poetics, Longinus: On the Sublime, Demetrius: On Style*. Cambridge Mass.: Harvard University Press. pp.143–307.

Lovecraft, H. P., 1927. The Call of Cthulhu. In: S. Jones, ed. 2008. *Necronomicon: The Best Weird Tales of H. P. Lovecraft*. London: Gollancz. pp.201–225.

Lovecraft, H.P., 1921. The Defence Remains Open!. In: S. T. Joshi, ed. 1985. *In Defence of Dagon*. West Warwick, RI.: Necronomicon Press. pp.21–33.

Lovecraft, H. P., 1921. The Defence Reopens!. In: S. T. Joshi, ed. 1985. *In Defence of Dagon*. West Warwick, RI.: Necronomicon Press. pp.11–20.

Radford, C. and Weston, M., 1975. How Can We Be Moved by the Fate of Anna Karenina?. *Proceedings of the Aristotelian Society Supplementary Volumes*, 49, pp.67–93.

Ralickas, V., 2007. "Cosmic Horror" and the Question of the Sublime in Lovecraft. *Journal of the Fantastic in the Arts*, 18(3), pp.364–398

Saler, M., 2012. *As If: Modern Enchantment and the Literary Prehistory of Virtual Reality*. New York: Oxford University Press.

Shaffer, T.H., Wolfson, M.R. and Greenspan, J.S., 1999. Liquid Ventilation: Current Status. *Pediatrics in Review*, 20(12), pp.134–142.

The Abyss. 1989 [DVD] USA: 20th Century Fox.

Walton, K.L., 1978. Fearing Fictions. *The Journal of Philosophy*, 75(1), pp.5–27.

Walton, K.L., 1990. *Mimesys as Make-Believe: On the Foundations of the Representational Arts*. Cambridge, Mass.: Harvard University Press.

Weber, M., 1946. *From Max Weber: Essays in Sociology*. Translated and edited by H. H. Gerth and C. Wright Mills, 1946. New York: Oxford University Press.

Part 2

Depths of Desire

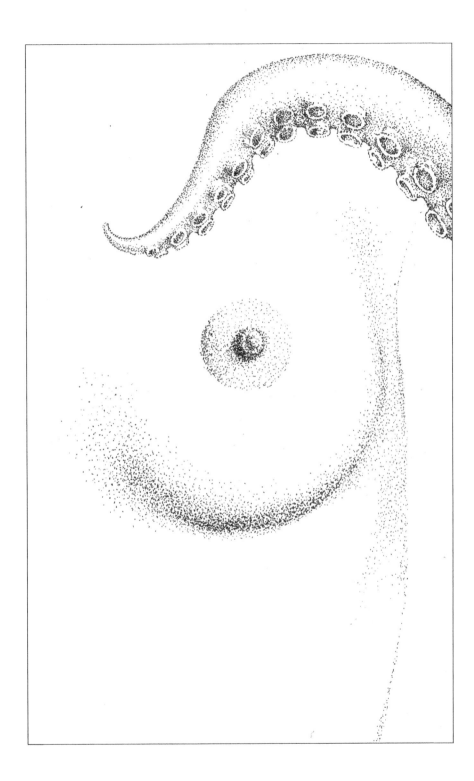

Chapter 4

Beauty and the Octopus: Close encounters with the other-than-human

Marco Benoît Carbone

The monster out there

Monstrous, sexualized octopuses abound in recent visual cultures, ambiguously embodying audiences' attraction to, and repulsion from, animality and otherness. Drawing from iconographic and psychoanalytic studies on the motif of the octopus, this study looks at fine and amateur art, film, animation, and pornography produced over the past decade, analysing perceptions of cephalopods as human-animal conundrums, whose physiology has often caused them to be understood as metonymically genital figures. The study identifies two recurrent motifs of gendered and sexualized body: the phallic raper, and the octopus-lady. The first figure can be outlined by looking at the popularization of Japanese artist Katsushika Hokusai's 1814 erotic woodblock painting, *The Dream of the Fisherman's Wife*, in which a lady engages in intercourse with two cephalopods (Hokusai 1996). The reception of this art work as a prototype of the phallic octopus took place in a sub-stream of art and pornography characterized by fantasies of monstrous intercourses between humans and tentacular entities. The second model, the octopus-girl, fuses octopoid features with female bodies and sexual attributes. Erotic comic books like the *Monster Girl Encyclopaedia* (Cross 2010), along with fine and amateur art, re-read monstrous-feminine figures from art and myth within this kind of representation.

The two foci allow a consideration of a broader continuum of sexualized and gendered reception of octopuses, ranging from fantasies of intercourse to one of animal-human hybrids and miscegenation. The popularity and variety of such tropes seem to suggest that this hotbed of imagination encapsulates both a series of varied fantasies, and underlying patriarchal, normative, and speciesist* ideologies that use and abuse the animal Other to project and

---

* The term denotes the prejudice produced by humans (in this case) towards another species. See Ryder (2004).

confront their own fears and anxieties. As philosopher Roger Caillois noted, cephalopods have "the privilege of setting our imagination in motion" (Caillois, 1970, p. 76). due to their oxymoronic appearance as a synthesis of human and non-human. In the placenta of the sea, mankind's phylogenesis almost seems to imaginatively revert to the formless, and thence beget a proliferating array of tentacular fantasies through which artists and readers can confront, embrace, or symbolically destroy the Other – the abject, that Kristeva defined as the place where established boundaries of the body might collapse (1982, p. 1). The octopus monster, while hailing from outside safe borders of civilization, thus remains within ourselves, activating the genital and prehensile fantasies of the naked ape.

Encounters with otherness

Today's visual cultures abound in fantasies and fears of close, sexually intimate encounters with animals associated with the alien and the other-than-self. In the art world, Hokusai's work could be argued to be the main drive behind the recent popularization of the octopus motif in popular culture. The growing popularity of traditional Japanese *shunga*, or wood-block pictures, through exhibitions featured in important museums world-wide,* probably helped propel circulating the broader production of Hokusai (Fig. 1), including the themes of octopus erotica frequently explored in his art tradition.

Contemporary Japanese artists like Masami Teraoka, Audrey Kawasaki and Yuji Moriguchi adapted them to new pop art sensibilities. Norwegian artist Rune Olsen and American artist Zak Smith developed the motif in art galleries in Europe and the USA. In addition to the art world, the rise of tentacle erotica as a commonplace of monstrous and weird pornography further popularized the octopus as a sex offender or genital figure. Some of the starkest examples can be found in animated and fantasy pornography: drawn and animated erotica featuring more or less explicitly rendered monstrous intercourses, including scenes where monsters rape women, have become widely and easily available on the Internet through image aggregators like *Tumblr, Pinterest,* and *deviantArt* and through pornographic websites like *PornHub* and *XVideos*. While octopus erotica reworks sources as diverse as Japanese netsuke statuettes and woodblock pictures, Picasso's art, horror film and animation from previous decades, and the art world, tentacle porn can also venture into more disturbing territory. In addition to rape narratives with animated monsters or live-action plastic props, the spoils of actual animals can be found photographed alongside human bodies as macabre sex toys as women engage with writhing masses of octopuses and tentacles.

The rise of this kind of imagery was received and amplified by media.

---

* See the 2013–2014 British Museum exhibition: http://www.britishmuseum.org/whats_on/exhibitions/shunga.aspx (latest access: 05/15/2017).

Tabloids like *Metro* and *The Sun* reported a man being jailed for owning octopus-porn. Magazines like *Glamour* also indulged in coverage of scandalous cases, detailing intersections between *shunga*, horror-erotic media, and tentacle-shaped dildos on sale on e-shopping platforms (Drell 2017). In natural science magazines, octopuses emerge as uncannily smart and eroticized non-human subjects. An article from BBC Earth discussed how an octopus avoided being eaten by the hungry female during intercourse, aligning the animals with the motif of the mantis-like, deadly femme fatale (Courage 2015). Another story discussed the octopus 'that strangled its lover' in a US aquarium (BBC Earth 2017). Tentacle erotica memes were disseminated on social media like Twitter and Facebook, or sites such as *Memecentral* or *Knowyourmeme* – where one can find countless examples of phallic tentacles and eroticized woman-octopus hybrids.

While fully developed in contexts that could be defined as hyper-specific or hyper-niche, such fantasies reveal a diachronically larger narrative that may include anything from 1950s pulp magazines to contemporary porn. Its recent resurgence may be due to the intensification of symbolic exchange in the Internet Age, which allowed easier percolation from niche content and unfiltered amateur media into mainstream audiences, but also offered artists and audiences chances to retrospectively define sexualized creatures and ambiguous and aberrant encounters from art, literature, and stories from previous decades and eras – from Hokusai's *shunga* to the Greco-Roman monstrous-feminine figures like Scylla – as consistent with the now-developed trope of tentacle erotica.

Across these many examples, the phallic raper and octopus girl models can be used as two general models around which to sketch a broader canvas that includes the varied body permutations of the sexualized tentacular figures of recent media cultures. This is, of course, not a study of marine biology.[*] Rather, the paper looks at octopuses in cultural perspective as, in Braidotti's term, constructed "nature-culture compounds" (Braidotti (2012: 49) – other-than-humans that serve iconographic motifs, metaphors, and forms that contrastively define normality. In this light, octopoid figures have provided bodies on which a variety of gendered and sexual anxieties have been projected, ranging from patriarchal normalization of rape culture and female objectification to more progressive, liberating and Dionysian non-heteronormative explorations of sexuality. Recent tentacle erotica and octopus girl motifs intercept more far-reaching representations of the marine expanses and tentacle creatures as fringe territories of alluring and yet frightening bodily transformations such as the ones that myths have encapsulated in mermaids and tritons. Octopus erotica's obsession with the bodies of tentacular creatures also resonates with the vaginal and phallic preoccupations traditionally approached by psychoanalytic studies. Sexualized cephalopod creatures are characterized by overtly explicit genital references

***

[*] In that regard, see Norman (2000).

and innuendoes, aligning themselves with intersecting mythographies of castrating mouths, annihilating wombs, and phallic fears traditionally seen as the inner subtexts of myths like those of the snake-headed, polyphallic Medusa or Scylla, which some of the novel tentacular fantasies actively receive and rework.

Ominous abysses: the reception of Hokusai's octopus lover

In 2009, an episode of *Mad Men*, the popular US series,[*] included a scene that featured Japanese artist Katsushika Hokusai's 1814 woodblock painting

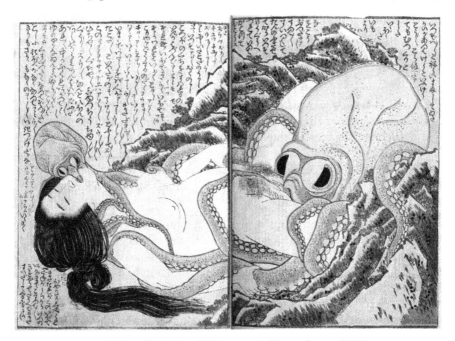

Fig. 1: Katsushika Hokusai, *Tako to ama*, in *Kinoe no komatsu* (1814).

Taco to Ama, also known as *The Dream of the Fisherman's wife*. In the scene, Japanophile Bert Cooper, the founding partner of a marketing firm, displays a very large painting of a woman ravished by two octopi. Hokusai's painting is, in fact, a 16 x 22 cm illustration included in a three-volume erotic print collections, *Kinoe no komatsu* (Hokusai 1996). It shows a young *ama*, or pearl diver, lying down on a beach while a large octopus entices her while lying over her, performing oral sex on the woman and caressing her body (Fig. 1).

Hokusai's painting is a *shunga*, an erotic painting produced in Japan during

[*]   Season 3, episode 2, 'Out of town', AMC: USA 2009; see Carbone (2013, pp. 21–42).

Fig. 2: Yanagawa Shigenobu, *Suetsumuhana*, 1830.

Fig. 3: *Diving Girl and Octopus*, Kikugawa collection.

the Edo period.* The term can be roughly translated into *spring pictures*.** Shunga pictures profusely used octopi as part of the larger production of *ukiyo-e*, a corpus of art focusing on the "floating world": otherworldly, uncanny encounters with macabre beings, often erotic-grotesque in nature, and involving women, man, and fantastic creatures that could sometimes metonymically represent genitalia. In Shigenobu's *suetsumuhana* (1830), an anthropomorphic octopus engages a pearl diver on a beach (Fig. 2). The folk motif was also to be found in *netsukes*, popular figurines, such as the one sculpted in 1773 by Katsukawa Shusho, in which a woman tries to dissuade a languid octopus from his insisting attentions (Fig. 3).***

In post-Edo times, Hokusai's octopus gained iconic status among arts enthusiasts. In recent decades, it became a symbol of the larger trope of tentacle erotica. The artwork was transposed in surreal, slightly horrific live action form in the fictionalized Hokusai biopic *Edo Porn* (1981, Japan, dir. K. Shindo), and reworked ironically in the production of contemporary Japanese artists like Masami Teraoka, where women languidly lying on beaches, about to elope with the octopuses, are sometimes shown to hand them condoms.

---

*   The Edo period is comprised between 1603–1868, corresponding to the shogun's Tokugawa family rule, and having Edo, the ancient Tokyo, as capital. On Edo art, see Singer (1998).

**   Other terms included *koshokubon* (erotic books), *makura-e* (pictures to keep under the pillow), *warai-e* (nice pictures), or *abuna-e* (or risqué). On *shunga*, see Screech (2009).

***   Currently in the Kikugawa collection.

Broader circulation of the motif in Western productions, however, could be said to have begun in the early 2010s, when Hokusai's art was understood as the iconic initiator of the visual trope of Tentacle erotica. Animation films like Kawajiri's *Wicked City* (1987), which featured female monsters with toothed vaginas and supernatural monsters with octopus-like tentacles raping female victims, enjoyed renewed popularity through the Internet. Japanese manga artist Toshio Maeda's apocalyptic erotic-action-horror animated series *Urotsukidoji* (1987–1994), *Demon Beast Invasion* (1990–1994), and *La Blue Girl* (1992–1993) used tentacles as fantasy phallic substitutes to circumvent industry prohibition of realistic representations of genitalia (Carbone 2013, pp. 23–25).[*] Around the same time, a vast series of animated, home-market adult animation products with scenes of tentacular porn became available alongside widely available Internet pornography. By the time Hokusai's painting was referenced in *Mad Men*, tentacle rape was already a cliché of Internet memes, and had been referred to ironically by TV shows such as *Family Guy*,[**] *Futurama*,[***] and *CSI*,[†] and later in blockbusters like *Prometheus* (2012, USA) and *007: Spectre* (2015, UK/USA). Through the combined reception of such texts, tentacular intercourse began to be discussed as a specific sub-set of pornography in media like Wikipedia, where a first dedicated page had been inaugurated in 2004 (Carbone 2013, p. 67n).

Tentacle rape that had already been lurking underneath the imaginaries of erotica and horror across different national contexts and audiences in earlier decades. Examples like horror/sci-fi *Galaxy of Terror*, produced by Roger Corman (1980, USA), and arthouse film director A. Żuławski's horror thriller *Possession* (1980, France/West Germany), featured, respectively, a scene of monstrous rape, and one in which a husband's jealousy transmogrified into a tentacular, horrific love rival. US pulp magazine stories and covers from the 1950s – such as *Men's Pictorial, Planet Stories, Spicy Adventures*, and *Weird Tales*) often revolved around fixed formulae in which monstrous animals confronted attractive women. Octopi featured among the top sexual aggressors, coveting attractive and passive female divers while the male hero rushed against the threat of the tentacular grips.

It is possible that such covers were partly inspired through the circulation of Japanese shunga motifs in post-War US, as a consequence of cultural contacts with Japan. Hokusai's art has indeed been discussed also in relation to the impact of *ukiyo-e* on European artistic avant-gardes, through the phenomenon of *japonisme*, and has been observed in works like Felicien Rops's *La pieuvre* (1900) and Picasso's *Woman and Squid* from 1900, in which the cephalopod approaches the welcoming woman's genitalia (Bru 2010). It

---

[*]   On Japanese regulations, see Bornoff (1992).

[**]   Season 10, episode 11, 'The Blind Side', Fox TV: USA 2012.

[***] Futurama. The Beast with a Billion Backs, USA: 20th Century Fox Home 2008.

[†]   Season 12, episode 1, '73 Seconds', CBS: USA 1011.

could also be argued to have inspired André Masson's 1944 illustrations for an edition of Victor Hugo's *La Pieuvre*, in which a firmly standing man, arms wide open, is seen from his back while an octopus, which faces the observer, voluptuously ensnares the man's body.

While a punctual historical account of Hokusai's impact in the West is beyond the remit of this study, it is fair to argue that *The Dream of the Fisherman's wife* (1814) was elected as the originator of the motif in the years surrounding the formulation of tentacle erotica as a recognizable motif for Western audiences in the 2010s.* Appropriations of Hokusai saw it as an artfully respectable but still alluringly ominous sexualized image that stood for the same 'genre'. In the context of *Mad Men*'s plot, a series about ruthless advertising chiefs and womanizers in rampant 1950s US yuppie culture, Hokusai's octopus in the room of a male senior CEO could be taken as an expression of monstrous, alpha male power. More markedly so, Jude Buffum's reworking of Hokusai in his video game aesthetics-inspired art work, *The Dream of the Octorok's Wife* (2010), is an example of recent reception that transform the octopuses into ominously malignant beings. Such reworkings are consistent with how the theme became a commonplace of weird, exotic, misogynistic media in the irony of Internet memes featuring Japanese schoolgirls ravaged by octopuses. Hokusai's reception cemented the cultural prototype of the octopus as the monstrous raper and eloper. As an animal hailing from the Sea, but often observed to walk and venture on land, as if transgressing the borders between our world and its own and thus as a potential invader of our cognitive safe space – as a news commentator noted ironically, "nothing is safe" (Koman 2015) – the octopus has lent his features to monsters from unfathomable dimensions, ranging from the ocean's abysses to their projection onto the dark recesses of the psyche.

Ambiguous crevices: the embraces of octopus women

Another recurrent sexualized octopoid motif is the octopus-girl, usually a hybrid monster with tentacles protruding from the lower half of the body. These representations suggest a more marked attention to anxieties related to female genitalia, interspecies intercourse, and miscegenation related to the female body's reproductive functions. As in the case of Hokusai's reception, the octopus ladies of the last decade emerged as the result of novel media formulations through the reception of existing motifs. The case of *Monster Girls Encyclopedia* is exemplary. An illustrated "compendium of knowledge concerning Monster Girls, or *mamonos*", designed by Japanese artist Kenkou Cross, this collection of erotic illustrations features female monsters from the traditions "of many countries, religions, history, literature and Japanese RPGs". Such creatures include mermaids, Medusas,

---

★ See Carbone (2013: 21–42) on how the transnational motif was orientalised as an example of perverse Japan by Western journalists and media.

Echidnas, succubae from the Greco-Roman myths, krakens from the Norse pantheon, and various other myth and literary traditions. Cross adopts the point of view of a scholar who travels around the globe and documents information on Monster Girls – described as the offspring of the carnal union between a "Demon Lord" and "the sultry, seductive, and sexy succubus race", in a narrative where forces of sex and chaos oppose the repression of a "theocratic Chief God".* The narrator finds "creatures that still walk on eight dagger-tipped legs or a million writhing tentacles, but at the same time have rockin' tits and a literally irresistible sexuality". Some of *Monster Girls Encyclopedia's* creatures rework marine monstrosities from previous myths as figures with tentacles writhing from their waist. Scylla, reworked after the Greco-Roman myth, is represented with an overflow of large tentacles and suckers with which she encircles and embraces her male suitors. She is described as a type of monster that launches "sudden tentacle attacks on men" in order to mate with them. The creature looks for a man "who strikes their fancy", and uses its tentacles in order "to force intercourse for the purpose of bearing offspring". Likewise, Charybdis is presented as an example of a species needing human men for food and breeding. The creatures are said to periodically need human men, thus generating whirlpools to entrap and entice them into intercourse. The Kraken – a sea monster from Norse myths, is presented as yet another kind of sexualized octopus girl with tentacles protruding in the place of her legs. All of these creatures result from the same mould of octopus-shaped fantasy. Hailing from the deep seas, the aberrant bodies of the octopus ladies peek at their audiences from beyond the borders of civilization and its sexual taboos.

Such representations are not exclusive of *Monster Girls Encyclopaedia* – rather, they are representative of a proliferating overflow of comics, animation, fan art, and other works reworking myth, fantasy and pornography. Japanese mangaka Horitomo's *My sister is a little Scylla* (2012) is "an eight legged monster girl" featured in a collection titled *Lamia of Love* (Horitomo 2012), in which hypersexualized, neotenic-looking girls sexually engage male protagonists and are used to explore scenarios of incest and miscegenation. On social media and image aggregation platforms like Pinterest or deviantArt, users share and compile collections of amateur art ranging from photorealistic hybrids to cartoonish sketches of alien-looking, feminized octopus figures. Fine art from contemporary artists like Toshio Saeki features, likewise, lurid, modern reworking of *ukiyo-e* themes, often focusing on images of violent and disturbing intercourse between men, women, and octopuses. In one of his illustrations, a bare-breasted 'octomaid' is shown naked while she mates with a young man, encircling him with her tentacles.

By liberally reworking and sexualizing figures from existing mythical canons, octopus girls explore the implications of hybridization between the

---

* A similar plot is in Urotsukidoji (1987–1994), T. Maeda & Takayama, West Cape/Team Mu: Japan.

human and the octopus figure. Recognizable names and figure work as catalysts for this particular sub-set of marine monstrosity, where both phallic tentacles and vaginal orifices – through the mouth of the octopus, coinciding with the creatures' genitalia, are fused onto a feminine body. Such transformations and explorations are popularized through relentless exchanges between artists and audiences: their circulation is international-ized by the Internet and social media's catalogues of iconography. A notable consequence of this process is that, given how many social media allow users easy ways to upload their own material, as well as relative anonymity, sexualized and pornographic explorations could proliferate unbridled in the broader sphere of Internet circulation. Tracing these transformations can be a daunting task, due to their sheer quantity and of the liberality of how professional or amateur artists approach them, ranging the manga aesthetics retained in strands of fantasy media to horror illustrators and amateur artists. It is fair to note, however, that octopus lady motifs capture a wide-spread fixation on such figures on the conflation of vaginal and phallic attributions of the animal-woman hybridized body.

The gendered lives of sex tentacles

Octopoid figures can be seen as motifs of otherness and monstrosity through which artist and audiences consume narratives of gender. The exploration of octopuses' monstrosity, and their hailing from the unfathomable dimen-sion of the sea, can thus be seen first and foremost in relation to specific concerns about the body. In this perspective, many of the examples dis-cussed so far reveal a male gaze that objectifies the feminine body and reveal an undercurrent of normalization of violence and rape culture. No matter how much Hokusai's women are represented as consensual and voluptuous, their encounters with tentacled ravager still cater to male pleasures in a far from gender-equal traditional society.* Likewise, pornographic renditions of *tentacle erotica* more often than not indulge in representations of rape. Toshio Saeki's renditions of females and octopi abound in depictions of rape and violence. Likewise, most of the tentacle porn available on the market exhibits rape narratives. In this perspective, the octopus' physiology makes it a suitable embodiment of an offender from darkness, with which male spectators are assumingly encouraged to identify. Tentacles work as means of coercion and phallic sexual predation, as if the ultimate embodiment of a patriarchal nightmare.

In the art world, such representation can at times become less violent, more female-positive, and include non-necessarily cissexual scenarios. Ken Wong's *Stay and I will Love Thee* (2013) and Audrey Kawasaki's *Enrapture* (2011) feature a sensual encounter with otherness, as does Rune Olsen's depiction of a muscular male with dreadlocks and a cephalopod, showing

---

* On Japan's Edo period, see Screech (2009).

that the motif can also encapsulate more sex-friendly, non-binary, and non-normative explorations and fantasy of sexuality.

The motif of the octopus girl is also largely embedded in rape culture. In the *Monster Girls Encyclopaedia*, reverse-rape myth-narratives are scripted to satisfy male youths' insecurities. Octopus girls are said, on the one hand, to be "extremely lustful": when they suck a man into their nesting holes, "they spread their vagina open with their own fingers and tempt the man". And yet, on the other hand, sexualized fetishization is accompanied by their description as "insecure and starving for affection". Visual clues such as blushing are used to portray the girls as lustful but, at the same time, embarrassed by sexual experiences. Such technique are standardized textual strategies that scholars of animation products have acknowledged as markers of a female character's winnable resistance to sexual advances, and frequently accompany representations of rape, where they are signal the victim's supposed ultimate willingness to be approached by the attacker (Allison 1996, pp. 147–160).* The implicit lewdness made explicit by the markets is thus seen to 'authorize' male insistence. Encounters between Scyllae and human males are described to "regularly end in hot, sticky reverse rape" – a narrative that could be read as designed to satisfy the reader's unconfessed, prohibited desires. Overall, the texts can be argued to not only provide sexually curious and insecure readership with a masturbatory playground, but also with scenarios that normalize the removal of consent assessment in the male fantasy.

Still, once again, heteronormative and male-centred narratives seem to not exclude possible exceptions or more ambiguous readings. The monstrous encounters between a female biologist and the titanic Cthylla (a literary pastiche between the Greco-Roman Scylla and H. P. Lovecraft's Cthulhu) in supernatural literature writer Tina Jens's story 'In her Daughter's Darkling Womb' describes the protagonist as she artificially inseminates the monster while controlling a "spermatophore" device through what is defined as "an hour of flirting and teasing" (Jens 1997, p. 79). Adult pulp tales like *Caught by Scylla* (Dare 2009) seem to target female pleasures as the male model protagonist is sacrificially thrown by his sailing mates in the clutches of the octopoid monster to satisfy her appetites. Alongside the prevalently and patently misogynistic narratives of tentacle erotica, female-oriented pornography inspired by tentacle erotica has also been filmed by female directors for female-oriented sex fantasies.

In this light, the motif of the octopus offers a territory for conceptions of the body, gender, and sexuality not only to be confronted normatively against the Other, but also potentially collapsed within a domesticated fantasy. Tentacles are signifiers though which artists explore power and gender relation in potentially destabilizing ways, through interrogations that chal-

---

* On Japanese manga as a medium and style, in relation to Japanese society, see also Boissou (2010) and Brenner (2007).

lenge the normative boundaries of bodies and species (Carbone 2013, pp. 92–93). In this light, cephalopods inspire many such a fantasy. As Roger Caillois noted, the octopus has "an enormous, isolated, entirely deformable head placed directly on a radiating array of arms" (Caillois 1970, p. 98) – thus explaining its transformation into a lewd and sexually hyperactive creature in phantasy. As a "primordial character", to borrow Needham's formulation (1994), tentacles could be said to variously short-circuit the binary between the human and the non-human, embodying transgressive superimpositions, paradoxes and oxymora. Crawling, tentacle creatures offer both deep otherness and evident sexual connotation on a surface, figurative level. The tentacle is a piece of anatomy that is far removed from our own as a species, and yet can be aligned to our prehensile as well as genital abilities. Scientific magazines recurrently report how certain species of cephalopods have a ghost-like appearance (Dell'Amore 2016), and the fact that octopuses can also walk on land. Their sexual connotation, likewise, are modelled after their being perceived as manipulators and body intruders: tentacles stand as their erotic as well as a repugnant metonymy (Carbone 2013, pp. 91–95). In the motif of the octopus girls, tentacles surround purportedly feminine genitalia, making them symbols in which vaginal and phallic qualities may co-exist.

The cephalopod on the couch

Psychoanalytic approaches to myth-figures and iconography have often stressed the presence of hidden sexual meanings behind motifs such as phallic snakes and vaginal crevices. Sigmund Freud popularized views that associated male genitals with oblong objects and female genitals to doors, passages, and chasms (1940). Freud also used Greek myths such as that of the monstrous-feminine Medusa to explain his analysis of culturally re-pressed sexual anxieties. For Freud, female Greek monsters displayed the terrifying genitals of the Mother; the snakes on the Gorgon's head embodied her phallic qualities, while her mouth stood for the fear of castration of the folk motif of the vagina dentata (Freud 1941) (Csapo 2005, pp. 98–102). Relatedly, psychoanalyst John Flügel related ancient octopus forms of Minoan and Greek art to symbols of a castrating vulva (Flügel 1924). The phallic offenders and octopus women of tentacle erotica seem consistent with such readings, not just because the texts would symptomatically reveal to the analysis the presence of universal of the unconscious mind, but because such innuendos are explicitly formulated at the surface level of the texts, and openly offered to their audiences.

At a figurative level, as noted by psychoanalyst E. Schnier, the tentacles of octopuses make them suitable to endow markedly polyphallic features, which he related to a Freudian interpretation of the oral stage of infants

(Schnier 1956, p. 15).* The octopuses of Hokusai and the other cephalopods from *ukiyo-e,* tentacle erotica, and octopus porn are endowed with bouquets of phallic, prehensile appendices, capable of immobilizing and penetrating their victims with multiple arms. Such features are shared by octomaids, who are encircled with phallic tentacles, and whose centre of the radius from which the tentacles erupt can also be read as a vaginal element, corresponding to the octopus's mouth. The presence of a powerful beak in the physiology of cephalopods' minds thus endows octopus girls with potentially castrating vaginae dentatae: octomaids may be seen as phallic, uterine, castrating, and penetrative.

The genital connotations of the octomaids also align them with ideas of annihilating wombs, capable of suckering in and potentially destroying the victims, or reverting them to a state of unity with the generative body of the mother. Again, such elements are not suggested based on a psychoanalytic treatments of the texts' symptoms – they are explicitly present in the texts. Particularly lurid illustrations in comics show young children and boys as they appear to be suckered back by tentacles into the vaginas of octopus women. Looking at these fantasies, one could think the character is confronted with a womb threatening or promising to re-absorb him or her, even though the polyphallic element also suggests a meeting of the figure of the mother in a reversed birth/coitus situation. Such interpretations are consistent with studies on the consumption of anime products suggesting that certain texts may be designed to cater to a young male readership in order to soothe and overcome a latent Oedipal complex in relation to their mother.** In Freud's traditional conceptualization, the Oedipus complex defined the children's sexual attraction to a parent. Freud suggested that the womb symbolized the pre-Oedipal stage of development, when felicity was expressed in being one with the mother.***

In other fantasies, monstrous-intercourse is related to the ensuing fantasy of monstrous offspring, and with preoccupations with motherhood and miscegenation as the result of mating between humans and monsters. In *Monster Girls'* plot, humans and monster girls generate hybrids. Octopus girls are said to receive "constant marriage proposals", and vignettes from the books series portray scenarios of pregnancy. Many other examples of fan art across web-sites enter openly pornographic representations of pregnant monstrous creatures, often accompanied by the presence of children. Japanese artist Yugi Moriguchi's *Noise of Waves* (2005) depicted a woman ambiguously ensnared by an octopus while she strokes her pregnant womb. Omar Rayyn's *Contessa with Squid* depicts a Medusean lady with tentacles

---

*   The study was inspired by a woodblock by Japanese artist Kuniyoshi.

**   For a psychoanalytic take on erotic manga and anime see Allison (1996). On the complexities of audiences see Shamoon (2004).

*** On Freud's theorization and its limits, see Csapo (2005, p. 102).

protruding from her head in lieu of the snakes of the Greco-Roman monsters, holding a baby squid in a motherly stance.

Such sexualized she-monsters seem tocater to the hotbed of unbridled fantasies of interbreeding and bodily proliferation as much as to patriarchal symbolic order in which the body of the woman is objectified and addressed as the site of culpable interbreeding and miscegenation. Animalistic hybrids have often represented the bestial side of humanity (Dombrowski 2014, p. xv). Genealogies of monsters and deities – hybrids like the Greco-Roman Minotaur generated by Pasiphae and the Bull, or the story of Leda and the Swan – worked as manifestations of the perceived unbridled generative powers of nature. These fantasies can thus be approached – borrowing Braidotti's post-human approach to matter – as an interrogation of *bios* against *zoe*, where the first term denotes life organized anthropocentrically, confined by cultural norms, and he second stands for the wider scope of animal life, explored by fantasy (Braidotti 2012, p. 60). As biologist Dekkers argued, "art and culture are permeated by physical love for animals" (Dekkers 2007, p. 154). Animality has always been related to monstrousness and otherness, in which mankind projects fantasies not only about itself, but also to trespass inter-species boundaries.

Animals, for Rosi Braidotti, are "nature-culture compounds" qualifying as "vectors of post-human relationality" (Braidotti 2012, p. 49). The octopus girls of this study seem to probe zoophilic and monstrophilic fantasies in which ideals of normative humanism are shattered and leave room for ambiguous perspectives: what McCormack defined as "the excesses, potentialities, and infinite protean configurations of form and flesh available in nature" (McCormack 2012, p. 293). Such operations open to both reactionary and potentially liberating, scandalous possibilities in relation to mankind's Others: tentacle erotica could be seen more broadly as a dimension of representation and discourses about body proliferation, germination, and miscegenation (Carbone 2013, p. 104–5).

In and out of the Sea-Womb

Fantasies of interbreeding and miscegenation seem to bring to extreme consequences the *what if* of fantasies of hybrids and bodily permutation. Oliver Wetter's cover of *Cthulhurotica* (Cuinn 2010), a collection of supernatural, weird erotic stories influenced by the creatures of the Lovecraftian *mythos*, represents a woman whose head turns into a medusean bouquet of tentacles. The creatures of *Monster Girls Encyclopedia* explore some of the many combinations of human and animal traits that one can find in the larger motif of the octopus creature. Other body permutations – easily searchable in the many user catalogues of online platforms like Tumblr – shift tentacles and feelers to the mouth; in others, human arms and legs co-exist with tentacles, partially or completely replacing the human limbs; in others yet, creatures range from anthropomorphic octopuses to masses of writhing tentacles. In many scenarios, hybridity offers adaptation to the marine element: representations of sirens and octopus girls show the sexualized maidens in their aquatic settings, enticing their suitors to join them underwater.

This study suggests that through such experimentation artists are reading the theme of the sea as if it were a placenta of the imagination, ripe with opportunities to explore the germinative powers of nature. This interpretative key could be consistent with traditional psychoanalytic treatments of the sea and ocean as metaphors of motherhood. Freud (1920, p. 12) noted that in dreams "birth is almost regularly represented by some reference to water". Kristeva compared the mother as the all-encompassing sea of pregnancy and infancy, prior to the child's entry into language: in 'The maternal body', she reflected on motherness as a bodily growth principle (Kristeva 1975, p. 409). In her poem *Ocean 1212-W* (1962), Edith Plath speaks of the motherly pulse of the sea. Psychoanalyst Ferenczi (1924) believed that any episode of sexual life can be interpreted as a return to the amniotic fluid. Czech psychoanalyst S. Grof even believed that the intrauterine state of the foetus could be associated with a consciousness of the ocean as an aquatic life form comparable to that of a whale, fish, or jellyfish (Grof 1975). In Grof's model of psychological experience (1975, 1988), unconscious 'perinatal matrices' orient the symbiotic unity of the foetus with the maternal organism that is the ocean or the cosmos. Michel Odent, a clinical experimental psychologist, thought water was critical to life because the human fetus grows in the amniotic fluid, and because he saw humans as a kind of primate that, even though related to land animals like chimpanzees, had adapted to land-sea interface (Odent 1993, p. 187; and 1990).

Through this reading, this study does not suggest that the character of the case study's reception of the theme of the octopus is entirely situated at the level of the archetypically or biologically universal unconscious, irrevocably diagnosing that the sea from whence monstrous octopuses emerges is indeed, and for all, always the mother. Rather, the study suggests that the visual cultures that these cases drawn on rely on cultural views of the sea that have been culturally imbued with such association, regardless of whether or not the artists used them warily or unconsciously in psychoanalytic mode.* Art critic C. Morris described the Sea, while discussing painter John Marin, as one of the "elemental big forms" that the artist "cannot possibly avoid", given how culturally the sea has provided its images and symbolism to the arts and literatures (Morris 1955, p. 327). If one looked at the sea like C. G. Jung, water would reveal itself as one of the main archetypes of mankind, symbolizing totality and a principle of "ubiquitous and all-pervading essence" (Jung 1970, p. 278). More circumstantially, this study sees

---

* Such critiques have been levelled at psychoanalysis as a circular model (Schneider 2009, p. 2), a critique that stems from the universalistic way in which Freud conceived of dreams, art and the unconscious as places where one could avoid the "censorious activity which is directed against the unacceptable of the unconscious wish-impulse" (Freud 1920, pp.1).

interrogations of marine hybrids and symbolic reception of the aquatic element as a myth, understood, as in Csapo (1955, p. 327), as resulting from social and cultural transmission, and aimed at exploring specific anxieties.

In this perspective, psychoanalysis captures important symbolic and cultural processes. Psychiatrist Michel Odent thought that myths such as the aquatic-ape theory – first proposed by M. Westenhofer, who claimed (1942) that *homo sapiens* emerged when our ancestors had to adapt to the sea – are useful to explain our cultural relation to the sea.* For Odent, sirens are the most universal legend, and "there is no wonder that water is such a powerful symbol" attracted mankind, given how "a liquid milieu" has been imprinted deeply in our individual and collective experience (Odent 1993, p. 192). Seen in cultural and historical rather than archetypal or positivist-reductionist terms, this theory is interesting because of how it encapsulates the aquatic and the deep as the dark end, the uterus of monsters, and the womb of fears. In such fantasies, water is the place where we cannot see, where otherness proliferates, and from whence the wriggling and writhing of the indistinct – from which we ultimately descend, as a species, in the wider scope of Nature – stares back at us enticingly.

The impact of the sea on imagination can be conceptualized as a process both experiential and cultural. Edith Plath, who was raised in Winthrop-by-the-Sea in Massachusetts, recalls to have for a time as a child believed "not in God or Santa Claus, but in mermaids" (Plath 1963, p. 21). A study on Hokusai's imagination by art critic H. Focillon remarked how, in the critic's view, such fantasies of octopus intercourses could only be inspired by the artists' upbringing in a marine environment, where divers would bring back edible monsters from the sea (Focillon 2003, p. 114). Still, in many of the examples of this study, one could argue that the sea is above all a mediated, represented motif, that various cultural traditions continue to receive as the element in which to locate such monstrous figures of abjection and otherness as the tentacular, pseudo-anthropomorphic, alien octopus.

Conclusions: the monster within

As a concluding remark, this study aims to point out the relation of human imagination to sexualized octopuses as symbolically received animals. In a way, as discussed, cephalopods emerge as weirdly anthropomorphic aliens from the watery element we associate with the unfathomable or the unconscious itself. Moreover, animals are also figures of abjection, pushed by culture into a dimension of irreducible otherness. Philosopher Rosi Braidotti argues that humans establish Oedipal relation with animals, framed by the habit of saturating their representations with projections, taboos and fantasies, while also taking for granted free access to their bodies (Braidotti

---

* Such theses were further popularized by E. Morgan (1982).

(2012, p. 68). This ultimate entitlement towards the lives of Others has also been conceptualized by philosopher Jacques Derrida through his notion of *carnophallogocentrism*, understood as an ideology working at the level of symbolic, political, carnivore, and sexual supremacism (Derrida 2006). In the perspective of this study, the animal is a sex worker of the imagination, as well as a laboured body destined for human consumption.

Such processes are visible in how octopi have been represented as well as treated by humans, both historically and in octopus erotica. French writer Michelet, in his novel *La Mer*, saw the octopus as an "eternal larva" (1861, p. ix) – a gelatinous and horrific foetus that breathed out murder. In Lautréamont's *Chants*, the octopus is a malignant devilish creature whose form is taken by Maldoror to challenge the Creator (1869, Ch. II, pp. 15). In Victor Hugo's *Les Travailleurs de la mer*, the animal emerges from the blackness of dreams and the freakishness of nature (1866, Book V, Ch. 2). In Verne's *twenty-thousand leagues* (1870), octopuses are prominent monsters of the deep – a view that goes back to myth and early marine cartography. The fact that his physiology can be compared to human sexual fantasies has prompted a selective attention to its purported reproductive fixations: in recent times, Jean Painlevé's and Geneviève Hamon's short film *Les amours de la pieuvre* (France 1965) depicted its mating in an aquarium while resorting to the same grim descriptions, ominous bleeps, and themes one can associates with the tentacular space invaders of science fiction. Caillois observed that octopi became malignant in the West especially though eighteenth century science and literature, through works such as an essay by D. de Montfort (1875), which defined the animal as a "devil"; as Caillois argued, the creature was harmonious and benevolent in Mediterranean antiquity and in folk tales and arts of pre-modern Japan (Caillois 1970, p. 88).

Caillois also noted that the "persistent fascination and hyperbolic horror eventually exercised by an animal" did not detract from noting that it was, after all, "more edible than terrifying" (1970, p. 88). The reality of the cases observed in recent times and within tentacle erotica suggests that the image we carve out of octopuses is more akin to a reflecting mirror. So-called artists like Daikichi Amano represent endless expanses of dead octopuses wrapping up naked women. A vast series of amateur photos, easily traceable on the Internet, reveal people's obsession with pictures of dead octopi placed above or inside their sexes. In octopus porn, the demonized, fetishized animal is smeared, consumed and vilified into the alien aggressors that have captured him or her for their own sexist and specieist pleasures. Dead octopuses are photographed in the mouths of naked models, when they are not eaten alive in restaurants serving alleged delicacies like the *san-nakij*. As indeed, while looking for monsters, we are the monsters.

References

Allison, A. (1996), *Permitted and prohibited desires: Mothers, Comics, and Censorship in Japan*, University of California Press.

Attwood, F. (2010), *Porn Studies: From Social Problem to Cultural practice*, in F. Attwood (ed.), *Porn.com: Making Sense of Online Pornography*, New York: Peter Lang.

Barai, A. (2016), 'Speaking the Space between Mother and Child: Sylvia Plath, Julia Kristeva, and the Place of Children's Literature', in M. S. Cecire, H. Field, K. M. Finn, M. Roy (Eds), *Space and Place in Children's Literature. 1789 to the present*, London and New York: Routledge, pp. 39–56.

BBC Earth, "The octopus that strangled its lover to death", http://www.bbc.co.uk/earth/story/20140916-the-octopus-that-strangled-its-lover-to-death (latest access: 15/05/2017).

Boissou, J. M. (2010), *Manga: a historical overview*, in T. Johnson-Woods (ed), *Manga. An Anthology of Global and Cultural Perspectives*, New York: Continuum.

Bolton, C. (2005), *Anime Horror and Its Audience*, in J. McRory (ed.), *Japanese Horror Cinema*, Edinburgh: Edinburgh University Press.

Bornoff, N. (1992), *Pink Samurai. An Erotic Exploration of Japanese Society*, London: Harper and Collins.

Brenner, R. (2007), *Understanding manga and anime*, Westport: Libraries Unlimited.

Braidotti, R. (2013), *The Posthuman*, Cambridge: Polity Press.

Bru, R. (2010), *Tentacles of Love and Death: From Hokusai to Picasso*, in M. Hayakawa, *Secret Images. Picasso and the Japanese Erotic Print*, Thames & Hudson, London.

Caillois, R. (1970), "The Logic of Imagination: Avatars of the Octopus", *Diogenes*, 18: 74–98.

Carbone, M. B. (2013), *Tentacle Erotica. Orrore, seduzione, immaginaripornografici*, Milano-Udine: Mimesis.

Courage, K. H. (2015), 'How male octopuses avoid being eaten by hungry females", *BBC Earth, http://www.bbc.co.uk/earth/story/20150223-mysteries-of-cannibal-octopus-sex* (latest access: 15/05/2017).

Cross, K. (2010), *Monster Girls Encyclopaedia*, Japan: Anime Comics.

Csapo, E. (2005), *Theories of mythology*, Maldon MA and Oxford: Blackwell.

Dare, I. (2013), *Caught by a Scylla*, amazon.co.uk: Amazon Media.

Dekkers, M. (1994), *Dearest pet: on bestiality*, trans. P. Vincent, London and New York: Verso.

Dell'Amore, C. (2016), "Watch an Amazing 'Ghost Octopus' Discovered in the Deep Sea", *National Geographics,* http://news.nationalgeographic.com/2016/03/160304-ghost-octopus-science-animals-oceans/.

Derrida, J. (2006), "Is there a philosophical language?", in L. Thomassem (Ed), *The Derrida-Habermas Reader*, Edinburgh: Edinburgh University Press.

Dombrowski, D. A. (2014), "Philosophical Vegetarianism and Animal Entitlements", in G. Lindsay Campbell, *The Oxford Handbook of Animals in Classical Thought and Life*, Oxford: Oxford University Press, pp. 535–555.

Drell, C. (2017), "Everything You've Ever Wanted to Know About Tentacle Porn", *Glamour*, April 25, http://www.glamour.com/story/everything-to-know-about-tentacle-porn (latest access: 15/05/2017).

Hokusai, K. (1996), *Kinoe no komatsu / Katsushika Hokusai*, Tokyo: Gakken.

Flügel, J. C. (1924), "Polyphallic Symbolism and the Castration Complex", *International Journal of Psycho-Analysis*, Vol. V, No. 2, pp. 155–196.

Focillon, H. (2003), *Hokusai*, Milano: Abscondita.

Freud, S. (1920), *A General Introduction to Psychoanalysis*. New York: H. Liveright (available at: https://archive.org/details/generalintroduct1920freu, latest access: 15/05/2017).

Freud, S. (1941) [1922], "Medusa's Head", tr. J. Strachey, *International Journal of Psychoanalysis*, 22, 69. Available at http://home.utah.edu, latest access: 4 May 2016.

Grof, S. (1975), *Realms Of The Human Unconscious: Observations From LSD Research*, New York: Viking Press.

Horitomo (2012), *My sister is a little Scylla*, Japan: Anime Comic.

Hugo, V. (1866), *Les travailleurs de la mer*, Paris/Bruxelles/Leipzig: Librairieinternationale Lacroix. Book V, Ch. 2.

Jung, C. G. (1956), *Mysterium Coniunctionis: An Inquiry into the Separation and Synthesis of Psychic Opposites in Alchemy,* London: Routledge.

Koman, T. (2015), Watch This Terrifying Octopus Crawl Around on Land, Never Feel Safe, www.Cosmopolitan.com, http://www.cosmopolitan.com/lifestyle/news/a50395/octopus-crawls-on-land/.

Kristeva, J. (1975), 'Motherhood according to Bellini', J. Kristeva, K. Oliver, *The Portable Kristeva*, Columbia University Press.

Kristeva, J. (1982), *Powers of Horror. An essay on abjection*, tr. L. S. Roudiez, New York: Columbia University Press.

Lautréamont, comte de, I. D. (1869), *Les chants de Maldoror*, Paris: Imprimerie Balitout.

MacCormack, P. (2012), *Posthuman Ethics. Embodiment and cultural theory*, Farnham and Burlington: Ashgate.

McClure Smith, R. (1996), 'I Don't Dream about It Any More': The Textual Unconscious in Jean Rhys's "Wide Sargasso Sea", *The Journal of Narrative Technique*, Vol. 26, No. 2 (Spring, 1996), pp. 113–136.

Michelet, G. (1861), *La Mer*, Paris: Hachette et Cie.

Monfort, Henry of (1875), *The octopus or the Devil-Fish of fiction and fact*, London: Chapman and Hall.

Morgan E. (1982). *The aquatic ape*. London: Souvenir Press.

Morris, H. C. (1955), "John Marin: the Sea as Symbol", *Western Humanities Review*, Issue 9, pp. 327–331.

Needham, R. (1988), *Primordial Characters*, University of Virginia Press, Charlottesville.

Norman, M. (2000), *Cephalopods: A World Guide*, Conch Books, Hackenheim.

Odent, m. (1990), *Water and sexuality*. New York: Penguin.

Odent, M. (1993), "Man, the Womb and the Sea: The Roots of the Symbolism of Water", *Pre- and Peri-natal Psychology Journal;* Spring 1993; 7, 3, p. 187–193.

Plath E. (1963), "Ocean W–1212", *The Listener*, August 23, 1963, p. 21.

Ryder, R. D. (2004), "Speciesism revisited", *Think*, Vol. 2 (6), pp. 83–92.

Schnier, J. (1956), "Morphology of a Symbol: The Octopus", *American Imago*, 13, pp. 3–31.

Screech, T. (2009), *Sex and the Floating World. Erotic Images in Japan 1700–1820. Second Edition. Expanded and Updated*. London: Reaktion Books.

Shamoon, D. (2004), "Office Sluts and Rebel Flowers. The Pleasures of Japanese Pornographic Comics for Women", in L. Williams (ed), *Porn Studies*, Durham and London: Duke University Press, pp. 77–103.

Singer, R. T. (1998), *Edo: art in Japan 1615–1868*, Washington: National Gallery of Art.

Verne, J. (1870), *Vingt mille lieues sous les mers*, Paris: Hetzel Éditeur.

Westenhofer, M. (1942). *Der eigenweg des menschen*. Mannstaedt.

Chapter 5

The Octopussy: Exploring representations of female sexuality in Victor Hugo's *The Toilers of the Sea* (1866) and *The Laughing Man* (1868)

Laura Ettenfield

In popular nineteenth-century writings, such as Tennyson's 'The Kraken' or Jules Verne's *Twenty Thousand Leagues Under the Sea*, the octopus is portrayed as a signifier of uncanny presence in a supposedly alien seascape; yet in Victor Hugo's fiction the octopus also represents the fear of female carnal and social independence. Historical Western portrayals of the octopus – including Pliny's description of a gigantic octopus in *Natural History* (circa 77–79AD), Bishop Pontoppidan's account of a kraken in *The Natural History of Norway* (1755) and Olaus Magnus' somewhat confused, quasi-mythological reference to the kraken and sea serpents on his *Carta Marina* (1539) – have all represented the creature as a huge, unfathomable monster which endangers mankind. This perception of the octopus persisted in British cultural understanding, as numerous newspaper articles published in the last three decades of the nineteenth century contained sensational headlines such as 'Attacked by an Octopus' (1879, *The Dundee Courier & Argus*) or 'Fight between a Diver and an Octopus' (1888, *Pall Mall Gazette*); but after the publication of Victor Hugo's *The Toilers of the Sea* (1866) and *The Laughing Man* (1868) the supposedly dangerous octopus also became associated with female sexuality. In contemporary France, Hugo's novels associated the animal octopus with sexually and financially promiscuous females – monstrous women who supposedly endangered men's wallets and sexual supremacy. The portrayal of women as octopus-like, with pervading tentacles and an ominous, fleshy, consuming centre, indicated the perceived threat that the autonomous nineteenth-century woman posed to patriarchal society. Hugo re-formed the Western literary octopus from a threatening presence which must be fought to a detestable indicator of female sexuality and autonomy which must be controlled.

Victor Hugo wrote *The Toilers of the Sea* (1866) from his sea-view desk at Hauteville House while exiled in Guernsey. Hugo's work, and particularly his fictive representation of an octopus, captured the imagination of nineteenth-century society, as Brighton Aquarium's naturalist Henry Lee indicates:

> ... public attention was never particularly attached to it [the octopus] until, within the last few years, Victor Hugo brought it again into notice by the publication of his "*Les Travailleurs de la Mer.*" Since then it has been constantly exhibited in aquaria, and "Octopus" has become a household word. (Lee, 1875, p.xv)

Hugo's fictional propagation of the octopus meant that this elusive subaquatic creature, traditionally associated with danger and aggression – as in the Lernean Hydra myth – became the subject of domestic discussions.

In fact, Hugo's novels were so successful in their portrayal of woman-as-octopus or octopus-as-woman that this definition of women and octopuses as sexualised life-sucking beings permeated beyond social and cultural understandings into nineteenth-century language and scientific documents. In *The Toilers of the Sea* Hugo's terminology for the sea creature directs the reader's understanding of the animal: it is repeatedly named a 'devil-fish' or a 'pieuvre' (Hugo, 1866, p.211, 213). The phrase 'devil-fish' implies the octopus is inherently evil, charging it with demonic intention and agency; this usage of the term 'devil-fish' was directly contested in British newspaper *The Star*:

> It is but wanton ignorance and vulgarity to call the octopus a "devil-fish," when it has about it nothing diabolical or fish-like. It is simply a mollusc... Such a creature is in itself sufficiently wonderful without being invested with fictitious attributes. (*The* Star, 1871, n.p.)

This article, which condemns the demonization of the animal, had little effect on the interpretation of *The Toilers of the Sea*. Hugo's terminology persisted: Brighton Aquarium's naturalist, Henry Lee, published *The Octopus; or, the 'devil-fish' of Fiction and of Fact* nine years after *The Toilers of the Sea* was first published in French; and though in his preface Lee states that his aim is to 'observe carefully, to describe faithfully, to record facts rather than to propound theories', he nonetheless uses Hugo's term 'devil-fish' to add sensation to the title of his work (Lee, 1875, p.vii). Further to this, Lee also follows Hugo in his personification of the classes of mollusca:

> This "paper-sailor," then, whom the poets have regarded as endowed with so much grace and beauty, and living in luxurious ease, is but a fine lady octopus after all. Turn her out of her handsome residence, and, instead of the fairy

skimmer of the seas, you have before you what Mr. Mantalini would call a "dem'd damp, moist, unpleasant body" (Lee, 1875 p.5)

This depiction of the octopus as a feminised, extravagant creature who, without the material charms of her shell, is simply a 'moist' and 'unpleasant' monstrous female, can be traced back to Victor Hugo's *The Toilers of the Sea* 'which made the octopus famous' (ibid, p.11). Hugo's literary descriptions of the octopus have been so influential that the Guernsey term 'pieuvre' is now used widely in France after the word was included in the 1878 dictionary of the Académie Française, replacing the contemporary term *poulpe*. The example given was taken directly from Hugo's *The Toilers of the Sea* (Caillois, quoted by Brombert, 1984, p.153, 261). In France, the term *pieuvre* was also used in the nineteenth-century to signify a sexually promiscuous or money-grabbing woman. It is this association between sexualised animality and materiality which continues to permeate representations of independent women as wanton octopuses.

Gerard Cohen-Vrignaud argues that this representation of woman-as-octopus began with Hugo's *The Toilers of the Sea* and persists in popular culture. Cohen-Vrignaud points out the long-term effect of Hugo's negative representations of the octopus and female autonomy; he lists characters such as the whorish Ursula in Disney's *The Little Mermaid*, and Bond's '"daddy" issues' villain Octopussy as dangerous, sexualised characters who merge animality with sexual licentiousness and financial independence (2012, p.53, 32).* To this list I add Marvel supervillain Lady Octopus and even an episode of *Mad Men* which features a print of Hokusai's nineteenth-century erotic artwork 'The Dream of the Fisherman's Wife' (1814). The artwork, in which two octopuses perform sexual acts on a woman, is selected by character Burt Peterson '"for its sensuality"' though he goes on to explain that he is more interested in '"the man who imagined her ecstasy"' than the sexual hybridity the print represents (*Mad Men*, 2009). This comment refutes the sexuality of the female subject and focuses on the male creator; this Japanese artwork becomes indicative of the Western man's dismissal of female sexuality – it is merely a commodity which can be purchased, judged and fetishized, in line with Hugo's enduring legacy of undermining female independence.

In this chapter I focus on Victor Hugo and his two novels *The Toilers of the Sea* and *The Laughing Man*, both of which portray either the octopus as a wanton woman, or the nineteenth-century Western woman as an octopus. In his work 'On Octopussies, or the Anatomy of Female Power' Gerard Cohen-Vrignaud argues that the above stated Western pop-culture exam-

---

* It is worth noting that despite the significant plot differences in Fleming's short story and Glen's 1983 film, both stories portray the octopus or the octopus-woman as a sexualised threat: Fleming's anti-hero Major Smythe is dragged under the water by his 'Pussy' which he considered one of his 'people' who he 'intimately' 'loved' (1966; 2012, p.1–5); and in the film version Octopussy is a female criminal mastermind whose passion for stolen jewellery parallels only her sexual appetite for James Bond, as encapsulated by the film poster in which Octopussy entraps Bond in her numerous arms.

ples, which link female financial independence and sexuality with life-sucking octopuses, originate in Victor Hugo's *The Toilers of the Sea* and are designed to negate any instance of female sexual or financial autonomy. I will build on Cohen-Vrignaud's work to argue that Hugo further constructs his sexualised octopus-woman through the character of Josiana in *The Laughing Man* and that these representations go beyond popular culture to permeate even factual writings of the nineteenth-century octopus.

In *The Toilers of the Sea*, loner protagonist Gilliatt volunteers himself to rescue a steamboat's engine from a cluster of treacherous rocks far out at sea in return for the hand of wealthy ship-owner's niece, Déruchette. While precariously stationed on the rocks, the combination of extreme physical labour and growing destitution results in Gilliatt undergoing a transformative, somnambulant experience. In the scene preceding Gilliatt's climactic confrontation with the octopus we are told that 'Gilliatt awoke feeling very hungry' (Hugo, 1866, p.208). The blunt reference to the protagonist's physical needs seems somewhat out of place in Hugo's otherwise dreamy and philosophical novel. This sudden sensory description of Gilliatt's ravenousness becomes a discursive way of addressing his hunger for carnal experience; the abstinent Gilliatt has found his sexual appetite. It is with the prize of the wealthy and sexually attractive Déruchette in mind, then, that virginal Gilliatt searches to satisfy his carnal impulses. Instead Gilliatt encounters an octopus, and this submarine encounter can be viewed as a universal, masculinised wet dream of heterosexual male dominance over perceived licentious female autonomy.

Gilliatt's entrance into the submarine grotto of the octopussy's lair is described as 'wonderful', 'strange' and 'gloomy' to the inexperienced Gilliatt (Hugo, 1866, p.159, 158). The passage to the octopus' cavern becomes interchangeable with the female anatomy: it is 'more than an opening' which is 'never dry', but 'polished and slippery' with 'ruddy, blood-coloured stains on the walls' culminating in a womblike 'chamber resembling a sanctuary' (Hugo, 1866, p.209, 210). Intrigued rather than deterred by this sexualised environment, Gilliatt discovers 'a horizontal crevice in the granite' and 'plunging his hand in, began to grope about in the darkness' (ibid, p.210). Initially half-concealed in the rock, the unsuspecting octopus is probed by Gilliatt. Hugo warns that though one may wander into the octopus' lair 'filled with wonder, you may leave it paralysed with fear' (Hugo, 1866, p.212). Indeed, Gilliatt's groping invasion into the octopus' habitat reveals the most terrifying aspect of indulging heterosexual masculine curiosity – female reciprocation and autonomy. Gilliatt's journey into the octopussy's lair thus becomes an imaginative venture into nineteenth-century gendered sexual politics.

Physically, the sex of an octopus is not always apparent – their anatomy requires careful studying to determine whether it is male or female. In *The Toilers of the Sea*, there is no examination of the octopus to determine its biological sex. Instead the octopus is feminised due to its supposedly impalpable body: Hugo is confused by the octopus' 'orifice' or 'opening' which, like the human vagina, 'is the entrance and the exit'; he describes the octopus as 'a species of sticky, slimy, living creature', which again can be read as synonymous with female genitalia (Hugo, 1866, p.213). Gerard Cohen-Vrignaud observes that in the original French Hugo 'almost always' describes the octopus in 'grammatically feminine... gendered pronouns', blatantly attributing femininity to the octopus and painting the *pieuvre* as a feminised creature of sexual agency (Cohen-Vrignaud, 2012, p.39). Anthropomorphising her, Hugo recounts Denis Montford's allegation that 'the poulp has human passions' (Hugo, 1866, p.213), portraying the octopus with an agency which exceeds that of other sea creatures. Hugo also claims that the octopus 'has its passions and its submarine unions', and deliberately 'becomes phosphorescent' in order to make herself 'beautiful' (ibid, p.214). Cohen-Vrignaud notes that this description of 'the octopus is animated by a scandalous sexual activity, which means that she, much like a fallen woman, tarts herself up in an attempt to snare a mate' (Cohen-Vrignaud, 2012, pp.39–40). Hugo attributes sexual agency to the feminised octopus, then, only to debase and destroy her.

Gilliatt's newly discovered sexual appetite is met by the octopus's voraciousness, and Gilliatt experiences reciprocated feminised desire rather than masterful masculine sexual agency as Hugo tells how 'his arm was grasped, and a feeling of indescribable horror crept over him' (Hugo, 1866, p.210). Entwined in the suctioned limbs of the octopus, the carnally curious Gilliatt struggles to separate his body from the feminised creature's sucking hold. Hugo uses sensual, climatic language to describe their physical mergence: for Gilliatt 'a pang went through his body' and 'every nerve and muscle of his body [was made] to quiver' as 'it seemed as if innumerable minute mouths had fastened upon his body' (Hugo, 1866, p.211). Alongside this, Hugo narrates Gilliatt's revulsion for this intimacy with the 'repulsive shapes' and the 'strange pressures' of the *pieuvre* (Hugo, 1866, p.211). Cohen-Vrignaud explains that Gilliatt's contradictory response to the sensual struggle with the 'octopussy' is encapsulated by 'the way she bridges the dualities of pleasure and horror, empowerment and powerlessness, active subject and passive object' (Cohen-Vrignaud, 2012, p.33, 35). The octopussy's physical response to Gilliatt's groping hands is both alluring and repulsive: Gilliatt is intrigued and aroused by the 'slow undulations' (Hugo, 1866, p.212) of the animal, yet she also threatens sexual, life-ending consumption. The octopussy's physical prowess jeopardizes Gilliatt's search for sexual dominance.

Gilliatt soon learns the dangers of groping around in unknown passageways which appear similar to the female anatomy. Having felt and fondled the octopussy in her lair, she then fully reveals herself from the darkness of the crevice and we are told that 'Finally a huge slimy mass, round and flattened, issued from below the cavity' and Gilliatt 'gave himself up for lost' (Hugo, 1866, p.211). The horror of responsive animalistic female sexuality overcomes Gilliatt as his carnal curiosity exposes him to the full power of the independent female octopussy. Desperate to dominate over the hold of the octopussy, Gilliatt kills the creature with his knife at the moment of climax:

> ... he struck a decisive blow with his knife. There were two convulsions in reverse directions – that of Gilliatt and the pieuvre. It was like the meeting of two flashes of lightning. Gilliatt had plunged the point of his knife into the flat, slimy substance, and with a rapid circular movement, like the flourish of a whip, he tore off the head... It was all over in an instant. The creature dropped at once; the terrible folds relaxed; it fell like a mass of wet linen... Panting with his efforts, Gilliatt could see, on the pebbles at his feet, two shapeless masses of slimy matter... Fearing that it might seize him again in a last convulsive moment of agony, he hastily withdrew beyond the reach of its tentacles. (Hugo, 1866, pp.218–9).

The brutality of this climax kills female sexual response and restores Gilliatt's masculine dominance. Having convulsed with, plunged into, and then executed the octopussy, Gilliatt is represented as blameless in contrast to the supposedly predatory, sexualised female octopus. Hugo condemns the 'fearful creature' which he claims is 'full of cunning; it endeavours to stupefy its prey, and therefore seizes it and waits' (Hugo, 1866, p.218). So despite Gilliatt's feelings of hunger, his deliberate journey into the octopussy's cavern which is synonymous with female anatomy, and his thrusting grope into the octopussy's lair, Hugo nonetheless entirely blames the feminised octopus for Gilliatt's own purposefully invasive and penetrating sexual encounter.

Hugo's description of an octopus attack parallels heterosexual intercourse in which the human male is forced into passivity:

> You are struggling with a void... Your muscles swell, your sinews are twisted, your blood boils, and is horribly mingled with the slime of the creature... The hydra incorporates itself with the man, and the man with the hydra; you become one and the same... the poulp, horrible to relate, draws you into its system... drags you to him and into him; bound helplessly, glued where you stand, utterly powerless, you are gradually emptied into a loathsome receptacle, which is the monster itself. (Hugo, 1866, pp.214–5)

This is one of the few occasions (in the translation I have used, at least) where the octopus' gender shifts. Cohen-Vrignaud briefly refers to this problem in English translations, where the octopus becomes an 'it' rather than a 'she' as Hugo originally penned her, and like Cohen-Vrignaud I will overlook this temporary masculine pronoun in order to sustain the tenor of my argument (2012, p.39). After all, despite the use of the word 'him', this quotation is irrefutably rife with sexual allusion. For Hugo the disgust of this scene lies in the supposed passivity of the human male who is subjected to feminised intercourse, as the female remains an uncanny 'monster' and a 'loathsome receptacle' who takes power and agency from the sexually active male. This description of an encounter with an octopus, which is not Gilliatt's experience but is written in generalised terms, invites direct comparison between a fatalistic submarine animal attack and reciprocated female sexuality. The sexually knowledgeable female is blatantly demonised by Hugo.

In his aforementioned work, Henry Lee accounts for the so-called "devil-fish" and offers a scientific explanation for its sucking hold on Gilliatt: Hugo's octopus may well be a hen protecting her young rather than a sexualised 'highly-coloured' predator of virginal men (Lee, 1875, p.19). While the scene in *The Toilers of the Sea* is exceedingly erotic, Lee explains that this reciprocated grasp from the octopus is actually a typical demonstration of a female octopus guarding her young. Lee recounts an instance where he documented the nursing hen, recalling how she initially settled into 'a recess in the rock-work' (1875, p.56):

> Her body just filled the entrance to it, and she further strengthened its defences by dragging to the mouth of her cavern two dozen or more of living oysters, and piling them one on another to form a breast-work or barricade, behind which she ensconced herself. Over this rampart she peered with her great, sleepless, prominent eyes; her two foremost arms extended beyond it, their extremities colliding and writhing in ceaseless motion, as if prepared to strike out right and left at any intruder. She seemed never to be taken unawares, and was no more to be caught napping than a cunning middy "caulking it" in the middle watch. (ibid)

Lee's handbook on the octopus was allegedly an 'endeavour to compare the "devil-fish" of the author with the octopus of nature' (ibid, p.19); yet Lee himself could not help but write about the octopus in anthropomorphised terms. Having defended the hen, he then goes on to anthropomorphise and demonise her due to her gendered instincts, just as Hugo demonises his fictitious octopus:

> Her companions evidently felt that it was dangerous to approach an excited mother guarding her offspring, and none ventured to go within arm's length of her. Even her forlorn husband was made to keep his distance. If he dared to approach with intent to whisper soft words of affection into his partner's ear, or to look with paternal pride on the newly-born infants, the lady roused herself with menacing air, and slowly rose till her head over-topped the barrier; ... a dark flush of anger tinged the whole surface of the body; the two upper arms were uncoiled and stretched out to their utmost length towards the interloper; and the poor snubbed, hen-pecked father, finding his nose put out of joint by the precious baby, which belonged as much to himself as to its fussy mother, invariably shrank from their formidable contact, and sorrowfully and sullenly retreated, to muse, perhaps, on the brief duration of cephalopodal marital happiness. (ibid, p.57)

Like Hugo's narrative, this description endows the octopus with a selfish intent which purportedly follows sexual knowledge – the octopus here is depicted as a monstrous, unchaste, and overbearing female whose aggression is linked to self-indulgent motherhood and misandrist feeling. So while Lee claims his intention was to 'indicate the points on which M. Hugo's representation of his "monster" is either substantially correct, partly true, or entirely unreal', Lee nonetheless continues to personify, and thus misrepresent, the actual animal (ibid, p.19).

It is notable that Hugo's fictionalised – and highly sexualised – account of Gilliatt's encounter, does nonetheless pertain to some facts about the behaviour of the real octopus. It is even more significant that the behaviour of the female octopus in this instance does in fact relate to female independence: the hen is capable of protecting her offspring autonomously. The behaviour of Hugo's fictionalised female octopus reflects the natural process of a hen defending her young; yet Hugo's writing of the octopus instead attributes her actions to sexuality and promiscuity rather than to instinctive or maternal behaviours. Lee did little to prohibit this misrepresentation of the octopus, as he outlines early on in his handbook that there is little difference between 'the florid conceptions of the novelist, and the scarcely less romantic, though truthful, description of the naturalist.' (Lee, 1875, p.10). Although Lee described Hugo's writing of the octopus as 'fallacious', Lee himself is unable to extricate his scientific discoveries from the cultural understanding of the octopus. He writes of the creature that 'there is a repulsiveness about the form, colour, and attitudes of its captor which invests it with a kind of tragic horror.' (ibid, p.10, 24). Lee disputes Hugo's claim that the feminised octopus is void inside, with only a singular 'orifice in the centre of its tentacles' (Hugo, 1866, p.213), yet Lee gained this knowledge by actually repeating Gilliatt's fictional probing and penetrating the animal:

> ... if anyone, believing the fictionist, were to place his finger in the small circular orifice at the base of the arms... [a] sharp nip might perhaps teach him that it has not only muscles, but a mouth and head also. For just within the oral cavity lie, retracted and hidden, but ready for use whenever wanted, a pair of horny mandibles which bite vertically... (Lee, 1875, p.25)

Lee refutes Hugo's fictive octopus, then, only to perform his own groping investigation into the real one. He portrays the octopus' body as an animalistic *vagina dentata*, which Cohen-Vrignaud explains is a myth which 'imagine[s] women's parts as a frightening and sometimes toothed mouth that spreads death and destruction.' (Cohen-Virgnaud, 2012, p.34). Lee's testimony does little to diminish the demonization of the so-called 'devil-fish'. Instead he admits that to analyse completely *The Toilers of the Sea* 'is beyond my powers' – despite spending two chapters investigating this fictitious representation (Lee, 1875, p.31). Hugo's quasi-philosophical treatise on the octopus leaves the naturalist perplexed, as he admits: '[o]ne can only wonder what it all means' (ibid).

Although Gilliatt's *petite morte* came at the expense of the octopussy's actual death, the closing scenes of the novel manifest the danger of female independence for Gilliatt. Having saved the steamboat's engines, Gilliatt goes to claim his prize, Déruchette, only to find in his absence that she has chosen to marry another man. While Gilliatt survived the sexual autonomy of the octopus, he fails to endure the reality of Déruchette's independent sexual and financial decision to marry someone else. Unable to face this rejection Gilliatt drowns himself in the sea: the independence of the sexualised woman comes at the cost of his life.

In Hugo's fiction the link between female autonomy and the octopus is more explicit in *The Laughing Man* (also known as *The Man Who Laughs*) which Hugo wrote just two years after *The Toilers of the Sea*. The comparison of female sexual deviance and financial independence with a life-sucking octopus is fully developed in *The Laughing Man* through the character of Duchess Josiana. Josiana is repeatedly represented as a spider, which Victor Brombert argues 'unavoidably brings to mind the giant *pieuvre*' of *The Toilers of the Sea* (1984, p.193). Thus Josiana is both spider and *pieuvre*: she is a predatory, fear-inspiring creature with eight legs who entraps and consumes her victims in her lair. This depiction of women as sexualised predators can also be seen in other nineteenth-century fictional representations of women, such as in Gustave Doré's illustration of Arachne for Dante's *Purgatorio* in his *Divine Comedy*. However, I will focus on how Hugo represents Josiana as an octopussy by emphasising her blatant animalistic sexuality and wealth. Kathryn Grossman has condemned Josiana as a 'wicked temptress' who represents 'material impulses' (Grossman, 2012, p.98), yet Josiana is actually an example of how female independence poses a direct threat to patriarchal power. Grossman's critical response to Josiana indicates that the fear of Hugo's literary octopussy still dictates how feminine sexual and social liberation is perceived today.

The Laughing Man tracks the mutilated protagonist, Gwynplaine, as 'the lost boy' who is abandoned as a child and brought up as a poor player in a travelling theatre. It is during one of his performances that we are introduced to the octopussy Josiana. Seated in the usually empty space reserved for nobility, the Duchess is described by Hugo as 'pink… [and] of the purple, and one felt that she did not fear the blush' (Hugo, 1868; 1900, p.220), just as the colour-changing *pieuvre* 'blushes' (Darwin, 1859, p.17) and 'like human beings… turns pale when exhausted, and flushes red under the influence of anger or excitement' (Lee, 1875, p.29). Similarly, the Duchess gives out an 'irradiation' which 'overflowed' (ibid) like Gilliatt's 'frightening' phosphorous polyp (Hugo, 1866, p.214), and the 'slightly phosphorescent' octopus which Darwin kept (Darwin, 1859, p.18). She is, most importantly, a 'dazzling creature' whose eyebrows were 'blackened' with 'ink' (Hugo, 1868; 1900, p.220) and her one blue eye and one black eye associate her sexualised gaze with the inkiness of Gilliatt's animal octopus which 'has two large but indistinct eyes, resembling the colour of the sea' (Hugo, 1866, p.213), and Jeffrey's nineteenth-century factual account of the animal octopus whose 'merciless eyes' convey an 'almost fiendish expression' (Jeffrey, 1865, p.144). Hugo describes Josiana as 'the effect of a vision', and she is also named a 'phantom', a 'spectre' and an 'apparition'; like the octopus, her presence is associated with fluid impalpability rather than actual concrete existence (Hugo, 1868; 1900, p.221, 222, 224). Her obvious wealth and oozing sexuality are confirmed for the virginal Gwynplaine by a note she sends to him in which she declares:

> You are hideous; I am beautiful. You are a player; I am a duchess. I am the highest; you are the lowest. I desire you! I love you! Come! (Hugo, 1868; 1900, p.231)

Josiana's categorisation as an octopussy is complete: there can be no denying her material independence or sexual appetite. Henry Lee claims that the animal octopus possesses 'an instinctive desire to lay hold on anything moving within reach' (Lee, 1875, p.34); it is clear that Hugo's depiction of Josiana's erotic invitation to Gwynplaine likewise presents her as a sexually threatening yet simultaneously alluring octopussy who wants to capture and consume the virginal protagonist. Gwynplaine reinforces this reading of Josiana as a dangerous creature from the depths with the declaration of 'What! From the depth of the impossible had this chimera come!' (Hugo, 1868; 1900, p.233).

Having initially refused the Duchess' note, the discovery of Gwynplaine's patronage as the long lost Lord of Clancharlie the following day leads to him being taken directly to the palace where Josiana lives. In a scene reminiscent of Gilliatt's deliberate journey into the *pieuvre's* lair after dreaming of Déruchette, Gwynplaine instinctively wanders to the Duchess's chambers. As in *The Toilers of the Sea*, the interconnected passages and chambers of Josiana's palace link to the female anatomy: the sexually inexperienced Gwynplaine's confusion regarding the 'unknowable depths', the 'receptacle of mysterious disappearances' and the 'secret and bewildering' inner workings of the palace, illustrate his sexual ignorance and his curiosity as he 'explored every passage he came to' (Hugo, 1868; 1900, p.326, 327). Eventually, after purportedly being lost, Gwynplaine is 'encompassed by a net of wonders' as he stumbles into the watery lair of the octopus-woman, signalled by 'a gentle noise... like dropping water' (ibid, p.328).

Entranced by the sounds and potential sights of the Duchess' bathroom, Gwynplaine ventures down the sexualised 'dark, narrow passage' of the virgin Duchess's quarters (Hugo, 1868; 1900, p.328); he experiences what Hamilton-Paterson describes as the 'inexorable', 'downward tug' (Hamilton-Peterson, 2013, p.45) of curiosity towards the sea-monster. Yet this sea monster is one of Hugo's imaginative creations and therefore does not just endanger human life, instead she is a self-sufficient, resolute woman who is sexually and financially unrestrained and who can be perceived as a threat to nineteenth-century patriarchy. Hugo's description of Josiana's lair associates her once again with the octopus: she has an 'octagon' bathroom with 'eight small Venetian mirrors'; like the octopus she basks in water, luxuriantly allowing her bath to overflow (Hugo, 1868; 1900, p.329). Gilliatt's devil-fish hides in a wall crevice (Hugo, 1866, p.210), as does the actual animal octopus (Lee, 1875, p.56), and Josiana likewise can be spied through 'an opening in the marble wall' covered only by a 'fairy-like' curtain which is 'transparent' and comparable to a sheet of water (Hugo, 1868; 1900, p.329). Like Gilliatt's dualistic response to the *pieuvre*, Gwynplaine is similarly torn between arousal and fear:

> Through the centre of this web, where one might expect a spider, Gwynplaine saw a more formidable object – a naked woman. Yet not quite naked... Her dress was a long chemise... so fine that it seemed liquid. (Hugo, 1868; 1900, p.330)

As she lies there, vulnerable, asleep, unaware she is being watched, it is actually Gwynplaine who becomes the monster; he has taken the place of the predatory octopus, watching an unwitting Josiana through a crack in the curtain. Hugo narrates how 'the moral force which has been preserving the balance gives way, and down we go' (ibid, p.332), implying that Gwynplaine's penetrative invasion into Josiana's privacy is not attributable to the protagonist, but to some uncontrollable force of immorality or sexual instinct. So despite being asleep during Gwynplaine's deliberate invasion into her private rooms, and despite Gwynplaine gawping at Josiana's naked vulnerability, Hugo nonetheless continues to represent Josiana as a predatory octopus – a sexualised monster by which Gwynplaine is subjected. Josiana is not dragging Gwynplaine down: Gwynplaine is *choosing* to satisfy his carnal curiosity. Yet once again, the 'formidable' octopussy is blamed for the male protagonist's sexual desire (ibid, p.330).

Hugo bluntly categorises Josiana – in contrast to his refusal to classify the *poulpe* in *The Toilers of the Sea* (1866, p.215) – as representative of all womankind. He states how the sleeping Duchess is defined through her likeness to anti-patriarchal historical female figures, as 'Messalina was perhaps, present though invisible, and smiled, while Diana kept watch' (Hugo, 1868; 1900, p.331). By comparing Josiana to the virginal Diana who killed the man who saw her nakedness while she was bathing, and also associating Josiana with the executed Messalina's perceived promiscuity and influence, Hugo's arachnid-octopus-woman embodies a generalised fear of female anatomy, dangerous sexual temptation, and the larger societal issue of the potential political and sexual autonomy of women. Hugo's allusion to Messalina and Diana link the female body and feminine independence with danger at the male's expense, supporting Cohen-Vrignaud's assertion that 'the pleasures women must give are not just a sign of their weakness but also the possibility of their power' (Cohen-Vrignaud, 2012, p.35); after all, it is

Josiana'a sexual and financial power which allegedly threatens Gwyn-plaine's newfound place in patriarchal society. Josiana is Hugo's ultimate octopussy: she poses a carnal and material threat to Gwynplaine who suddenly finds himself on equal ground with this strong, independent Duchess.

The potential equality between Gwynplaine and Josiana is distorted by Hugo's narrative, as he maintains that it is Josiana who is the sexualised manipulator of this situation. Rather than acknowledging the sexual perver-sion of his wandering protagonist, Hugo instead reinforces Josiana as an octopussy who threatens the purity of Gwynplaine: 'There she was in that lonely room – asleep, far from succour, helpless, alone, at his mercy – yet he was in her power!' (Hugo, 1868; 1900, p.333). Although Kathryn Grossman acknowledges that the 'virginal temptress' 'is neither impure nor chaste, simply bored and jaded' (2012, p.114), the octopussy nonetheless continues to be connected with regressive animality and this assertion that Josiana is merely 'bored and jaded' refuses the Duchess any autonomous agency and is instead redolent of a predator playing with its prey before consuming it. When Josiana awakes and speaks of sexual revolution, independence and her desire to 'Bring the highest and the lowest together' (Hugo, 1868; 1900, p.337–8), Hugo deliberately prohibits the planned sexual liberation of both Josiana and Gwynplaine. The octopussy's plans of sexual empowerment are blotted into nothingness through octopus ink itself, as Hugo exerts his phallic pen to rewrite Josiana into subservience. Informed of Gwynplaine's newfound social place through a letter signed by the Queen, but composed by two male characters – and of course written by Hugo himself – Josiana's equality is overwritten by multiple masculine pens. She is forced back into chastity and material dependence as the Queen's letter commands that 'Gwynplaine shall be your husband, and that you shall marry him.' (ibid, p.343). The prospect of a sexual relationship between the two is no longer illicit and thus takes away Josiana's sexual *and* financial agency: to marry Gwynplaine entails physical consummation and financial dependence and prohibits her from making her own decisions. Hugo portrays Josiana as an octopussy and then utterly restricts her autonomy. This control of her sexual and financial independence encapsulates Cohen-Vrignaud's notion of 'the unsettling possibility that female autonomy might make male anatomy redundant' (Cohen-Vrignaud, 2012, p.32).

And in a way, Gwynplaine is made redundant. While he is lusting after the octopussy, his supposedly beloved (though temporarily forgotten) Dea falls fatally ill and Gwynplaine escapes the palace just in time to watch her die. Overcome by the knowledge that he was creeping over an octopussy rather than caring for his soul-mate, Gwynplaine drowns himself. Gilliatt's death is attributed to Déruchette and Gwynplaine's suicide is supposedly Josiana's fault: Hugo holds the female octopussy responsible for the deliberate sexual-ised actions of both his male protagonists. Grossman states that 'Gwynplaine's temptation by Josiane's material charms threatens to obliterate his devotion to the higher ideals' (Grossman, 2012, p.98, 110); and so it is again the 'temptation' and 'charms' of the octopussy which take the blame for the protagonist's suicide, despite Gwynplaine's deliberate entrance into the Duchess's chamber and Gilliatt's purposeful invasion of the octopussy's lair. The suicide of Hugo's protagonists in itself reinforces the demonization of Gilliatt's feminised octopus and the Duchess Josiana. In *William Shakespeare* Hugo claimed that 'To be dead is to be all-powerful' (Hugo, 1864, n.p.), and Gilliatt and Gwynplaine's self-destruction is actually self-empowerment which ensures that the feminised octopus or the octopus-woman are blamed for their deaths. This depiction of octopussies as fatalistic, sexualised, autonomous manipulators portrays feminine independence as deathly perilous, and thus upholds nineteenth-century patriarchal values.

In these two novels, then, Hugo leaves a lingering legacy of the octopussy which endures. Cohen-Vrignaud states that 'men inflate their own power by mocking women's autonomous anatomy' (Cohen-Vrignaud, 2012, p.33), and this is evident in both *The Toilers of the Sea* and *The Laughing Man*. These texts illustrate Hugo's determination to portray financially and sexually independent women as degenerative, linking female desire to ravenous, predatory octopuses. Hugo's work succeeded in both undermining female autonomy and demonising the animal octopus. After the publication of *The Toilers of the Sea* Cohen-Vrignaud describes how 'a new social type was born, the wanton woman who manipulates men's desires and extorts his male privilege by instrumentalizing her "octopussy"' (Cohen-Vrignaud, 2012, p.33), and I argue Hugo's *The Laughing Man* further reinforces this categorisation of women as financially consuming predators who are sexually licentious. Gilliatt's and Gwynplaine's sexually resonant experiences with octopussies demonised both the woman and the creature, yet the male protagonist's need for total dominance came at a refusal to acknowledge female sexuality and independence.

For Hugo himself, the fear of female independence and sexuality was a very real one. Put in the real-life context of Hugo's own experiences, his reputation as an egotistical womaniser persists, yet what is perhaps less well known is that Hugo suspected his own wife of infidelity, and after the birth of his daughter Adèle, Hugo himself went through a period of sexual repression and abstinence (Brombert, 1984, p.66). His anxieties regarding female sexuality can be further illustrated through the recollection of one of his dreams in which a naked woman is tied on a wheel and rotated around (Brombert, 1984, p.194), the movement of her limbs and the exposure of her orifices calling to mind the many tentacles of the *pieuvre*. Hugo's dream eerily matches his description in *The Toilers of the Sea* of how octopus limbs 'resemble the spokes of a wheel' (Hugo, 1866, p.212–3); and indeed, it seems that Hugo's sexualised octopus-woman haunted his own sleep, as his daughter recorded in her diary that he 'could not go to bed without a kind of dread, that he complained of waking up with a "sacred horror" of his nightly visitations.' (Brombert, 1984, p.237).

Likewise, Hugo's authorial smattering of the self on the page through his inked illustrations can be viewed as an attempt to redefine and control female sexuality. Many of his artworks, which were produced while in exile in Guernsey, contain undeniable sexual overtones. Works such as 'The Mouth of Darkness' (1856) which is an illustration of a gloomy cavern aesthetically similar to the vagina-like grotto in *The Toilers of the Sea*, and 'The Snake' (1866), which depicts a dark phallic snake with blood erupting from its mouth, were composed around the time Hugo was writing *The Toilers of the Sea* and *The Laughing Man* and provide a visual representation of the anxieties contained within his writing: reciprocated feminine sexuality, and masculine redundancy. Perhaps his most striking illustration, *La Pieuvre* (1866) – again, note the feminine pronoun – illustrates Hugo's manipulation of the octopus, as her tentacles curl around themselves unnaturally in order to present his initials at the top centre of the image, placing himself above the unnecessarily demonised octopus. Victor Brombert has commented that 'Hugo's graphic work was for him an important form of self-expression' which 'parallels his written work, at times precedes and inspires it' and 'often displays an obsession with his own name or initials.' (Brombert, 1984, p.xi). His *La Pieuvre* embodies all Brombert's assertions: the depiction of an octopus, created in octopus ink, twisted to champion his initials definitely parallels his fictional control and contortion of octopus-women. In his artwork and in his fiction, Hugo reinforces and reminds his viewer and reader of his own patriarchal dominance as the 'paternalist figure' of nineteenth-century French fiction (Cohen-Vrignaud, 2012, p.36).

The octopussy, then, was created by Hugo in order to undermine female autonomy and the octopus became a genuine symbol of fear through which he successfully undermined female independence. Hugo was 'widely considered the national poet-laureate, whose every work was a guaranteed sensation', and he used this status to pen the perceived growing independence of women as regressive, dangerous, and abhorrent (Cohen-Vrignaud, 2012, p.36). Hugo was hugely successful in this endeavour – so successful, in fact, that he not only triumphed in demonising the woman and the octopus, but he also succeeded in scaring himself into practising abstinence and having nightmares of vulnerable, sexualised octopus-women. In a letter composed by Hugo he claimed that 'I, too, am an octopus' (ibid, p.54) – yet he possessed something that he deliberately denied nineteenth-century women: unbridled sexual promiscuity and financial independence.

References

Attacked by an Octopus (1879) *The Dundee Courier & Argus*, 8 September, n.p.

Brombert, V. (1984) *Victor Hugo and the Visionary Novel*. Cambridge: Harvard University Press.

Brombert, V. (1988) *The Hidden Reader: Stendhal, Balzac, Hugo, Baudelaire, Flaubert*. London: Harvard University Press.

Cohen-Vrignaud, G. (2012) 'On Octopussies, or the Anatomy of Female Power'. *Differences*. 25 (1). pp.32–60.

Darwin, C. (1859) *The Voyage of the Beagle*. New York: P F Collier & Son. Available from: https://ia800306.us.archive.org/25/items/voyageofbeagle00darwuoft/voyageofbeagle00darwuoft.pdf [accessed 20 April 2017].

Fight between a Diver and an Octopus (1888) *Pall Mall Gazette*, 17 December, p.9.

Fleming, I. (1966; 2012) 'Octopussy'. *Octopussy and The Living Daylights*. London: Vintage. pp.1–46.

Grossman, K. M. (2012) *The Later Novels of Victor Hugo: Variations on the Politics and Poetics of Transcendence*. [Accessed online]. Oxford: Oxford University Press. Available from: ttp://www.oxfordscholarship.com [accessed 11 May 2016].

Hamilton-Paterson, J. (2013) The Monsters Within. *Aquatopia*. Tate, pp.44–48.

Hugo, V. (1864) *William Shakespeare*. Translated from the French by Melville B. Anderson. London: George Routledge & Sons. Available from: ttps://archive.org/stream/williamshakespea00hugouoft/williamshakespea00hugouoft_djvu.txt [accessed 27 April 2017].

Hugo, V. (1866) *The Toilers of the Sea*. Translated from the French by an unnamed translator. London: Walter Scott Limited.

Hugo, V. (1868; 1900) *The Laughing Man*. Translated from the French by an unnamed translator. London & Glasgow: Collins' Clear-Type Press.

Jeffrey, G. & Voorst, V. (1869) *British Conchology*. Vol. 5. [Online]. Available from: ttp://ia600206.us.archive.org/28/items/britishconcholog05jeffr/britishconcholog05jeffr.pdf.

Le Pieuvre (1871) *The Star*. 30 November. n.p.

Lee, H. (1875) *The Octopus; or, the "devil-fish" of fiction and of fact*. London: Chapman and Hall. Available from: ttps://ia800205.us.archive.org/7/items/octopusordevilf00leegoog/octopusordevilf00leegoog.pdf [accessed 18 April 2017].

Mad Men series 3 (2009) *Out of Town*. New York City: AMC, 16 August, 22:00.

Octopussy (1983) Directed by John Glen. California: MGM. [video: DVD].

The Octopus.* (1875) *The Pall Mall Gazette*. Issue 3358. 22 November. pp.9–10.

Chapter 6

Psychedelic Deep Blues: the Romanticised Sea Creature in Jimi Hendrix's '1983 … (A Merman I Should Turn to Be)' (1968), Tim Buckley's 'Song to the Siren' (1968) and Captain Beefheart's 'Grow Fins' (1972)

Richard Mills

Introduction

The three songs under discussion are cultural texts that foreground male fears concerning the unresolved tension between male and female binaries. All of the artists are male musicians in the rock, folk, blues and jazz traditions of late-1960s music-business culture. As such, their lyrics sometimes resort to gender stereotypes; however, the imagery and characterisation of mermaids and sirens in these songs are ambivalent actualisations of sexual politics.

All three songs are characterized by doubt, ambivalence and exoticism concerning the mermaid/siren other. Buckley sings 'I'm as puzzled as the oyster/I'm as troubled as the tide' ('Song to the Siren', 1968) putting the fear and tension of all three songs into sharp relief. As we shall see, I will discuss Matthew Schneider's contention that the idealistic lyric palette of 1960s counter-culture has its roots in the Romantic revolution of the 1790s when literature and culture changed dramatically, but the latter's othering of the enigmatic feminine sea creature enshrined a chauvinist conceptualization into the literary and cultural canon.

My application of Schneider's thesis, that the 1960s counter-culture is informed by the Romantic poetic imagery and tropes, is primarily discussed through Beefheart, Buckley and Hendrix, but it is germane to this essay that I trace the 'Romanticized feminine mystique' from Coleridge through the Victorian Romantic female stereotypes of Tennyson and Yeats (women are evil succubi or innocent virgins to both poets); to Eliot's male-devouring mermaid in the modernist period; to The Beatles' Romantic dream-woman others (Julia and Lucy in the Sky). Shelia Whiteley's work shows that artists such as Donovan and The Beatles create fantastical female others that are sexist products of the 1960s counter-culture and these dream women are directly contemporaneous with and shed light on my discussion of Beefheart, Buckley and Hendrix.

My conclusion uses the words and imagery of popular musicians such as Beyoncé, Lady Gaga and Madonna, and the poets Carol Ann Duffy and Caitríona O'Reilly, to put this male stereotyping of the feminine other in sharp relief. This piece comes to praise and not bury the artists under consideration. By emphasizing the incipient sexism of the 1960s cultural revolution, we have a better understanding of the great artistic achievement of Beefheart, Buckley and Hendrix, while being aware of the gender politics which is a questionable aspect of their discography.

The 1960s Counter-culture and Romanticism

Matthew Schneider, who sees strong links between the nineteenth-century Romantics and the 1960s counter-culture suggests that:

> Victorianism, Modernism, and Postmodernism did not supersede Romanticism [...] However desperately novelists like Joyce and William Faulkner struggled to free their chosen art from what they saw as the limitations of Dickens' nineteenth-century 'realism', the Modernists still proceeded from the central Romantic article of faith: the validity, even the sanctity, of the perceptions and experiences of ordinary individuals (Schneider, 2008: 20).

If I substitute the words 'ordinary individual' with 'Romantic egotist who is given over to the grandeur of romantic hyperbole', then, we have Hendrix's Thanatos merperson diving into the depths of lyrical grandeur: his transsexuality motivated by a macho desire for an impersonal and irresponsible union with the id. Again, as Schneider, demonstrates:

> What is Joyce's *Ulysses* if not an attempt to endue everyday life with the epic grandeur that pre-Romantic culture reserved to kings and magistrates. Even the most cynical and purportedly 'revolutionary' of today's conceptual and performance artists are motivated by the desire that urged Lord Byron both to live and write in a scandalous and satiric mode: to shock the middle class (Schneider, 2008: 20).

To put it simply, a watery death is a bold romantic gesture from Keats through Yeats to Shelley, and mermaids are the exotic goddesses whose function is to act as repository for the romantic male ego. The speaker in Hendrix's song may be transsexual, but any progressive feminism here is compromised by the death drive of a phallocentric 1960s music industry, where even the most creative minds (Beefheart, Buckley and Hendrix), are colonised by Romantic linguistic exaggeration.

Jimi Hendrix: A Merperson… I Should Turn to Be

Jimi Hendrix's '1983… (A Merman I Should Turn to Be)' imagines the singer and his lover escaping a world corrupted by materialism and militarism by becoming merpersons and living under the sea, having escaped the 'killing noise' (Hendrix, 1968). Of the three lyrics Hendrix's is the most progressive as the speaker in the text embraces an aquatic utopia of sexual union.

Hendrix's sea goddess is in the transatlantic roots of rock Romanticism. That is, an eroticised feminine 'other' whose identity is predicated on male desire. The song's imagery of sea, sirens and mermaids is in the lyrical tradition of British Romanticism, which implies a 'Life before the invention of civil society was…an uninterrupted bliss of solitude…the Romantic avoids crowds, and is happiest when alone in a pristine wilderness' (Schneider, 2008: 19). Here Hendrix uses the mermaid trope to imagine his escape to a watery nirvana; the mermaid and merman turning into merpersons: a very progressive gender bending idea for 1960s rock culture. However, Hendrix's sexual utopia is couched in Romantic lyrics that demonstrate a solipsistic egotistic death drive. In a sense, his merperson is may transgress heteronormative culture, but the male ego desire is a clichéd and Romantic immolation. The song is putting into effect a typical Romantic self-absorption; and this type of self-obsession has been a strain in English literature from Byron, Shelley and Keats, through Yeats to The Beatles and the 1960s counter-culture. For instance, Yeats's early Romantic poetry embodies macho melancholy, 'A mermaid found a swimming lad/ Picked him for her own/ Pressed her body to his body/ Laughed; and plunging down/ Forgot in cruel happiness/ That even lovers drown'(Yeats, 1997: 117).

On its release, Hendrix's second album *Electric Ladyland* (1968) was banned from several British record shops in York, Hull and Bristol. The UK covers had Hendrix surrounded by nineteen naked women. In fact the decision to release the album cover had nothing to do with Hendrix. His British record company, Track, was behind the release. The label's boss, Chris Stamp, offered girls from a local speakeasy £10 each to appear nude on the cover. The cover was an attempt by the label to generate some controversy to help sell the album; however, the record didn't need any publicity as it was one of the most eagerly awaited releases of the year and the controversy was limited to a few British tabloids. Hendrix hated the cover and wrote an impassioned letter to the record company asking for it to be replaced (which it eventually was).

Hendrix's response spotlights the sexual politics of the 1960s music business. The sexist objectification of women was de rigueur in counter-cultural hippie politics of 1968. In fact, it is remarkable that Hendrix complained in such a pre-PC cultural climate. His protest does underscore the progressive lyrics in the song – admittedly Hendrix is revisiting the hackneyed romantic troupe of the eroticised goddess, but his underwater pairing is a transgressive mingling of genders in a marine psychedelic fantasy. Many artists from this period, including The Beatles ('Girl' and 'Run For Your Life') and Cream ('The Tales of Brave Ulysses') lapse into casual sexism that is reinforced by two hundred years of Romantic stereotyping of men being devoured by malevolent female sea creatures. Hendrix's female other is not an evil succubus, but an equal partner in his aquatic escape.

Given the sexual politics of the period, Hendrix cannot go too far in his transgression of gender binaries as his lyrics are very much a product of Romantic aesthetics and 1960s counter-culture sexism. In fact all three male singers in this chapter produce beautiful poetic fantasies, but their lexicon is a patriarchal lyrical palette that stereotypes gender. A poem entitled 'The Mermaid' by Caitríona O'Reilly demonstrates the extent to which male poetics enshrine the female as an erotised other. In the poem, the mermaid's hair and face:

> Look more like P.T. Barnum's Freak of Feejee
> piscene and wordless, trapped in the net of a stare.
> She has the head and shrivelled tits of a monkey,
>
> the green glass eyes of a porcelain doll, a pair of praying-mantis hands,
> and fishy lips open to reveal her sea-caved mouth,
> her rare ivory mermaid-teeth (O'Reilly, 2006: 40).

Tim Buckley, Happy/Sad: the Romantic Doomed Troubadour

Tim Buckley's 'Song to the Siren' does not offer a deconstruction of binaries, but a series of romantic images concerning the speaker's Eros/Thanatos drives. The mermaid/siren figure is an evil creature lulling the doomed sailor to a watery grave. The lyrics depict the speaker as victim, the male hare to the female fox. Buckley's lyrical embroidery prescribes sexual annihilation in a Romantic and self-absorbed manner. The siren's 'singing eyes' tempt the speaker in the song to a doomed romantic union, the speaker lying 'broken' on the rocks at the end of the song (Buckley, 1968).

Given the narrative of Buckley's short and traumatic life, it is a harrowing and prescient romantic piece that is beautiful Romantic poetry. But the siren's function is that of devouring mother who demands sacrifice: a stock cliché of Romantic verse. Simone de Beauvoir sees the male death drive as predicated on male fear, and as her words demonstrate, an inability to deal with real people: the woman is a mythological other who demands self-sacrifice:

> In the deeps of the sea it is night: woman is the *Mare tenebrarum*, dreaded by navigators of old; it is night in the entrails of the earth. Man is frightened of this night ... [This] threatens to swallow him up. He aspires to the sky, to the light, to the sunny summits, to the pure and crystalline frigidity of the blue sky; and under his feet there is a moist, warm, and dark gulf ready to draw him down; in many a legend do we see the hero lost forever as he falls back into the maternal shadows – cave, abyss, hell (de Beauvoir, 1997:179).

The lyrics to 'Song to the Siren' were not written by Tim Buckley but by his artistic collaborator. 'Buckley often wrote to words by Larry Beckett, a friend and former bandmate turned poet and academic. Inspired by Homer, Shakespeare and a woman whose name he won't reveal' (Aston, 2011). It is very revealing that the woman in the song remains unnamed. Larry Beckett, who was steeped in the canon of English literature, was responsible for the superb but unashamedly Romantic lyrics. Buckley added the melancholy blues. Beckett remembers that, 'He had this incredible gift for matching melody to language. It's the way the melody falls and lifts, like the images, and repeating a figure as he's making a plea. Meanwhile, the bass line is dropping and eroding as if the sea is eroding his plea' (Beckett, cited in Aston, 2011). The two men responsible for the song's composition are explicitly influenced by transatlantic Romanticism – the speakers' woes drown out any attempt to delineate a mental picture of the siren other.

Hendrix (Slight Return)

Hendrix's work too was characterised by a death wish that was often expressed in a starker and minimal manner. In the song 'I Don't Live Today' (Hendrix, 1967), the romantic marine imagery of the merman is replaced with a melodramatic and Romantic death wish; the song's lyrics are a plea to be 'executed' and the speaker feels he is living in a 'grave'. These lyrics are a terrestrial variation on the Thanatos of 'Song to the Siren' and '1983...'. Hendrix is the speaker in the poem who longs for the grave and who doesn't find redemption in the erotic goddess of the sea. However, as Charles Shaar Murray points out, too-literal interpretations regarding artists' Romantic death wishes are frequently unrealistic constructions of a shallow media and lazy biographers. Buckley's and Hendrix's premature deaths were the result of Romantic stereotyping of creative artists, a Romantic cliché indeed, 'Gifted people who die young invariably become the focus of romantic necrophilia. They are adopted like Christ-substitutes, dying for "our" collective sins, depicted as somehow too beautiful or too sensitive to live. In real terms, they are either stupid or unlucky' (Murray, 2012: 158).

Charles Shaar Murray's consummate book on Hendrix makes it clear that his relationship to women was 'a deep, abiding and complex one' (Murray,

2012: 85); and that the sexual politics of three artists here is partly a product of the rock cultural machine of the 1960s: each artist has an intricate relationship to feminism that often rejects chauvinism. For instance, although the mermaids featuring in their songs are distant eroticized love goddesses, they usually have power over their male suitors. In Hendrix's work 'The feminine ideal that haunts most of his most powerful songs is no geisha, slave or groupie. She is stronger and wiser than he is, and she is his only hope of salvation' (Murray, 2012: 91). However, Murray glosses Hendrix's occasional dark side by saying his violence was due to 'heavy pressure' and this led to 'frightening displays of violence directed at whoever was unfortunate enough to be in his way, be it Noel Redding, a female companion, Swedish cops or anybody else' (Murray, 2012: 89). Hendrix sometimes acted in a chauvinist manner and Beefheart's and Buckley's lyrics opened a window on to the sexual politics of the counter-culture.

Captain Beefheart: Ironic Blues?

Captain Beefheart's desire to take up with a mermaid is the most idiosyncratic of the three songs and his melancholy is couched in surreal irony. The speaker's metamorphosis to half-fish and half-man expressed a deep sadness and, as in Hendrix's '1983...', a desire for escape from a brutal world. Beefheart spoke of his aquatic carnal desires in *Sounds* in 1972, 'I'm a sexy, healthy male – I've got blood running everywhere. I have a group of men, who play men's music, to women. Other men can enjoy it too, but it is definitely to women because I'm playing to a receiver' (cited in Froy, 1999). Beefheart wants to return to a pre-human and natural state, but the mermaid is again described as a 'receiver' of male desire and the irony and originality of the song (although postmodern and witty) is firmly couched in the lyrical trope of the Romantics. The speaker in the song 'grows fins' to elope with a mermaid and Beefheart deliberately reverses the symbolism of sirens luring men to their watery graves with their singing, by stating that song was him 'singing to women'. This is a funny and subversive twist in gender stereotypes, but for the word 'receiver' which casts doubt on the song's interpretation as a transgressive text.

'Grow Fins' by Captain Beefheart does little to deconstruct a male/female binary with lyrics such as 'Ya said ya had it together once/ Now yer head's around the bend/ I'm tellin' ya, woman/ Ya better get it back together again' because, the speaker in the song threatens, if his woman does not 'get it together' he will jilt her for a mermaid: 'I come home late/ 'N I stumbled 'n swore/ Ya won't even give me a hug/ Ya had my things all laid out by the door/ I'm leavin'/ I'm gonna take up with ah mermaid/ 'N leave you land lubbin' women alone' (Beefheart, 1972).

However, there is an irony here the other two songs seem to lack. For instance Charles Shaar Murray points out that the perceived sexism of early blues lyrics was often a thinly veiled attack on white racists and not their partners. Likewise, Beefheart's desire to elope with a mermaid is framed in blues irony.

From Sirens to Street Corner Girls

Tim Buckley's 'Song to the Siren' has the most vicious and vengeful female other in the lyrics. The speaker's attitude in the song is that the siren will metaphorically and literally rip him to pieces. Hendrix's saving grace is that he will shape-shift into a merman, whereas Beefheart hides behind postmodern irony concerning sexual politics. Buckley, and lyricist Beckett, redeem the unreconstructed sexism of the music industry by showing the male protagonist to be passive in the song. The mermaid other tempts the poor unsuspecting troubadour to his sunken fate.

Buckley characterised the lyrics on his later album *Greetings From L.A.* (1972) as proto-feminist. The album opens with the line; 'I went down to the meat rack tavern'; the album's ending finds Buckley looking for 'a street corner girl' to 'beat me, whip me, spank me, make it all right again'. Buckley explained his reasoning to Chrissie Hynde when she interviewed him for the NME in 1974. 'I realised all the sex idols in rock weren't saying anything sexy — no Jagger or [Jim] Morrison. Nor had I learned anything sexually from a rock song. So I decided to make it human and not so mysterious' (Hynde, 1974).

In fact these lyrics are exoticism masquerading as realism; the 'street corner girl' conforms very neatly to a stereotyped description of a prostitute. If the phrase 'street corner' is substituted with 'siren', you have a protagonist who uses and abuses the 'meat rack tavern', but it is acceptable as the male is the passive partner. However, the victim relates to their partner in the crudest and meanest sexual language that presents the prostitutes as an admittedly aggressive female other who is faceless and nameless, like his sirens, and is hanging on display in the meat rack. Again Buckley inhabits a lyrical and performative palette of a music business that couches women as mysterious and exotic sirens. Buckley sings about real women, but his words are no different to the posturing of Jagger or Morrison, his 'real' depiction is predicated on the prostitute/siren other. Buckley's attitude may be liberal, but the music business is founded on institution sexism and crude sexual stereotypes.

Beefheart, Buckley and Hendrix have complex attitudes to the women in their personal lives, but the narrative of the music industry in the 1960s and 1970s is a less complex organism. These three artists are have an intricate and labyrinthine attitude to gender, but finding their way out of this maze is difficult in an era so dominated by Romantic cliché. In a sense, each artist should be not be judged by our historical standards, but they should be contextualised with reference to a crude and philistine music industry that encouraged gauche and lazy sexism.

Sheila Whiteley describes the 1960s music as having

an evangelical purpose [...] establishing common cultural and political bonds. The counter culture's marginalisation of women in rock is therefore particularly disturbing. [...] both the lifestyle and the musical ethos of the period undermined the role of women, positioning them as either romanticized fantasy figures, subservient earth mothers or easy lays (Whiteley, 2000: 23).

All three categories coalesce here. The artists' songs are fairytales where mermaids and sirens are remote, fanciful romantic images that reflect the male's unconscious desires. Whiteley acutely discusses the romantic imagery that was prevalent in 1960s rock culture. 'The genre is full of exotic fantasy figures such as Donovan's Jennifer Juniper, The Beatles' Lucy in the Sky with Diamonds and Julia who are 'etherealised and inscribed within a dreamlike and unreal world, detached from reality, defined by the male as a fantasy escape *from* reality' (Whiteley, 2000: 35, emphasis in original). The mermaids in '1983...' and 'Grow Fins' fall neatly into this category of the 'etherealised' other who dwells in the surrealistic deep blue sea and a creature whose agency and autonomy are a threat to the male who wants fulfillment with a romantic nonentity who lacks the light and shade of a real character, an unreal being without identity and individuality.

Buckley's exoticism, however, is based on dread of the female or *'femme castratrice* of Freudian theory' (Whiteley, 2000: 38; spelling amended to Barbara Creed's original phrasing, cited here). It is imagery which appears in the Hendrix song 'Dolly Dagger', where the lyrics are not the psychedelic goddess-figure whimsy of '1983...', but a female devourer of young men, a creature who 'drinks her blood from a jagged edge'. This is no transgressive female proto-feminist vampire, but a crude stereotype of faceless women who represent male desire. Cream's 'Strange Brew' also puts into effect the demonic female as 'siren, one whose physical allure spelt death to man's transcendental soul' (Whiteley, 2000: 38). The song refers to the female as a 'witch' and she is couched in Romantic sea imagery worthy of Coleridge, 'on a boat in the middle of a raging sea'. If we read Tim Buckley's 'Song to the Siren' in the light of Whiteley's critique of Cream's misogyny, we have a song where the demon sea creature is 'soulless, one who fascinates desire but who must be repelled for fear of self-destruction' (38). Admittedly, 'Song to the Siren' is a song of fragile poetic beauty, but the siren protagonist represents a dark side to the counter-culture's sexual politics, a culture where 'rock music in the late 1960s embodied the patriarchal imaginary of the madonna–whore binary'. (Whiteley, 2000: 41).

As I have suggested earlier in this chapter, my analysis of these three songs is prompted by admiration of their music and their lyrical poetry; however, it is clear that the rock institutions, the machinery of the music business, then and now, gives men a platform to disseminate lyrics that are in the transatlantic tradition of Romanticism where the feminism is often ignored by a male lexicon that promotes exotic goddesses instead of real people. In

2016 Björk wrote that the rock industry remains reactionary; as I suggested, Beefheart, Buckley and Hendrix are not sexist or misogynist, but their industry was and is, and their casual gender stereotyping opens a window on this culture. 'Women in music are allowed to be singer songwriters singing about their boyfriends,' Björk wrote, 'If they change the subject matter to atoms, galaxies, activism, nerdy math beat editing or anything else than being performers singing about their loved ones they get criticized. Journalists feel there is just something missing ... as if our only lingo is emo' (cited in *The Guardian*, 2016).

Peter Doggett's analysis of the counter-culture is as damning as Whiteley's. His work shows that the institutional sexism was altogether more insidious than rock stars writing whimsical songs about mermaid dream goddesses and exotic lank-haired Pre-Raphaelite princesses. The 'entire pop industry was controlled by men, for the profit of men, at the expense of young women. Either they paid by buying records, posters and concert tickets, or else they joined the queues of hopefuls who waited outside the hotel bedrooms of (for example) the Beatles' (Doggett, 2007: 69). If we replace The Beatles' names with those of Beefheart, Buckley or Hendrix, their romantic othering of mermaids seems disingenuous at best. In fact the counter-culture was so loaded in favour of men that Doggett goes on to argue that 'pop was erected (I choose the verb carefully) on exactly the same (im)balance of power as society itself' (Doggett, 2007:70).

The treatment of women in songs, when it wasn't blatantly misogynist as in The Rolling Stones' 'Stupid Girl' and 'Out of Time' (where both the women in the song are broken by constant male aggression and a sapping under-mining of their independence and individuality), was romantic exoticism, what Betty Friedman (1963) called the 'feminine mystique'. The term correctly described the lyrical politics of Beefheart, Buckley and Hendrix; although Friedman saw 'mystique' as something positive, it took later feminists such as Germaine Greer to deconstruct this 'mystique' or male exoticism and point out that feminists needed to break away from 'the romantic idealism which had pervaded the Feminine Mystique' (Marwick, 1998: 690) and warned women 'that they did not realise, as she put it, how "much men hate women"'(Marwick, 2007: 690).

Beefheart, Buckley and Hendrix wrote songs of romantic exoticism that marginalised women as supernatural goddesses and not real people. However, as I have stated earlier, as individuals their lives and work are very nuanced, complex and intricate with regard to their relationships to women. But I have endeavoured to untangle this knot and separate their personality from their work. In their work all three create romantic submersible goddesses who use their sensuality and supernatural powers to tempt men into the deep blue sea. In their work they fail to realise real people or, at the very least, recognisable fictional characters (whatever Buckley says to the contrary in *Greetings From LA*). But separating their personality from their work proves to be a Gordian knot; no amount of untangling frees these artists from the ineluctable fact that their lyrics are colourful representations of a male dominated music industry. All three artists' songs broadly fit into the description of psychedelic rock (and the etymology of 'psychedelic' is from the Greek *psyche* meaning mind and *delos* meaning reveal), so what these lyrics show is a whimsical obfuscation of institutional sexism. What their work demonstrates is the extent to which the gendered clichés of English literary Romanticism live on in a culture that codifies reductive gender demarcations (think of James Bond, Harry Potter, The Beatles, The Stones and most heavy metal bands).

Rock and Romanticism

Schneider writes that 'the poems of [a] small group of writers – Blake, Burns, Wordsworth, Coleridge, Byron, and Carroll – was gathered in by the hungry maw of nineteenth- and twentieth-century popular and mass culture and repackaged as the intellectual background against which ordinary life is lived today' (Schneider, 2008: 199). Now it is unfair to judge people of the past by today's standards, but since Beefheart, Buckley and Hendrix are such near contemporaries, and in this regard the music business seems to have changed very little since the 1960s, we are comparing today's standards by a past that was dominated in the Romantic period, and the 1960s by male exoticism and Romanticism. My thesis also does not concentrate on the huge gains made by feminism in the 1960s, but rather shows that the poetic diction and tone of today's male rock songs eroticises the other and is part of the male symbolic code. My chapter is a critique of the aesthetics of rock songs that inherit hackneyed romantic imagery when they could write words that open up new possibilities for engaging with a discussion of gender. Whiteley has shown that contemporary women artists since Madonna have made art that addresses the contemporary world, but unfortunately the lyrics of great artists such as Beefheart, Buckley and Hendrix undoubtedly fall into the counter-culture binary of angel or whore.

As we have seen, the three songs concern men searching for sub-aquatic love with mermaids. Tennyson's 'The Mermaid' has a female speaker who desires sexual union with a merman; nevertheless, the imagery and theme is the same as the songs we discussed in this chapter. The strands of Romanticism are prevalent in all three songs, a male fantasy of underwater love in rococo, male romantic imagery. In the manner of Tennyson, Beefheart and Hendrix want to transform into mermen. Buckley wants to make the same transformation, but sees mermaid love as erotic immolation of self. All three lyrics are in the tradition of Anglo-Irish sea shanty and nineteenth-century Romanticism, but Beefheart's words are couched in rhythm and blues stylings. So, all three are complex artists, who in the creation their songs focus on fantasy gender relations that put the reality of sexual politics into sharp relief. The work here is occasionally transgressive and ironic concerning gender, but in the manner of Tennyson or Yeats, we have the dream female positioned as a repository of male desire and the male death drive. The words of Tennyson's poem show that Beefheart, Buckley and Hendrix inherit male escapist imagery from the last two hundred years of Romantic verse:

> From the diamond-ledges that jut from the dells;
> For I would not be kiss'd by all who would list
> Of the bold merry mermen under the sea.
> They would sue me, and woo me, and flatter me,
> In the purple twilights under the sea;
> But the king of them all would carry me,
> Woo me, and win me, and marry me,
> In the branching jaspers under the sea.
> Then all the dry-pied things that be
> In the hueless mosses under the sea
> Would curl round my silver feet silently, All looking up for the love of me.
> And if I should carol aloud, from aloft
> All things that are forked, and horned, and soft
> Would lean out from the hollow sphere of the sea,
> All looking down for the love of me (Tennyson, 1994: 11–12).

The desire here is the Romantic id of the ocean; Beefheart, Buckley and Hendrix too drift into the floridas of their collective ids, and like Tennyson, their death is a male fantasy of escape into the arms of the devouring female, who is a generic, faceless, fantasy sea creature: an exoticised other which is a dominant feature of the 1960s hippie id.

Beefheart and Hendrix's lyrics are ecstatic and fanciful sexual unions with mermaids, whereas Buckley's song is characterised by a certain sexual inadequacy and fear of a devouring sea beast. Buckley's lyrics are a romantic melodrama in which he is portrayed as victim. Buckley's 'Song to the Siren' is a hallucinatory poem in the tradition of Coleridge's 'Kubla Khan'; 'Song to the Siren's 'shipless oceans' are traumatic dream lyrics that end in death. The resonances from Coleridge's work are explicit, 'Alph, the sacred river', flows for 'five miles meandering' before a 'tumult in a lifeless ocean' (Coleridge, 1963: 51). Buckley's melancholy watery poetics in which 'lifeless' is reminiscent of 'shipless', put a Romantic loneliness into effect, and a cure for this isolation is drowning. This fear of the other is a trope that is expressed in T. S. Eliot's 'The Love Song of J. Alfred Prufrock'. In this poem the speaker has 'heard the mermaids singing, each to each'. 'I do not think that they will sing to me', he adds morosely.

> We have lingered in the chambers of the sea
> By sea-girls wreathed with seaweed red and brown
> Till human voices wake us, and we drown (Eliot, 2012: 3).

In a sense, the mermaid/siren figure is a poetic device that endures through folk song, Romanticism, modernism, postmodernism (Beefheart) to late

20th century song. The female sea creature remains such a seductive metaphor in the history of transatlantic folk history because male songwriters can couch their own doom at the hands of a female seductress.

There is considerable debate about the difference between mermaids and sirens. In my chapter the terms mermaid and siren are interchangeable as over the centuries mermaids and sirens merged into the same creature. Mermaids were originally benign half-women and half-fish creatures, while sirens were a malign hybrid of a bird with women's heads luring sailors to their death. Whether the objectification is a siren or mermaid, the three artists under consideration here are products of a rock culture which prescribes sexual union with a woman–fish hybrid as panacea for 'deep psychedelic blues'. Each of these whimsical marriages is couched in a mix of ironic blues clichés or male lyrical Romantic imagery: a strand in Atlantic, Anglo-Saxon culture that resonates from Keats to twentieth-century rock culture.

However, it is important to draw a distinction between the three artists' music and their lyrics. It is fascinating that the lyrics to Beefheart's 'Grow Fins' have very little of the Romantic male angst that we see in Buckley and Hendrix. On the other hand, Beefheart's music is typical Howlin' Wolf-like 12-bar blues and he exhibits none of the avant-garde stylings of the other two texts. Buckley and Hendrix draw from romantic imagery, but the words are underpinned by music which inherits classical and jazz influences. Hendrix's solos in '1983...' are extreme rococo psychedelic experiments which have moved a long way from their Delta Blues origins. 'Song to the Siren', especially in the *Starsailor* album version (following earlier performances, including on television), is much closer to avant-garde jazz than it is to the folk and blues origins of most 1960s rock culture. Nevertheless, the mermaids are made into a male fetish and a Romantic othering that has been a central in theme in male poetry regardless of metre and rhyme scheme. Structure and form may change, but from Coleridge's ballads to T.S. Eliot's fragmentary modernism, the stylistics are a drama of male ego eddying into the mysterious depth of the female id.

Mrs Beast

If we compare 'Song to the Siren', Tennyson and T.S. Eliot to a feminist poem and if the sexual roles are thus reversed, we can see how preposterous the poetic performance of the doomed male lover is. Carol Ann Duffy's 'Mrs Beast' describes an aquatic encounter in which the mermaid has agency.

> ...The Little Mermaid slit
> Her shining, silver tail in two, rubbed salt
> Into that stinking wound, got up and walked,
> In agony, in fishnet tights, stood up and smiled, waltzed,
> All for a Prince, a pretty boy, a charming one
> Who'd dump her in the end, chuck her, throw her overboard.

...

What you want to do is find yourself a beast. The sex
Is better (Duffy, 1999:72).

The poem is a fairytale reminiscent of Angela Carter's (1995) *The Bloody Chamber*, in which female sexuality is the focus and is described in graphic terms from a woman's perspective. Duffy's words demonstrate that when roles are reversed, the faceless watery nymphs of romanticism seem lazy and ridiculous.

It is important to stress that Beefheart, Buckley and Hendrix are giving performances expected of a chauvinist 1960s rock culture. All three artists in the private lives were fairly happy individuals, not doomed poets and not misogynist; however, their cultural milieu did not have the lyrical palette for painting colorful feminist characters. The peace and love generation was characterized by very politically incorrect lyrics. For instance, Ian MacDonald illustrates this tendency of the counter-culture, writing about The Beatles' 'Run for Your Life': 'Lennon produced a lazily sexist lyric unmitigated by saving irony'. And MacDonald goes on to how 'grimly threatening' the song is with the 'I'd rather see you dead little girl than to be with another man' refrain (MacDonald, 2008: 161). In this cultural climate it unsurprising that Beeefhart, Buckley and Hendrix lapse into lazy gendered rhetoric, but in their defense, the three songs under consideration here are performances for poetic effect and they are mimicking the sexist exoticism which was general in 1960s and early 1970s culture at large.

In pop music terms, it was only with artists such as Beyoncé, Yoko Ono, Madonna and Lady Gaga that we were offered pop lyrics and videos in the spirit of Carol Ann Duffy's writing. In 'Cherish', Madonna is surrounded by handsome merboys. Beyoncé 'believed she was a mermaid in a past life: "I'm always happy when I'm surrounded by water. I think I'm a mermaid, or I was a mermaid. The ocean makes me feel really small, and it puts my whole life into perspective"' (Adickman, 2012). Lady Gaga in her video, 'donned a tail for her "You and I" music video in 2011' (Adickman, 2012). As Matthew Schneider demonstrates, 'Rock Romanticism', is the prevalent artistic expression of our post-modern age, but rock music was slow to give a platform to female artists who subvert the male death wish with funny and satiric art that views mermaids as emancipatory post-feminist icons.

It is important to stress that fandom and performativity are crucial in any discussion of gender roles in popular culture. In fact counter-cultural male hegemony was subtly inverted by female fandom. Hendrix's and Buckley's sexuality was often enjoyed by women: the female gaze often appropriate and change male performances into male objectification. Hendrix's stage act was often highly sexual and he writhed, pouted, swivelled his hips and flashed his tongue in the manner of a male stripper. Buckley's pretty boy looks were also appropriated by female sirens into emancipatory feminist sexuality that transgressed the sexism of the counter-culture. Beefheart's 'Grow Fins' and his stage persona were less overtly sexual than the other two performers, but it is wrong to homogenise an audience; his appeal may have been largely male, but audiences are a mess of contradictory people and the female gaze might have twisted his bluesy ironic sexism into new areas depending on the receiver of the performance.

Nevertheless, although performativity may have caused a status inversion between the male gaze and the female gaze, lyrically very little has changed with boy bands singing songs about erotized mythical female saviours such as Robbie Williams's highly romanticized 'Angels'. If we compare the lyrics of contemporary boy bands we still see ethereal goddesses being the object of male sentimental and idealistic impulses.

Conclusion

In sum, Hendrix's and Buckley's songs feature lyrics by doomed troubadours in the Romantic tradition of Keats and Shelley. Beefheart is an ironist, which makes him more postmodernist in his approach to lyrics: 'Grow Fins' is a blues parody whereas Hendrix and Buckley's pieces are an outpouring of melodramatic emotion; and the three songs represent a powerful dilemma in rock culture poetics. Is each lyric a nuanced and complex negotiation with the watery feminine other? Or is each song an idealized death wish for briny goddesses? In a profound sense, these pieces of poetry are narcissistic songs predicated on the male ego and a 1960s creative industry that drowned political progressiveness with crude cliché.

To conclude, Beefheart, Buckley and Hendrix are sui generis artists whose work is among the most innovative and intelligent, both lyrically and musically, in terms of experimentation, of their era. Few artists in the popular music field have reached such artistic heights. Bowie, Eno and The Beatles have occasionally matched their off-centre approach; other comparisons would come from jazz, names such as John Coltrane and Miles Davies. So the intention of this chapter, for all its acknowledgement of the sexism of the context in which they worked, is also to celebrate their sublime work.

Bibiography

Adickman, E.A. (2012), 'The Mermaids Of Pop: Lady Gaga, Beyonce, Madonna And More', *Idolator*, 29 May [online], ttp://www.idolator.com/6543822/mermaid-lady-gaga-beyonce-katy-perry (accessed 20 February 2017).

Aston, M. (2011), 'Song to the Siren's irresistible tang', *The Guardian*, 17 November [online], ttps://www.theguardian.com/music/2011/nov/17/song-to-the-siren-classic (accessed 28 February 2017).

Carter, A. (1995), *The Bloody Chamber and Other Stories*, London: Vintage.

Brabazon, T. (2012), *Popular Music: Topics, Trends & Trajectories*, London: Sage.

Coleridge, S.T. (1963), *The Complete Poetical Works of Samuel Taylor Coleridge*, Oxford: Oxford University Press.

de Beavoir, S. (1997), *The Second Sex*, London: Vintage.

Duffy, C.A. (2010), *The World's Wife*, London: Picador.

Dogget, P. (2007), *There's A Riot Going On: Revolutionaries, Rock Stars and the Rise and Fall of '60s counter-culture*, Edinburgh: Canongate.

Eliot, T.S. (2009), *Selected Poems*, 80th Anniversary Edition, London: Faber and Faber.

Friedan, B. (1963), *The Feminine Mystique*, New York. W.W. Norton.

Froy, S. (1999), 'At the Crossroads with the *Spotlight Kid*', *Perfect Sound Forever*, February [online], ttp://www.furious.com/perfect/beefheart/spot2. html (accessed 9 April 2017).

Guardian, The (2016), 'Björk on Sexism: "Women in music are allowed to sing about their boyfriends"', *The Guardian*, 21 December [online], ttps://www.theguardian.com/music/2016/dec/21/bjork-sexism-open-letter-music-industry-facebook (accessed 9 April 2017).

Hynde, C. (1974), 'Tim Buckley: How a Hippie Hero became a sultry Sex Object', *New Musical Express*, 8 June [online], ttps://www.rocksbackpages. com/Library/Article/tim-buckley-how-a-hippie-hero-be-came-a-sultry-sex-object (accessed 20 March 2017).

Marwick, A. (1998), *The Sixties: Cultural Revolution in Britain, France, Italy, and the United States, c.1958–c.1974*, Oxford: Oxford University Press.

MacDonald, I. (2008), *Revolution in the Head: The Beatles' Records and the Sixties*, London: Vintage.

O'Reilly, C. (2006), *The Sea Cabinet*, Newcastle: Bloodaxe.

Shaar Murray, C. (2012), *Crosstown Traffic: Jimi Hendrix and Post-War Pop*, Edinburgh & London: Canongate.

Schneider, M. (2008), *The Long and Winding Road From Blake To The Beatles*, New York: Palgrave Macmillan.

Tennyson, A. (2004), 'The Mermaid'. In *The Complete Works of Lord Alfred Tennyson*, London: Wordsworth.

Whiteley, S. (2000), *Women and Popular Music: Sexuality, Identity and Subjectivity*, London: Routledge.

Yeats, W.B. (1997), 'A Man Old and Young', 'The Mermaid'. In Edward Larrissy (ed.), W.B Yeats, *The Major Works*, Oxford: Oxford University Press.

Discography

Captain Beefheart (1972), 'Grow Fins', *The Spotlight Kid*, Reprise, Track [Album]

The Beatles (1965), 'Girl', *Rubber Soul*, Parlophone, Track [Album]

The Beatles (1965), 'Run For Your Life', *Rubber Soul*, Parlophone, Track [Album]

The Beatles (1967), 'Lucy in the Sky with Diamonds', *Sgt Pepper's Lonely Hearts Club Band*, Parlophone, Track [Album]

The Beatles (1968), 'Julia', *The White Album*, Apple, Track [Album]

Tim Buckley (1970), 'Song to the Siren', *Starsailor*, Straight Records, Track [Album]

Tim Buckley (1972), 'Move with Me', *Greetings From LA*, Straight Records, Track [Album]

Tim Buckley (1972), 'Make it Right', *Greetings From LA*, Straight Records, Track [Album]

Cream (1967), 'Tales of Brave Ulysses', *Disraeli Gears*, Reaction, Atco, Polydor, Track [Album]

Cream (1967), 'Strange Brew', *Disraeli Gears*, Reaction, Atco, Polydor, Track [Album]

Donovan (1967), 'Jennifer Juniper', Pye [Single]

Jimi Hendrix (1967), 'I Don't Live Today', *Are You Experienced*, Track [Album]

Jimi Hendrix (1968), '1983… A Merman I Should Turn to Be', *Electric Ladyland*, Reprise, Track [Album]

Jimi Hendrix (1971), 'Dolly Dagger', *Rainbow Bridge*, Reprise, Track [Album]

Lady Gaga, (2011), 'You and I', 'Streamline', *Kon Live*, Interscope, Track [Album]

Madonna, (1989), 'Cherish', *Like a Prayer*, Sire, Warner Brothers, Track [Album]

Robbie Williams (1997), 'Angels', Chrysalis [Single]

Part 3:

Aquatic Spaces and Practices

Chapter 7

Fan Totems: Affective Investments in the Sea Creatures of Horror and Science Fiction

Brigid Cherry

Monsters, and the celebration of monsters, are central to horror and fantasy fandom. It is therefore important to consider the role which monstrosity plays in the affective investments viewers make when watching horror and similar genres or categories of fiction. For fans of horror, science fiction and fantasy, affective investments in the storyworld are often tied up in emotional responses and in particular the way viewers enjoy the feelings associated with being vicariously frightened. But my previous studies of horror fans suggest that such viewing pleasures also involve feelings of empathy, identification and attraction towards monstrous entities (Cherry, 1999 & 2017). Female viewers, for example, might find human and human-like monsters such as vampires, werewolves, and Barkerian monsters (Pinhead, Candyman) appealing, even erotic. But many other categories of monsters exist – many of them far from being recognisably human in form or behaviour. Inhuman monstrosity does not, however, preclude fans from also developing affinities with such creatures. It is therefore worth exploring fans' affective investments in these non-human examples of monstrosity further, not least to aid understanding of patterns of taste and behaviour within fan communities and the role monsters play in signifying fan interest.

If non-human monsters are not a bar to fans' affective investments in the objects of their fandom, it is important to consider how such pleasure and desire operates in relation to fan identity. Affective investments in non-human monsters and their incorporation into fan identities can therefore be explored in order to illustrate this by drawing on examples of monstrous sea creatures in popular culture. Non-human monsters are varied of course, but representations of aquatic creatures in horror and related genres provide key examples in this category in particular since they inhabit an alien and inhospitable (to humans) environment. A case in point is steampunk fandom and its association with the octopus, but mermaid culture, fandoms that privilege eldritch horror (and Lovecraft in particular), and the popular taste for killer shark movies are also applicable in terms of affective investments in aquatic monsters. Desire in this instance includes not only seeking out viewing pleasures, but also extends to the desire to be with and be the monster. The status of fans as producers of their own texts allows fans – through various producerly activities such as fan art – to create their own images of the monster and extends through prop-building, costume-making and cosplay into areas of performance. This links to the Deleuzo–Guattarian idea of becoming-animal (1987, 274–5), in this instance through fans' performative activities.

Through such popularity and circulation within fan culture, monsters come to be adopted by fan communities and are thus accorded totemic status. The adopted animal is not always a monstrous entity or creature of course, but particularly within horror and fantasy fandoms, a totem may be an entity that personifies fear in the narrative or storyworld. In particular, mythic sea creatures such as the kraken or giant squid, the mermaid, the sea serpent, the giant whale and the killer shark, as well as Cthulhu who is associated with the submerged city of R'lyeh, offer appeals to fans. Since being frightened is a desired emotional affect from viewing horror and related genres, the monster comes to represent the pleasures and affective investments fans make in the storyworld. The totem is not simply displayed as a signifier of fan interest in particular texts, but is incorporated into the fan identity itself with a number of activities practiced by fans that facilitate a sense of becoming-monster.

Modes of affect and the sea creatures of the horror genre

The first step in a monster becoming totemic arises in the way the attraction to monstrous entities is central to personal fan histories (or biographies) as a desire to be with and be the monster. Emotional affect is an extremely important element in the range of experiences sought by horror fans – not least the frisson of fear. Fear in this context is not a negative emotion. Experiences of childhood viewing and reading often underlie the adult taste for particular genres and modes of affect, as well as the fascination with monstrous creatures. As Daniel Shaw (1997) has stated there are unique pleasures to be gained from being horrified. Discussing Noel Carroll's philosophy of horror (1990), he counters the idea that the emotion of art horror – namely, revulsion – is 'unproblematic, unpleasant and uncomplicated'. Shaw observes that:

> My son Patrick loves the monster, and not just when the monster is lovable (like Frankenstein is at certain moments) [...] he loves to be chased by just about anyone that he can get to chase him. He loves to be scared, and is constantly (and ineffectually) sneaking up behind someone and acting like a monster.

Obviously, one anecdotal observation is not sufficient proof of an observable trend, but this suggests that viewers, even – perhaps especially – young ones, enjoy watching monsters, enjoy being (vicariously) scared, and even enjoy playacting – in other words, being or becoming – the monster. Shaw goes on to propose that: 'any satisfying account of the reasons why so many of us love horror fictions has got to recognize that our primary source of pleasure is the monster, or horrific human, which we relate to in a profoundly ambivalent fashion'. Certainly the findings from my own empirical studies of horror film audiences and fan cultures shed light on the affective investments made by fans in monstrous creatures.

The fans in my study often date their enjoyment of monsters and liking being scared to an early age, sometimes younger than five (Cherry, 1999). This does not mean though that they were viewing horror films as children. The books, films or television programmes triggering such a reaction were most likely to have been fairy tales, classic children's novels, and films or TV programmes for children or family audiences (and sometimes less explicit, older or tamer adult material).

It is not at all unexpected that fans report these experiences: Marina Warner (2014) has highlighted the way traditional fairy tales have elements in common with horror literature and many nursery tales contain horrific sequences. Harold Schechter (1984: 69) argues that a common source links fairy tales and horror; he suggests 'the "symbol-inventing" level of the mind, a reservoir of primordial images, is the matrix of all folk-dream and myth'. Given that sea creatures are so prevalent in the kinds of children's entertainment that horror fans cite as formative (and assuming that like Shaw's son they take pleasure out of playacting the monsters), we might then look to further analyse the ways in which fans seek to incorporate aquatic monsters into their own fan identities and the fan communities they participate in as acts of becoming-monster.

Indeed, fans name a wide variety of formative texts that they still feel affective investments in as adults. Many of these contain significant examples of sea monsters: amongst fairy tales and classic children's fiction *The Little Mermaid* (Ron Clements & John Musker, 1989), *Pinocchio* (Ben Sharpsteen & Hamilton Luske, 1940) and *Peter Pan* (CyldeGeronimi, Wilfred Jackson & Hamilton Luske, 1953) stand out (all also in the Disney catalogue, whilst monstrous versions of mermaids are found in the live action *Peter Pan* (P.J. Hogan, 2003)).

Doctor Who (BBC, 1963–) is mentioned most frequently and there are several stories from the 1960s to the present day with sea creatures; notable occurrences are found in 'The Underwater Menace', 'The Sea Devils' and 'Fury from the Deep', as well as a significant number of other aquatic creatures including versions of the Loch Ness monster, a Siren-like virtual medical programme, giant crabs, alien vampire crustaceans, humanoid fish, marshmen, space-faring reptiles with gills and fins, sky sharks, star whales and sea-slug like aliens.

Jules Verne, John Wyndham and H.P. Lovecraft are often mentioned authors known for *20,000 Leagues under the Sea* (1870) with its giant squid (and another Disney adaptation, this time live action), *The Kraken Wakes* (1953), and the Cthulhu Mythos (1931),* respectively. Other mentions include Gerry Anderson's puppet animations – *Stingray* (1964–5) has its merman king, his daughter Marina and the Amphibian henchmen – and Ray Harryhausen who has animated a giant octopus, a giant nautilus, a giant crab, and a rhodosaur, as well as the kraken from *Clash of the Titans* (1981). It might be concluded therefore that scary elements in children's entertainment are important precursors to fans' later affective investments in aquatic horror.

Given the range of sea creatures in these formative texts, the importance of monsters from the deep and their pivotal role in the history of horror and fantasy should not be forgotten (though perhaps they are less widely explored – like the ocean depths themselves – than the iconic and quite often recognisably human monsters of the genre such as Frankenstein's creature, the werewolf, the vampire, zombies and the walking dead, and the various stalkers of the slasher genre). Films that represent this category of monsters include Roger Corman's first film as producer, *Monster from the Ocean Floor* (WyottOrdung, 1954), the Stephanie Rothman film he produced later, *Humanoids from the Deep* (Barbara Peeters & Jimmy T. Murakami, 1980), *It Came From Beneath the Sea* (Robert Gordon, 1955) and other films with Ray Harryhausen's famous stop-motion creatures; *Jaws* (Steven Spielberg, 1975), *Sharknado* (Anthony C. Ferrante, 2013), *Orca the Killer Whale* (Michael Anderson, 1977), and of course the cult classic, *Creature From the Black Lagoon* (Jack Arnold, 1954). The latter illustrates the significance of the sea and other bodies of deep water as a semiotic and psychoanalytic trope in the horror genre. David Cronenberg's (1984: 57) introduction to the Toronto Festival of Festivals, on the Black Lagoon as representation of the unconscious, illustrates this:

For me the imagery of *The Creature From The Black Lagoon* was always perfect because the Black Lagoon is the dark pool of the unconscious and of course there are creatures within it. The exercise is to jump down into the Lagoon to see what is going on down there and to say 'hello' to the creature.

Psychoanalytic readings of horror films have not been uncommon, of course, but once we have dived down and said hello to the creature – faced our repressed anxieties and desires – what relationship can we subsequently have with the monster? In moving beyond (or at least complicating) this idea of the Black Lagoon (and its Creature) as a representation of the unconscious, it is pertinent to explore audience responses to monstrous entities, particu-

---

* Cthulhu incorporates the kraken's physical characteristics in the squid-like tentacles around the mouth.

larly by considering how viewers, particularly horror and science fiction fans, make affective investments in monstrosity beyond the appeals of recognisably human – and often physically attractive – monsters. This is a key factor in the fans' affective investments and the creatures' resultant totemic status.

What is important to note here is that even animalistic, monstrous creatures can elicit viewer empathy, if not identification, as the (unnamed) Girl (played by Marilyn Monroe) in *The Seven Year Itch* (Billy Wilder, 1955) illustrates. Upon leaving the cinema where she has just seen *The Creature From the Black Lagoon* she says:

> 'Didn't you just love the picture? I did. But I just felt so sorry for the creature. At the end.'

> 'Sorry for the creature?' her date replies. 'Why, d'you want him to marry the girl?'

> 'He was kinda scary looking. But he wasn't really all bad. I think he just craved a little affection. You know. Being loved and needed and wanted.'

My own research indicates that many horror fans are indeed similarly attracted to monsters, feel sympathetic towards the monster or empathise and even identify with them, even where that monster has no or few human features. For these fans, such pleasures often originate – as for Daniel Shaw's son – in childhood. That some viewers become attracted to monsters in childhood is a significant factor in understanding their appeal. One notable observation when analysing forms of monstrosity that fall broadly into non-human configurations (or as in the case of the mermaid, for example, are part-human, part-animal), is that they are clearly not attractive, sexually appealing monsters. Rather they are sometimes monstrous animal forms with no or few human characteristics. Or they are hybrid creatures, part-human or with humanoid forms. Some might hold appeal, as the mermaid does (though even the mermaid, despite often being portrayed as attractive and sexually alluring, might confound sexuality with her fish tail), but most *are* 'kinda scary looking'. Nonetheless, all such creatures have a place of importance not only in the fans' affections, but in some cases as significant tropes within related genres that come to be privileged by fans, and in some cases to represent the fandom itself.

The aquatic monster as intertext in steampunk

The examples mentioned above illustrate the ways in which sea creatures might be pivotal in a developing attraction to horror. They create an experience of fear as a positive and pleasurable emotional affect, constructing empathetic responses to monstrosity, identification with the monster, and a desire to be and be with the monster. How then might this be useful in respect of understanding the role of the monster in fan identity and imaginative play, or its resultant totemic status in horror and science fiction fandom? The aesthetic qualities of monsters (including such elements as make-up, visual effects, set design, animation, music, dialogue and performance) construct affective responses, responses that those with a developing taste for horror and related genres embrace.

These responses thus contribute to the affective investments that fans make in the text and in the fandom that surrounds it. It is significant also that many of these creatures have come to acquire the status of iconic images within the genre. Moreover, this gives them additional standing within the fan community. Iconic status can be linked to the way in which the concomitant interests of the fans – fairy tales, myth and folklore – and their formative tastes – scary elements in children's literature, films and television programmes – also work as intertexts in the cult media and genre texts that interest the fans. An important factor in this is the influence of such formative texts on producers of key texts.

Take for example, Alan Moore's comic book series *League of Extraordinary Gentlemen* and its spin-off *Nemo* (1999–2015). The main characters in the storyworld, which is initially set in the late nineteenth century, derive from Victorian fantasy fiction – H. Rider Haggard's Allan Quartermain, H.G. Wells' Invisible Man, Robert Louis Stephenson's Dr Jekyll, Bram Stoker's Mina Murray/Harker, and most notably – especially since the character was central to the spin-off series – Verne's Captain Nemo. The comic, itself a key example of the steampunk aesthetic, can thus be categorised as belonging to the steampunk genre (although it is much wider in terms of its generic and historical scope) and is popular with members of the steampunk fandom. Moore's work references the aquatic environment of Verne's novel and Nemo's encounter with the giant squid. Furthermore, this also allows Moore to draw on other intertexts – this is a characteristic of the series as a whole (namely, bringing various fictional storyworlds together). *League of Extraordinary Gentlemen: Black Dossier* (2007) and *Nemo: River of Ghosts* (2015) include a colony of creatures like that from the Black Lagoon films that, it is also suggested, are related to the Silurians (and thus to their sibling-species the Sea Devils) from *Doctor Who*. Moreover, references are also made to Kutulu (a deliberate misspelling of Cthulhu) and the sinking of R'lyeh.

Similar connections are made within the wider genre. In the *Doctor Who* novel *All-Consuming Fire* (Lane, 1994), the Sea Devils are said to worship Dagon, the sea god of the Lovecraftian Great Old Ones. Eldritch horror fans might thus also connect the Sea Devils (who somewhat resemble Cthulhu with their winged crests and beaked mouth and being awoken from their slumber in the depths) to the aquatic humanoids the Deep Ones in 'The Shadow Over Innsmouth' (Lovecraft, 1931) who also worshipped Dagon. These intertexts are further referenced in other popular works of the steampunk genre, such as when the artist D'Israeli illustrates a splash panel in the comic *Scarlet Traces: The Great Game* (set during the war with Wells'

Martians) with a mural (a map of the solar system) depicting (amongst other alien inhabitants of the inner planets from keys texts in the science fiction genre) a Sea Devil and a Silurian – they are shown as the inhabitants of a Pangean-era Earth. In yet another example of a Lovecraft intertext, the seminal steampunk novel *Infernal Devices* (Jeter, 1987) features aquatic humanoid creatures who mate with humans to create hybrids just as the Deep Ones do. Steampunk can thus be seen as a source of important intertexts that provide moments of pleasure for fans of storyworlds featuring aquatic monsters. It links Vernian fiction, 50s horror cinema, *Doctor Who* and Lovecraft. The intertextual referencing of such cult media reinforces and feeds back into the appeals of such creatures for this fan community.

Fan totems and imaginative play

Given such significant intertexts in the steampunk genre, it is only to be expected that affective investments in such creatures will transfer into the associated fandom. The cephalopod has thus become a totem of steampunk fandom. Precedents for the adoption of animal totems are already present within fan communities. One emblem of vampire fandom (if a now rather clichéd one) for example is the bat (a monstrous form that the Gothic vampire has been known to transform into). The bat or a batwing shape can be incorporated into jewellery, buttons on clothing or embellishments on shoes, displayed in the home on clocks, mirrors or candlesticks, and be used as a graphic to adorn vampire fan websites or in fan tattoos. Similarly, the *Harry Potter* and *Game of Thrones* fandoms adopt the heraldic animals of the school and family houses from the respective storyworlds. Fan communities might thus adopt monsters or monstrous creatures as symbols of their fandom with accessories, personal possessions and household items taking the form of the monster, and the monster or features of the monster adorning various material artefacts or profiles on social media and websites. In some respects this can be read as a commodification of fandom, but it also illustrates the ways in which monstrous entities can be incorporated into fan identities.

Why then has the cephalopod* come to be so prevalent in steampunk fandom? It is not quite as simple as linking this directly to Verne's kraken. This is only one instance in a genre of nineteenth-century fantasy fiction that forms a precursor to steampunk (which only came to prominence as a literary genre in the 1980s, as a film aesthetic in the 1990s and as a performative subculture in the 2000s). The adoption of animal totems does not derive simply from the presence of the creature, but from the way that characters in the narrative are associated with them (Dracula can transform

---

*   It should be noted that although the squid is of a different order to the octopus, the two creatures have been somewhat conflated, with the curvier octopus adopted as the key design element in the steampunk aesthetic.

into a bat; Harry Potter has the trait of courage and is sorted into the House with the lion as its totem).

In *20,000 Leagues Under the Sea*, Captain Nemo has to fight the kraken, but Nemo's Nautilus in Alan Moore's *League of Extraordinary Gentlemen* – and thus Nemo himself as master of his ship – is the kraken. Its external design takes the form of a giant squid. The top of the main middle section resembles the squid's mantle, with fins at the aft shaped and positioned just as a squid's are. The top of the forward section resembles the head of the squid with the curving arms and tentacles forming a design across the extended front part of the submarine. Large viewing windows are in the position of the eyes. The Nautilus' tentacles are hydraulic arms capable of fluid movement that can manipulate or retrieve underwater objects and are used in loading and unloading supplies when in dock. In *The Black Dossier*, it is described as being like 'some new, unearthly creature [...] two undersea leviathans, a kraken and a whale, locked in an embrace that was mortal or else amorous.' Taking on the semblance of the kraken in form and function represents a totemic embrace of the power and menace of the monster. Nemo not only signals his ascendancy over the kraken by defeating it, but by becoming-kraken. In *The League of Extraordinary Gentlemen* he is thus possessed of its characteristics – its size, strength, maneuverability, and dominance of the seas.

It might be concluded from this that the kraken thus links to the masculinity of steampunk with its emphasis on steam-driven technology, but this gendering is not straightforward. It is Nemo's daughter Janni who is the Captain Nemo of the *Nemo* series and she functions in the same role as her deceased father. In this way, she is both becoming-kraken and becoming-male. A similar conjunction of becomings occurs in The *Parasol Protectorate* novels (Carriger, 2009–2012), popular amongst female steampunk fandom. Although many of the scientists in The Order of the Brass Octopus – a scientific organisation in the storyworld – are male as might be expected in the Victorian era, one of its members is Genevieve Lefoux, a female engineer and the owner of a hat shop with her inventor's workshop in the basement beneath. As the name of the Order suggests, its members associate themselves with the octopus, having octopus tattoos and working octopus designs into the architecture and décor of their buildings. Lefoux has an octopus tattoo on the back of her neck to signify membership of the Order, but this inscription on her body (just as Nemo inscribes it on the Nautilus) is also her becoming-octopus. In a parallel act of becoming-male (like Janni she is already in a prominent masculine role), it is notable that Lefoux also dresses in male clothing. Moreover, in *Heartless* (Carriger, 2011), Lefoux builds an octomaton – a giant steam-driven vehicular machine shaped like an octopus wearing a bowler hat (which houses the control cabin). It is described as 'the world's biggest automated cephalopod' and 'a giant tiptoeing octopus' that looks 'almost as though it floated atop the cloud of steam that gushed forth from under its mantle to swirl about its tentacles'. It 'walks' with its tentacles just as live octopuses do on the seabed. Like Nemo's Nautilus, the vehicle has eight tentacles capable of independent movement, each with a weapon that can kill vampires. Lefoux and Nemo are both identified with their totemic creature and their vehicles' design features symbolise their affinity with it.

Gender in these examples is problematized – with female characters being associated with the technological (and traditionally masculine-coded) world. Representations of femininity and female sexuality are also encoded in contrasting representations of the cephalopod totem, as illustrated by Otto and Victoria from Brian Kessinger's picture book *Walking Your Octopus: A Guidebook to the Domesticated Cephalopod* (2013). This demonstrates how the empathetic connection or the desire to be with the monster that many fans experience can be represented by the domestication of the monster. Thus the octopus is here depicted as the pet or animal companion to the young Victorian lady. The cover shows Victoria in a bustled and trained dress accessorised with pocket watch, parasol, goggles and top hat (all key elements of the steampunk style) walking Otto on a leash just like a pet. Otto was adopted from 'a local cephalopod rescue' and – like a cat – prefers playing with an empty box rather than the toys Victoria provides (one of which is a Cthulhu figure). As a pet substitute, she takes Otto for walks, plays with him, feeds him, exercises him (on a penny farthing ride), and dresses him up in funny costumes for photographs

There are parallels here with advice on caring for pets (of which *Walking Your Octopus* is a pastiche) and with the 'fur baby' culture populated online by cat photos and videos. But *Walking Your Octopus* also draws on the sensual aspect of the octopus and depicts an eroticised relationship between Otto and Victoria. Victoria shares her bath with Otto, he laces her corset, pulls suggestively at her bloomers on a trip to the beach, and wrestles prospective human suitors away. This suggests the sensuality if not the sexuality of the octopus (as Laura Ettenfield and Marco Carbone explore elsewhere in this book) and illustrates the point that strong female characters in the steampunk text are of paramount importance to female steampunks. Indeed, there are many examples of Victoria cosplays incorporating various kinds of stuffed or toy Ottos.

It is perhaps worth asking why the steampunk fandom adopted the octopus over the squid as their totem, given that the squid has more basis in the genre through *20,000 Leagues under the Sea* and *League of Extraordinary Gentlemen*, and whether this reveals a gendered preference. The widespread fascination with the octopus rather than the squid (which is presented in its giant form as spectacle) is certainly relevant in the perceived 'cuteness' of the octopus and the way stereotypes of women's relationships with their pets (particular cats) is pastiched in *Walking Your Octopus*. Victoria's relationship with Otto is certainly encouraging of this viewpoint and Victoria, representing Victorian femininity, has a domestic relationship with the octopus. This is not straightforward or unproblematical gendering, however, and as with the female Captain Nemo and Madame Lefoux, Victoria exhibits independence, autonomy and agency. However, by and large the octopus is a generic trope associated with female characters in the steampunk genre.

Regardless of the issues of gender representation, though, it is clear that the fan responses to steampunk texts and the appearance of cephalopods (or rather cephalopod designs for personal vehicles) within the genre contributes to the growing profile and popularity of the octopus amongst fans and worked to elevate the octopus to totemic status. On The Steampunk Empire website fans themselves discussed the question of why the octopus was their favourite 'monster'.* Fans linked the adoption of the octopus as an unofficial totem of steampunk firstly to appearances of cephalopods in Victorian and Edwardian science fiction and fantasy: not only *20,000 Leagues Under the Sea*, but the air kraken in Arthur Conan Doyle's 'The Horror of the Heights' (1913), HG Wells' tentacled Martian invaders in *The War of the Worlds* (1898) and Lovecraft's 'outlandish horrors' (even though Lovecraft was writing in the 1920s and 30s). This suggests that fans seek out intertexts that draw on features of the cephalopod, and also boundary cross, expanding their classification of cephalopod to include other similar creatures from non-aquatic environments, even aliens and demonic entities, that share some characteristic with the octopus. But a more significant indicator of why the octopus in particular has become a totem of steampunk fan culture are its real-world attributes, both physical and behavioural. One fan says that it 'looks like it's wearing a helmet and goggles, and the tentacles remind me of the mechanics of gears with many individual items working in unison'. Another says it is because 'they are tool using invertebrates. It's a gadget loving cephalopod!' This reflects the characteristics of the steampunk genre and fan culture. The octopus has meaning to steampunk fans because they see themselves in it.

The Deleuzo–Guattarian notion of becoming-animal is pertinent here. As Anna Powell (2006) has discussed, becoming-animal is found in the transformations and hybrids of myth and fairytales, and of horror cinema. For Deleuze and Guattari, this is related to cycles of desire. The desire to be with and be the monster does not necessarily end at the end of the film or story. Fan activities can incorporate becoming-monster into the imaginative play undertaken during cosplay and in fans' everyday lives too. If fans are anything like Daniel Shaw's son (and they are), playing at being the monster arises out of responses to popular cultural texts; this completes a cycle of desire related to being with and being the monster. Producerly and performative activites such as cosplay allow fans to be dress up and act as fictional characters, but becoming-monster is not restricted to costumed activities. Fans also participate in acts of 'everyday cosplay' where they can incorporate

* See The Steampunk Empire forum, ttp://www.thesteampunkempire.com/forum/topics/question-why-is-the-octopus (accessed 14 April 2016).

the monster into everyday clothing or styles. In a recent research study of fan handicrafting (Cherry, 2016), it was observed that images of the fan totem were often incorporated into the material objects that the fans make.

Imaginative play and becoming-animal

Through the examples of giant cephalopods in the steampunk genre, the octopus has come to symbolise steampunk fandom and culture. It permeates a wide-range of fan arts and crafts, including material objects – clothing and accessories – that can be worn, and can thus signal fan affinities and be incorporated into the fan identity, enabling acts of becoming-animal. Countless examples of steampunk-style octopus and tentacle jewelry, t-shirts, hats and masks are available on e-commerce sites such as Etsy. Some steampunks have octopus tattoos, sometimes mechanical, sometimes wearing top hats and monocles. The steampunk fans on the Ravelryhandicrafting site formed their own version of Team Brass Octopus in communal knitting events and gave themselves code names similar to those used by the characters in *The Parasol Protectorate* novels. These activities complete the cycle of desire and the process of becoming-animal in terms of fan identity. The adoption of animal totems by fan cultures such as this also illustrates how totems feed into the producerly activities of fans. Fans are inveterate remediators of texts – they write their own fiction and draw on their favourite elements of the text as fan producers. Accordingly, they produce material objects that allow them to own, pet, wear and dress up as their own favourite monster. Many examples of knitted and crocheted fan art incorporate fan totems and these illustrate the ways fans incorporate becoming-monster into their everyday lives.

Returning to Daniel Shaw's observation of his son, children like to play at being monsters. Well, so do fans, at the very least in the way fans incorporate monstrous creatures into their fandom as animal totems through their fan art. In terms of responses to representations of monstrosity it is understandable that fans of monsters in particular might want to be the monster through dressing up and play-acting. The vampire fans in Mellins' (2013) study for example form a style community as well as practising cosplay, dressing up in Victorian styles of clothing and wearing vampire fangs. But even outside of attractive monsters that offer association with erotic appeal, other horror monster fans do exhibit similar behaviours in terms of performative fan activities. Zombie walks, for instance, invite fans to dress up (with distressed clothing and make-up emulating the decayed flesh of the corpse) as the 'walking dead' and join a horde of fellow fans in urban meet-up events or pub crawls.

However, whilst vampire fans can easily adapt vampire costumes whether Gothic or modern in terms of fashion or performative style, and zombie costumes are variants of everyday dress, distressed for a special dress-up occasion, with other monsters such performative behaviours might not be so possible (at least outside of fan conventions or other specialist cosplay arenas). Non-human creatures and monstrous entities with less resemblance to the human form are not necessarily easy to perform in cosplay and do not easily carry over into everyday life. It is hard to conceive, for example, how an eldritch horror fan might dress to resemble Cthulhu as easily or as frequently as a vampire fan can adopt the Gothic style of a Hammer vampire (at least outside of cosplay). However, fans and fan communities do incorporate non-human creatures or aspects of creatures into their fan identities; such behaviours (becoming the monster by dressing up, cosplaying or immersing oneself in a style culture) might also be extended into everyday life. In practice, fans of many kinds adopt clothing or styles of dress that signify fan affiliations outwith performative activities at fan conventions, clubs or meet-ups. Many fans wear everyday items of clothing sporting a logo or picture (on a t-shirt, for example) or incorporate copies of a single item of clothing worn by their favourite character on screen into their usual attire. But more importantly, such behaviours can move beyond personal dress practices into the wider spheres of fan culture. Mechanisms thus exist within fan cultures for being with and being monsters whether the monster take a human form or not, and whether performance and performative styles are easily achievable or not.

Soft toys, of course, have long been amongst the material objects created by handicrafters. In the context of fan culture, these are not only for children. Such objects allow fans to possess (and pet) their own monster, recreating – in the case of the octopus – the relationship between Victoria and Otto. The Dandy Sir Cephalod pattern[*] is popular with steampunk fans, for example. The octopus in this pattern is cartoony – resembling the rounded head and short, fat arms of the flapjack octopus, and thus offers a cute design that has a child-like aesthetic appeal.

There are a number of octopus and squid patterns available for fan handicrafters, from the more anatomically authentic to the playful or whimsical. But the Dandy Sir Cephalopod pattern is directly aimed at steampunk fans with instructions for steampunk accessories including a knitted stovepipe hat, an embroidered monocle and a button handlebar mustache (with a link to the Etsy store where knitters can buy the specific wooden button). Some of the fan handicrafters who have made the pattern follow it closely, but there is also a wide range of customisation or modding (as might be expected from members of the steampunk culture). Some give their finished project a steampunk-style name on their Ravelry profile: Sir Squiddington Esquire, Aberforth the Cephalopod, Sir Sebastian the Cephalopod, and Sir Octavious, for example. Some paint or decorate the specified wooden button and some substitute a different style of button (a ceramic one, for instance) or make

---

[*] See Dandy Sir Cephalopod by Susan Claudino, ttp://www.ravelry.com/patterns/library/dandy-sir-cephalopod (accessed 10 May 2016).

various styles of moustache – some are embroidered, others appliquéd felt, and one project has an overlarge, stuffed moustache. Similarly, the monocle is customised, some are made from Modpodge (a decoupage glue) or modelling clay, and others make them out of the ubiquitous steampunk cogs or gears. And although the Dandy Sir Cephalopod is clearly male, some handicrafters have made female versions – with flowers, fascinators and parasols instead of stovepipe hats. Some steampunk knitters have taken part in communal knit-alongs to make a Dandy or other octopus, embellishing it with various steampunk accessories in order to win acclaim within the group.

Other members of fan communities have similarly undertaken crafting projects involving their fan totem. Eldritch horror fans make their very own crochet Cthulhu[*] and these have been the subject of craft-alongs at the Thought Bubble comic festival in Leeds in 2012 and displayed in the window of the Pulp Fiction bookshop in Edinburgh. Mermaid fans have a large number of mermaid patterns to draw on, not only the attractive or 'girlie' mermaid but also the Monster Mermaid[**] which plays on the darker side of the creature with pointy fin ears, mismatched eyes, and even fangs.

If such examples of fan art allow fans to be with their monster as a material, albeit inanimate, pet, they can also through their crafting projects become-monster. Fans of sea creatures are prolific in producing fibre art that not only allows them to play homage to their favourite monsters, or to make a display of their fandom, but facilitates becoming-monster too (at least through acts of imaginative play). Steampunk fans, for example, can be (as in be transformed into) the octopus with tentacled headwear suggesting the fan's affinity with the creature. For example, one hat design[***] evokes the mantle and head of the octopus as the crown of the hat with large buttons suggesting the eyes. Stuffed tentacles descend from the bottom of the hat on each side and around the back. To similar effect, they can knit a jumper[8] with an intricate and realistic colourwork design of an octopus. The mantle and head of the octopus cover the right front shoulder area and tentacles extend out covering the front of the jumper and around the back with one spiralling down the left arm. Through imaginative play this allows them not only to display their fan credentials (not to mention their craft skills), but be embraced by the octopus. In fact, the jumper pattern is titled 'Embrace Octopus' – the somewhat awkward grammar (it sounds like it should be a command) suggesting the knitter can both *embrace* the octopus and *be embraced* by it.

*   See Mr Cthulhu Amigurumi by Randy Lee, ttp://www.ravelry.com/patterns/library/mr-cthulhu-amigurumi (accessed 9 May 2016).

**   See Monster Mermaid by Jess Rollar, ttp://www.ravelry.com/patterns/library/monster-mermaid (accessed 12 May 2016).

*** See Octopus Hat by Randy Lee, ttp://www.ravelry.com/patterns/library/octopus-hat-2 (accessed 10 May 2016).

Similar examples are found in other fandoms. The Cthulhuclava* (a play of words on balaclava) allows Lovecraft fans to become-Cthulhu by wearing a design that covers the head and face with ridged brows above the eye holes and stuffed tentacles descending around the mouth. The photos displayed in the fan handicrafters' Ravelry projects demonstrate becoming-Cthulhu. In one, the choice of sea blue yarn and the beachside staging of the project photograph suggests Cthulhu emerging from under the waves. Corporate Cthulhu further illustrates the imaginative play (here taking the form of everyday cosplay) that provides a tongue-in-cheek connection between the everyday life of the fan and the Lovecraftian storyworld of the imagination. There is an uncanny disconnect between the monstrosity of Cthulhu in the form of the balaclava and the rest of the fan's clothing – an office 'uniform' of suit, shiny shoes and briefcase – as he walks down an urban street. This makes an ironic statement of fan status. More importantly, it demonstrates the ways fans bring what might otherwise be formalised cosplay at fan events into their everyday lives (more popularly, the Cthulhuclava is often worn by fans as they dress up for Halloween and fan events).**

Other examples of everyday cosplay include the mermaid fans who express their desire of becoming-mermaid by crafting their own mermaid's tail blanket*** – this can be used to keep warm when sitting or lying on the sofa and undertaking mundane activities such as reading or watching TV. It can also be sexualised as part of the imaginative play of wearing the mermaid afghan. The staging of the project photographs in one example emphasises the sensual qualities of the mermaid and seduction – the crafter is modelling her tail lying on the floor invitingly in front of the open fire.

Being with and being the monster in imaginative play can also have a macabre edge (albeit an ironic or amusing one too), as with patterns for shark blankets and socks. The Shark Week sock pattern† depicts a stuffed shark head biting off the wearer's foot – complete with red drop beads for the blood dripping from the shark's jaws. The Shark Blanket‡ can be 'worn' like the mermaid tails, having the tail at the foot end and the jaws encircling the torso so it looks as if the shark is swallowing the wearer whole. These patterns enable the user or wearer to imaginatively play at being devoured by the monsters of *Jaws* or *Sharknado*, despite – or perhaps because of – the gruesome nature of these films (horror fans do not just enjoy the frisson of

---

* See Embrace Octopus Sweater by Maia E. Sirnes, ttp://www.ravelry.com/patterns/library/embrace-oc-topus-sweater (accessed 9 May 2016).

** See Cthulhuclava by Anne-Marie Dunbar, ttp://www.ravelry.com/patterns/library/cthulhuclava (accessed 9 May 2016).

*** See Bulky and Quick Mermaid Blanket by MJ's Off the Hook Designs, ttp://www.ravelry.com/patterns/library/bulky—quick-mermaid-blanket (accessed 10 May 2016).

† See Shark Week by Lisa Grossman, ttp://www.ravelry.com/patterns/library/shark-week (accessed 12 May 2016).

‡ See Shark Blanket, Black Sheep Wools, ttp://www.blacksheepwools.com/shark-blanket-knitting-pattern-yarn-pack.html (accessed 26 May 2016).

fear, but the shock moments and instances of gore too). These projects, and the many more like them, are a source of pleasure for fans who willingly desire, embrace and play at being the monster. Through playful acts of everyday cosplay these examples of fan handicrafting facilitate becoming-monster.

Fan art and identity

In *The League of Extraordinary Gentlemen* Alan Moore not only ties together children's popular culture, classic horror cinema, and Jules Verne in a steampunk graphic novel, but depicts the totemic status of the kraken for Captain Nemo through the design of the Nautilus. Through affective investments in this and other texts, steampunk fans similarly adopt such creatures as totems of their fan community. This bringing together of concomitant tastes illustrates a fan life history from formative childhood tastes to the becoming-monsters of fan culture. The fascination with sea creatures and other monsters in fairytales, myths and legends and the enjoyment of watching monstrous entities in children's popular culture precedes (though does not predict) a taste for horror. The fans' affective investments in texts not only facilitate identification with monsters, but the imaginative play of becoming-monster. The attraction to human monsters – vampires, were-wolves in their human form, even seductively attractive serial killers such as Hannibal Lecter or Dexter – seems obvious. But as the desire for and to be decidedly non-human and inhuman sea creatures suggests, all monsters hold appeals. Just like Daniel Shaw's son, fans clearly want to be with and be *even* 'kinda creepy looking' monsters.

References

Carriger, G. (2011), *Heartless*, London: Orbit Books.

Carroll, N. (1990), *The Philosophy of Horror or Paradoxes of The Heart*, London: Routledge.

Cherry, B. (2017), 'Beauty, Pain and Desire: Gothic Aesthetics and Feminine Identification in the Filmic Adaptations of Clive Barker'. In S. NíFhlainn (ed.), *Clive Barker: Dark Imaginer*, Manchester: Manchester University Press, pp.111–126.

Cherry, B. (2016), *Cult Media, Fandom and Textiles: Handicrafting as Fan Art*, London: Bloomsbury.

Cherry, B. (1999), 'Refusing to Refuse to Look: Female Viewers of the Horror Film'. In M. Stokes & R. Maltby (eds), *Identifying Hollywood Audiences: Cultural Identity and the Movies*, London: BFI, pp.169–178.

Cronenberg, D. (1984) 'Appendix: Festival of Festivals' 1983 Science Fiction Retrospective'. In W. Drew (ed.), *David Cronenberg: Dossier 21*, London: BFI.

Deleuze, G. & Guattari, F. (1987), *A Thousand Plateaus: Capitalism and Schizophrenia*, Minneapolis: University of Minnesota Press.

Conan Doyle, A. ([1913] 1989), 'The Horror of the Heights'. In F.D. McSherry, M.H. Greenberg & C.G. Waugh (eds), *The Best Horror Stories of Arthur Conan Doyle*, Chicago: Academy Chicago, pp.60–79.

Edginton, I. (2006), *Scarlet Traces: The Great Game*, Milwaukie: Dark Horse Comics.

Jeter, K.W. (1987), *Infernal Devices*, New York: St Martin's Press.

Kesinger, B. (2013), *Walking Your Octopus: A Guidebook to the Domesticated Cephalopod*, Van Nuys: Baby Tattoo Books.

Lane, A. (1994), *All-Consuming Fire*, London: Virgin Books.

Lovecraft, H.P. ([1931] 1999), 'The Shadow Over Innsmouth'. In *The Call of Cthulhu and Other Weird Stories*, London: Penguin.

Mellins, M. (2013), *Vampire Culture*, London: Bloomsbury.

Moore, A. (2007), *The League of Extraordinary Gentlemen: Black Dossier*, Burbank: DC Comics.

Moore, A. (2015), *Nemo: River of Ghosts*, London: Knockabout Comics.

Powell, A. (2006), *Deleuze and Horror Film*, Edinburgh: Edinburgh University Press.

Schechter, H. (1984), 'The Bloody Chamber: Terror Films, Fairy Tales and Taboo'. In R.B. Browne (ed.), *Forbidden Fruits: Taboos and Tabooism in Culture*, Bowling Green: Bowling Green University Press, pp.67–82.

Shaw, D. (1997), 'A Humean Definition of Horror', *Film-Philosophy*, 1 (4) ttp://www.film-philosophy.com/vol1-1997/n4shaw [accessed 9 May 2003].

Verne, J. ([1870] 1992), *20,000 Leagues Under the Sea*, Ware: Wordsworth Classics.

Warner, M. (2014), *Once Upon a Time: A Short History of Fairy Tale*, Oxford: Oxford University Press.

Wells, H.G. ([1898] 2017), *War of the Worlds*, London: Pan Macmillan.

Wyndham, J. ([1953] 2008), *The Kraken Wakes*, London: Penguin.

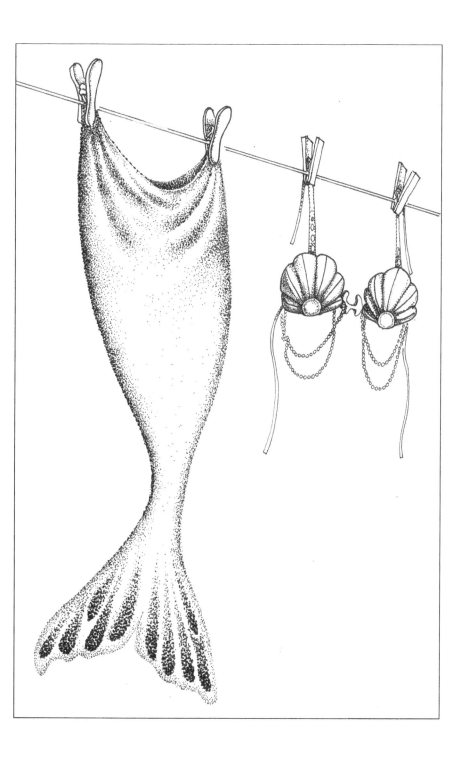

Chapter 8

Mermaid Spotting: the Rise of Mermaiding in Popular Culture

Maria Mellins

Since the beginning of cinema there have been a number of depictions of the mermaid in films like *The Mermaid* (director unknown, 1911), *Mr Peabody and the Mermaid* (Irving Pichel, 1948), *Miranda* (Ken Annakin, 1948), *Splash* (Ron Howard, 1984) and of course Disney's Ariel from *The Little Mermaid* (Ron Clements & John Musker, 1989). Currently, mermaids and their darker counterparts, sirens, have gained popularity and are emerging across different forms of media, fashion and lifestyle. Much like the vampire in recent years, there is an appetite for these human/fish hybrids, with films and TV series including Disney's *The Little Mermaid*, Polish horror film *The Lure* (Agnieszka Smoczyńska, 2015) and Freeform's television drama, *Siren*.

Reimaginings of the mermaid are not just confined to screen fiction, but can be found across wider lifestyle practices, as styling oneself as these beautiful creatures of the sea is no longer confined to screen sirens Annette Kellermann, Anne Blyth and Daryl Hannah, but has now been extended to high street trends. Mermaid fashion can be found across a number of popular clothing brands such as ASOS, which sells mermaid inspired merchandise carrying the slogans 'mermaid hair don't care', 'mermaid academy' and 'off duty mermaid,' and New Look, which offers mermaid tail socks, 'mermaid sparkle' body glitter, as well as mermaid knitted blankets. Styling the sea is even disseminating into more DIY fashion, as teal blue ombre hair colours and crimped 'beachy' hairstyles have become popular.

Whilst the recent proliferation of mermaid products has indeed permeated popular fashion and lifestyle trends, a smaller group of people with a fascination for these fantasy figures have gone one stage further, as 'mermaiding' has become a legitimate leisure activity and business opportunity. Mermaiding is a lifestyle, crafting process that is often linked to cosplay. It involves using a combination of free diving methods and underwater dolphin kick techniques, with the swimmers' legs bound together in a monofin tail. The WeekiWachee showgirls of Florida are perhaps the best known mermaid shows, and have been performing at the springs since the 1940s. However, currently a rapidly growing number of women and men are reaching for their fabric and silicone tails. In fact the U.S. Bureau of Labour statistics states that there are one-thousand professional mermaids working on a full time basis in America and whilst the UK mer-community is smaller, it is on the increase, and is supported by a developing British mer-industry. A growing number of mermaid swim schools have emerged, such as Mermaids UK in North Devon, and Mono-Fin Mermaids in Hastings, as well as tail makers and party planners. There are also lots of opportunities to get together and swim with other mermaids, take part in splash mobs, as well as attend larger community events like Brighton's annual festival, March of the Mermaids, and London based convention, Merfolk UK.

Through a combination of methods including questionnaires, interviews and online observations of primarily UK and North American mermaids on sites such as the UKMerpod, Mermaid Squad, MerNetwork and individuals' social media pages, this chapter will set sail on a 'mermaid spotting' boat tour, and will examine mermaid lifestyle and the motivations behind involvement in Mer. Shared values within the 'pod' community will be considered including those associated with beauty aesthetics, positive body image and common attitudes and ideals such as the role of the merman and issues of ocean environmentalism.

Finally, the increasingly professional nature of mermaiding provides a useful springboard for investigating the rising nature of 'professional' community members and their use of micro-economies. Drawing on previous studies by Sarah Thornton, Matt Hills and Brigid Cherry, this chapter will consider how the mer-community can be used as a case study to contribute to wider debates on the transforming nature of producers and consumers.

Mermaid Capital

Sarah Thornton's work on subcultural capital can be very useful to draw upon when considering shared aspects of the mer-community. Like Thornton's club cultures, the mermaid community includes people who experience the mermaid world in very different ways; for instance, the community contains both casual hobbyists who occasionally partake in mermaid swimming, as well as those who are professional mermaids that have created their own 'mersona', sit in grottos at charity events such as Whale Fest, model for underwater photoshoots, and take out large business grants to launch swim schools. Whilst the community is diverse, it is possible to identify shared qualities and behaviours that are valued within the community. A mermaid that possesses these qualities may be considered rich in subcultural capital, or as Matt Hills puts it, they may experience social status in the eyes of the fans (2010: 89).

In 'The Social Logic of Subcultural Capital' (1997), Thornton draws on the work of Bourdieu and his ideas of cultural capital set out in *Distinction: A*

Social Critique of the Judgement of Taste (1984). It is here that Thornton coins the phrase 'subcultural capital':

> Subcultural capital confers status on its owner in the eyes of the relevant beholder [...]. Subcultural capital can be objectified and embodied. Just as books and paintings display cultural capital in the family home, so subcultural capital is objectified in the form of fashionable haircuts and carefully assembled record collections [...]. Just as cultural capital is personified in 'good' manners and urbane conversation, so subcultural capital is embodied in the form of being 'in the know' (1997: 186).

During the course of this research, conversations with mermaids revealed common aspects of the community that many members held dear. Discourses about aesthetics, promoting empowerment, and environmentalism were particularly privileged by members of the community. Whilst simply having 'the right type of tail' or engaging with discourses around ocean activism does not necessarily translate to raising a mermaid's subcultural capital, when put together with a mermaid's increased visibility online, and a professional approach (such as owning your own swim school, or appearing in fashion videos and photography) celebrity mermaids are made. Before exploring this celebrification in more detail, it is firstly important to consider just what the community holds dear, and what works as subcultural capital.

Mermaid Style

The overall look of the mermaid, unsurprising, favours an excessive femininity, which includes long flowing hair, either natural or aided by wigs and hair extensions. Although there are short haired mermaids, many opt for long locks when mermaiding, and have commented that at children's events long hair covers cleavage and gives them something to play with whilst lounging in the sun in character. The sea shell bra top is a staple, and mermaids wear a selection of underwater iridescent make-up, crowns, hand fins, and hair jewellery.

Of supreme importance, is of course the mermaid tail. Many tails are inspired by Robert Short's fully functioning burnt orange tail design in *Splash* and (to a lesser extent) Disney's Ariel. Unlike cosplay mermaids who often perform in outfits inspired by existing media characters, most mermaids pride themselves on their individual stamp or 'brand' of mermaiding. This is not unlike other style communities like goths or steampunks, who privilege individual flair and DIY ethos.* Tails are created from a variety of resources, but two of the most common are fabric and silicone. Silicone tails are expensive, and cost between £2,500 and £6,000. Silicone is also difficult to work with, given that the tails are cumbersome (they can weigh over 15

---

* The cosplay community value these aspects too, but tends to be more focused on existing characters/media examples.

kilos) and fit snugly to the body; they can take a great deal of time and effort to put on. Due to the complexities of working with silicone, many mermaids outsource their tail to specific tailors like Mertailor, Finfolk Productions and Mermaid Creations. However, they maintain creative control to a point, as their bikini tops and in many cases their tails are designed by themselves. For instance, Hannah Fraser, a professional mermaid who has celebrity status amongst the community, has recently created her own tail, but collaborated with Abby and Bryn Roberts at Finfolk Productions for the 'pink lionfish' fins. Even for mermaids with less money and resources than Hannah Fraser, there are ways of customising the design. As Mermaid Lily-Rose asserts, one of the trends in mer-designs is elaborating on the fluke. The fluke is found at the end of the tail, where the monofin is located, and is used for diving or 'fluking'.

> There are different types of fluke design, a friend of mine has a new tail made by Finfolk production, his fluke is styled like the *Thirteenth Year*, which is a merman movie. It has been extended to match the movie.' (Mermaid Lily-Rose, Interview, 2016)

Therefore from looking at the aesthetics, certain shared ideals become clear. As these impressive and expensive tails reveal, the community do want to show their individual artistry, but they also enjoy partaking in a group 'spectacle' to be watched and looked at. In addition to this, whilst mermaids want to show off their performative bodies in this way, the intense work that goes into creating such looks (wriggling into a mermaid tail is a lengthy process) must remain hidden at all times as the community have a shared interest in maintaining a sense of verisimilitude. For instance, some mermaids will only swim in silicone tails as it makes them look more real, and others have adopted a mermaid name and have developed fully fledged 'mersonas' that have back stories as to how they became mermaids. So whilst mermaids don't really believe they are mythical creatures who have been swimming in oceans for thousands of years, they reimagine scenarios that allow them to dwell in the sea and look like 'real' merfolk.

> 'There is debate amongst the community between silicone and fabric tails. We've had events where children think that I am real, as opposed to the other mermaids, because I am wearing a silicone tail rather than the fabric tail. I feel much happier in a silicone tail as that to me looks the most real.' (Mermaid Lily-Rose, Interview, 2016)

The emphasis placed on 'realism' arises in another, even more interesting way within the community. The mermaid tail is a spectacle, an illusion to be upheld; however, in terms of a mermaid's upper body, there has been a great deal of discussion around being true to one's form and presenting 'real' women, especially in terms of weight and body shape. Feeling beautiful in a mermaid tail is something that is quite central to the community, and there are many instances where mermaiding is used to discuss body image. There has been a great deal of discussion in relation to the social media tag #bodypositivemermaid with responses ranging from comments that the mermaid tail makes women feel more confident, to entire photoshoots that have been commissioned to raise self-esteem and present a positive body image as demonstrated by Run Away Days, in collaboration with Bodyposipanda.

Threads that invite other merfolk to post images of themselves celebrating their bodies, regardless of shape and size, are common within the community. Reponses to such posts include people pinning photographs of themselves in imperfect poses to show what 'real' bodies look like. Photographs are posted with titles 'because mermaids have belly rolls too' and 'my tiny rolls' which provide a welcome contrast to women's bodies that are usually portrayed in fashion and advertising, which have been airbrushed and carefully posed.

> At mermaid children's parties, when the children have a photo shoot in a tail their parents will tell them to 'suck their bellies in' or to pull the tail up over their stomach. As someone who has struggled with body image issues it really hurts me to see little girls sucking their tummies in or covering their arms. I desperately want to show them that all mermaids/mermen are beautiful and that there is no one look/body type you have to have to be a mermaid! So I wondered if people could send me pictures of merpeople of all ages and shapes for me to create a picture wall showing that anyone can be a mermaid no matter what your age/gender/size. (Sophie, UK Merpod Group, 2017)

The mermaid's attachment to promoting a positive body image can also be noted on a wider scale as the 'Keep your thigh gap – I've got mermaid thighs' meme reveals. The meme that began as an Instagram post, 'If your thighs touch you're one step closer to be being a mermaid, so who's the real winner here?' was written in response to the 'thigh gap', a beauty ideal that deems a woman is attractive if she is thin enough to have a space between her inner thighs when her legs are pressed together. The mermaid thighs meme sparked a trend of curvaceous women uploading images of themselves with touching thighs, reminiscent of a mermaid's tail.

Therefore, whilst the community cannot always be harmonious, and like all communities has its antagonisms and disagreements, its members do present an overwhelmingly positive ethos when it comes to issues of body image (and this also extends to issues concerning ocean environmentalism). Discussion with mermaids revealed that women were often engaging with discourses of empowerment around the legend of the mermaid that are not only confined to positive body image, but relate to wider issues concerning femininity.

Gender and Empowerment

Femininity is an important area to consider within the mer-community. On the whole mermaids adopt an ultra-feminine identity or they invest in what Dunja Brill would term the 'cult of femininity' (2008: 41). In general, mermaids present themselves as safe and wholesome, much like the princesses imagined by Walt Disney. This is largely due to the fact that children are the principle market for professional mermaids; whether in the capacity of running a swim school, or (more commonly) performing at birthday parties as the special guest mermaid, interaction with children is key to the profession.

Despite this tendency for non-threatening feminine mersonas, performances of gothic, dark sirens do exist and there are several mermaids who adorn black/dark blue tails, body art and a more general 'goth' style. This is hardly surprising as siren mythology lends itself to the gothic. The siren, is imagined by the mer-community as simultaneously beautiful and dangerous, with her exquisite singing voice that lures sailors to their watery deaths. Steeped in folklore and a return to the past, sirens are truly gothic as they have 'a commitment to exploring aesthetics of fear', and their hybridity results in a 'cross contamination of reality and fantasy' (Spooner & McEvoy, 2007: 1; the authors are discussing the ideas of David Punter and Rosemary Jackson, respectively, in these two quotations). Brenda Stumpf's underwater photography is popular amongst community members and exemplifies the darker side to mermaids. Photographs include various watery nightmare scenarios of sirens with vampire teeth, stretching out skeletal, pale white hands, whilst black eyes stare down the camera lens. Other images contain beautiful, strong sirens wearing golden bikini tops, effortlessly pinning sailors, clad in historical dress, to rocks amidst a raging ocean; and warrior sirens, wearing suits of armour and wielding swords, enveloped by their dancing, fiery red hair.

As these images by Brenda Stumpf demonstrate, the community's representation of sirens maintains a sense of femininity, but also presents strength and power. Similar discourses of combining excessive feminine performances with a woman's strength and power were frequently noted amongst wider mermaids. One such example is from Mermaid Nessie, of the Halifax Mermaids. The Halifax Mermaids, owned by Raina the Halifax Mermaid, is a swim school with the remit to 'edutain' young girls. Their ethos is to teach girls to be strong, to help their self esteem and empower them.

> Raina did an empowerment workshop. It's wonderful seeing the smile on girls' faces when they first put on their mermaid tail. I still remember how happy I felt when I first put on the tail. We try to encourage girls to engage in physical activity. We know that girls aren't pushed in the same way as boys to engage in physical sports, so the mermaid tails are a way of doing this. (Mermaid Nessie, Interview, 2016)

This ideal of teaching girls positive messages of self-worth was echoed in interviews and questionnaire responses with language such as 'strong' and 'ridiculously powerful' being a common descriptions of the mermaid, but these terms are often used in conjunction with 'feminine.' Femininity, combined with strength, is therefore key to the mermaid identity.

Returning to Dunja Brill's (2008) work on the 'cult of femininity' and her study of the goth community, this term can be useful to draw upon in order to understand the complex gender relations that occur amongst merfolk. Brill's work demonstrates a preference in the goth community for feminine trappings such as long hair, skirts and make-up. Brill asserts that the goth community found these attributes 'sexy' and 'beautiful' but they were not only privileged amongst women. She notes that whilst the goths she interviewed also referred to men who adopted hyper-feminine looks (by growing their hair long and wearing make-up and skirts) Brill notes that the community may call these men 'androgynous' but they are more precisely described as adopting the 'cult of femininity' for both sexes (2008, 41).

> Goths of both genders tend to stress over and over again how 'sexy' and 'beautiful' they think long hair, skirts and make-up are. If sported by a male, such an effeminate look stands in stark opposition to traditional gender stereotypes of style and appearance. This opposition is further highlighted by Goth women often stating that they find traditional markers of male strength and attraction (e.g. bulging muscles) repulsive, and instead prefer ultra-skinny, frail guys – qualities normally deemed improper for a man in our culture' (Brill, 2008: 41–2)

The cult of femininity for both sexes within the mermaiding community does follow suit. The idealised image of a mermaid or merman often has long hair, make-up and a genderless tail. However, unlike the male goths of Brill's study who go in for more 'effeminate', 'ultra skinny' looks, some mermen also privilege a muscular torso and the 'markers of male strength'. Therefore, mermen's experience of gender is complex within the community. Whilst they do opt for styles associated with femininity, there is also an enforcement of masculinity, and the strength involved in performances is often underlined, with some men discussing the desire to 'compete' in mermaiding and call for it to be recognised as a sport. Merman Christian has recently worked as a model for the professional swim brand Finis, to promote their competitor monofin. The promotional material contains an image of him swimming bare chested and the slogan 'dare to take a dive'.

The role of the merman in the mer-community is a difficult one. On the one hand, mermen are an important part of the mer-community, and actually often experience more positive attention because of their rarity. For example, when talking about Merman Christian's performance at the Aquatron in Nova Scotia, responses have included praise for 'phenomenal' and 'amazing' merman performances who 'blew the audience away'.

We hosted a merman this summer. He worked a booking this year. Everybody loved him, he was amazing. A phenomenal performer who really blew me away. We don't have male mermaids here. (Mermaid Nessie, Interview, 2016)

However, there is also a perceived antagonistic response towards mermen from the wider public, which can make it difficult for professional mermen to experience the full range of opportunities on offer. For example, an article in Vice Media's *Broadly* entitled 'Anyone can be a Mermaid. The World of Professional Mermen' (Kale, 2016) was shared by the community. It presents accounts of Chris O'Brocki; Merman Christian; and the well-known merman behind the company Mertailor,* Eric Ducharme. During the interview, numerous mermen express the difficulties they experience at being men in a predominantly female industry. They ascribe the gender gap in the mer-industry to numerous reasons. Firstly, whilst there are merman movies like *The Thirteenth Year*, and popular merman characters such as Zac in shows like *Mako Mermaids*, there is an overwhelming lack of male mermaids or 'visible role models' in popular culture (Kale, 2016). By comparison, famous mermaid characters such as Madison and Ariel prevail. However, even more contentiously, the article suggests there is a perceived discomfort at seeing a male mermaid, and further, booking them for a children's party. Eric Ducharme comments that 'Without a doubt. A man in a tail is a scary thing for some people.' (cited in Kale, 2016)

> Although I've never experienced sexism in the mercommunity because we do not judge – we are more like family – there are some unhappy people out there who look at us mermen and say, 'That's not a merman. Merfolk are supposed to be women. (Maksim Merman the yellowtailed Seawitch, cited in Kale, 2016)

Whilst the experience of mermen is currently problematic, the mer-community is still relatively new and only time will tell how such complexities will play out. Although it is difficult to predict the future for these mermen, the announcement of a remake of Disney's 1984 film *Splash* may alter the dynamic once again, as the new version reimagines the story with a merman, played by Channing Tatum, at the centre of the narrative.

Hannah the Mermaid Activist

Having identified some key, shared interests in the mer-community including a striving for individualism but also verisimilitude in mermaid style; the use of the mermaid to discuss ideas of empowerment for women and young girls; and the presence of the cult of femininity for both sexes – but the complexities and paradoxical relationship this has for some mermen who also accentuate physical strength and power; this discussion will now move on to look at two high profile mermaids in more detail. Such case studies can contribute to wider discussions on the formation of subcultural celeb-

---

* Mertailor makes tails for a number of high profile performers including Lady Gaga.

rities, in the case of Hannah Fraser; and the establishment of micro-economies, in the case of Raina the Halifax Mermaid.

Australian born Hannah Fraser, or Hannah Mermaid as she is more widely known, is an underwater model and mermaid performance artist. Although WeekiWachee shows existed previously, Fraser is largely credited to be amongst the first of the modern, lifestyle mermaids and is certainly one of the earliest to utilise social media to connect with an audience. Fraser presents an elaborate display of mermaid style, which 'embodies' the valued look of the group (Thornton,1997: 186). With her long blonde hair and glittering collection of delicate bikini tops, Fraser fashions both femininity and realism. Her tail designs and body make-up are often intended to replicate the visual properties of marine creatures such as the tiger shark (in Tigress Shark) and Manta Rays (in Mantas [sic] Last Dance), demonstrating her knowledge and commitment to the ocean. Alongside her spectacular style, Fraser's richness in subcultural capital can also be attributed to her exposure online and at flesh and blood events, where she showcases her work as an underwater model and ocean activist. Looking at her social media, Fraser uses her Facebook, Instagram and Youtube accounts to display her showreel, and numerous videos and photoshoots of herself being interviewed by television networks, appearing in films such as *Twig the Fairy* and *The Mermaid Mystery*, or behind-the-scenes diving videos. Together with these promotional aspects that are intended to cultivate an audience for the Hannah Mermaid brand, the majority of Fraser's online content is also designed to draw attention to issues arising in ocean conservation. For instance, Fraser posts frequently about topical environmental issues, from sharing videos about edible six-pack rings that could save the lives of sea creatures and reduce plastic levels in the ocean, to campaigns to remove fluoride in water. More significantly, Fraser is also actively involved in staging underwater performance protests to raise awareness for environmental causes. For instance, in 2013 Fraser swam with manta rays to rally support against manta ray gill hunting. Similarly, Fraser's tigress shark dive in the Bahamas is amongst her most famous videos, which was created to oppose the global slaughter of sharks. The video presents Fraser complete with 'sea tiger' inspired body paint, wearing lead boots, which anchor her to the seabed as she is encircled by tiger sharks. Fraser does not wear any diving or protective equipment during her three-minute underwater dance in an attempt to change people's attitudes towards these marine creatures.

This sense of eco-activism is an issue that is also important to the wider community and is a movement that Hannah Fraser seems to be at the helm of, earning her the nickname 'activist mermaid'. For instance, such environmentalism is often at the forefront of mermaid activities. Examples of ocean activism within the wider community include: the emergence of mermaid grottos at events such as World Oceans Day; one-off photoshoots by members of the community aimed at fighting pollution and increased plastic levels in the ocean; to more wide-scale ventures such as Project Mermaid, a photographic project that aims to 'capture celebrities in mermaid form', which was set up in 2012 to raise awareness about ocean and beach conservation, with 50 percent of proceeds going to the Save Our Beach foundation.

> The connection to clean water and marine preservation is important to us. From an ocean that gives us so much, we must give something back.(Mermaid Anonymous , Questionnaire, 2016)

Alongside Hannah's ocean activism and publicity online, Hannah Mermaid's activities at flesh-and-blood events have cemented her position of celebrity mermaid. Matt Hills (2010) in his research of horror film communities suggests that flesh-and-blood contexts such as festivals and conventions are increasingly overlooked in studies which consider community members' subcultural capital. He underlines how attending socially organised events works to create and sustain subcultural capital as this allows attendees to be 'in the know' and relay their often 'privileged access' and experiences to other members of the community (2010: 89). Flesh-and-blood events are incredibly important for the mermaid community. The nature of mermaiding requires a physical and social response; therefore swimming at flesh-and-blood events is vital (unlike other communities that may be more concerned with intellectual pursuits and talking). Hannah Fraser's celebrification has meant that she has been invited to perform, and give speeches at high profile events within the community. For example, Fraser was a guest at the World Mermaid Awards in Las Vegas, and NC Mermania (an event hosted in North Carolina). So whilst her celebrity schedule does actually limit her time and involvement in the more low-key community activities such as organised swims, her privileged position at large-scale events is crucial to maintaining her high-profile status.

Raina the Halifax Mermaid and Micro-Economies

Another example of an individual who has become well known amongst community members is Raina the Halifax Mermaid. Whilst environmental issues are also at the centre of Raina's Canadian organisation, it is her business acumen that has elevated her to a celebrity-like status within the community. Raina has developed one of the most prestigious mermaid swim schools, in the Halifax Mermaids. Additionally Raina has also published three books including the aptly named, *Fishy Business: My Life as a Mermaid* (2014), which functions as a resource for anyone who wants to become a mermaid. With her Bachelor's in Education, Raina draws on her background in youth development to market her business to children and young adults who want to learn to swim like mermaids. Her business is continuing to flourish as the Halifax Mermaids won a $10,000 dollar business grant in 2016, which enabled them to purchase further equipment, and crucially some silicone tails. As well as achieving grants, the Halifax Mermaids have also attracted attention from researchers and Raina is now working with Dalhousie University's Capstone Project for what is being termed 'the first study on the functionality and engineering dynamics of mermaid tails' (Halifax Mermaids, 2017). Raina describes her business as 'a chance to use my education, flare for performance, love of the ocean, and the empowerment that comes from swimming in a tail' (Raina, Questionnaire, 2016). The school teaches technical swimming skills, but is also focused on empowering students and raising self-esteem. Drawing on the concept of edutainment, Raina takes a play-based approach to learning, and implements what she terms as the three I's framework, information, imagination and inspiration, to simultaneously educate and entertain children.

Raina has risen to such a prominent position within the mer-community largely due to the success of her business. Other factors, such as her company's commitment to ocean environmental issues, and having a positive ethos of empowerment and education for young people (Raina has been invited to host empowerment talks at various events) are also in keeping with ideals that the community hold dear. However, it is specifically Raina's business acumen that has made her so well known. Raina, like a growing number of mermaids across the globe, demonstrates the increasing ways in which community members can now use their interests and attachment to a community, not only to enrich their everyday lives but to develop their own, often highly profitable, micro-economies.

For instance, during her discussion of the micro-economy of fan knitting, Brigid Cherry researched the fibre arts. Her research of Ravelry online community for knitters, crocheters, spinners, weavers and designers reveals how such sites enable 'members to sell their own patterns via the site marketplace and offering opportunities for micro-businesses to advertise to niche markets' (2011: 149). As Cherry documents, this has led to a collapse of the division between social and commercial spheres. 'Such shared love of the text between the dyer and her customers is indicative of Humphreys's (2008) hybrid market environment in which there is no clear distinction between social and commercial economies, they co-exist in the same space' (2016: 171). In this way, the social community influences demand for what is being produced.

This is a trend that has also been noticed by Matt Hills (2002) in *Fan Cultures*, and more recently during his discussion of Dr Who fans (2010). Hills suggests that there has been an erosion of traditional consumer and producer roles.

> Fandom was thought of as essentially different from – and frequently opposed to – 'official' media production. And it was resistant 'poaching' that provided the key metaphor for this fan/producer difference. Fans were creative but relatively powerless; producers had power over 'official' media texts. Such a view was also carried through into John Tulloch and Henry Jenkins' study of *Star Trek* and *Dr Who* fans, *Science Fiction Audiences*. However, as Alan McKee

has argued, by the time of this book's publication, binaries between *Doctor Who* fandom and professional media production were already eroding [...]. In *Fan Cultures*, I explored similar issues (2010: 57).

Going back to the mer-community, wider examples of mermaid prosumers are plentiful. For example, one of the fastest growing companies within the British mer-industry is Mermaids UK. Lisa and Charlotte Bousted established this family-run business in response to the global rise of mermaiding. Mermaids UK are a one-stop shop for mermaiding. As well as running their own mermaid swim school, 'mer-cise' fitness classes and short course experiences, Mermaids UK can provide mermaid training for swimming instructors, swim school insurance, equipment and tail making services. Similarly, the community also includes tail makers, jewellery and accessory crafters, swim trainers, party planners and performers, who all frequently contribute to group conversation on UK Merpod and Mermaid Squad, both to advertise their businesses but also, crucially, to be part of the community. For many, these mermaid businesses are not simply a commercial enterprise, but a way of positioning the mermaid at the centre of people's professions as well as their lifestyle activities.

This sense of prosumption is clearly not limited to members of the mer-community, but is something that is part of modern life in the digital age. Since the advent of social media, a multitude of opportunities has arisen that allow people to connect, consume and produce. Research into the mermaid community, and case studies such as Raina the Halifax Mermaid and Hannah Fraser, are important as they can function as a microcosm to explore the changing nature of producers and consumers in the world around us. Another key reason that the mermaid community is such a rich, exciting area to research, is its relative newness – but fast-growing popularity. Mermaiding is happening right now. The community is growing and becoming increasingly sustainable. In his article 'Youth subcultures: what are they now?', Alexis Petridis argues that traditional subcultures may currently be faced with difficulty and may even be dwindling, as the internet 'doesn't spawn mass movements, bonded together by a shared taste in music, fashion and ownership of subcultural capital' but rather cultivates sporadic, fleeting cultures (Petridis, 2014). Mermaiding provides a contrast, as it may indeed have 'legs' for quite some time.

When introduced to the phenomenon of mermaiding, it might be dismissed by some as a short-lived fad; however, the draw of the mermaid for children and adults is undeniable. For children, especially young girls, mermaiding provides the opportunity for them to live out their fantasy in a real-life context, amongst their friends and wider community. And its ethos of empowering and educating young minds and teaching resilience, self-esteem and confidence is one that will undoubtedly attract their parents' investment. For adults, mermaiding invites people to bond both digitally and physically. It attracts people who have a close attachment to the mermaid legend, and others who simply love to engage in cosplay and alternative modelling. It also appeals to those who don't necessarily want to engage in mermaid style but want to train their inner core strength or practise free diving techniques, dolphin kick and butterfly strokes.

Conclusion

So where has this mermaid spotting boat tour taken us? We have encountered a number of sightings of the mermaid along the way. There have been the dark sirens of Brenda Stumpf's photographic reimaginings, who emit a strong and powerful femininity. There have been the eco-mermaids who dive underwater and swim with marine life to safeguard their futures and protest against ocean pollution. Body positive mermaids have emerged from the depths, as they celebrate women's curves and use the mermaid to discuss issues of strength and power and the importance of presenting images of 'real' bodies. We have also caught a glimpse of a merman or two, who experience mermaiding slightly differently to their sisters. Given the remarkable pace in which the community seems to be evolving, it will be intriguing to see where future voyages take us.

References

Bourdieu, P. (1984); *Distinction: A Social Critique of the Judgement of Taste*, London: Routledge.

Brill, D. (2008), *Goth Culture: Gender, Sexuality and Style*, Oxford: Berg.

Cherry, B. (2011), 'Knit One, Bite One: Vampire Fandom, Fan Production and Feminine Handicrafts'. In G. Schott & K. Moffat (eds), *Fanpires: Audience Consumption of the Modern Vampire*, Washington: New Academia Publishing.

Cherry, B. (2016), *Cult Media, Fandom, and Textiles: Handicrafting as Fan Art*, London: Bloomsbury.

Fiske, J. (2008), 'The Cultural Economy of Fandom [1992]'. In E. Mathijs & X. Mendik (eds), *The Cult Film Reader*, Berkshire: Open University Press.

Halifax Mermaids (2017), 'Mermaids for Science', Halifax Mermaids [online]; ttp://halifaxmermaids.weebly.com/mermaids-for-science.html (accessed 18 July 2017).

Hills, M. (2002), *Fan Cultures*, Oxon: Routledge.

Hine, C. (2000), *Virtual Ethnography*, London: Sage.

Hodkinson, P. (2002), *Goth: Identity, Style and Subculture*, Oxford: Berg.

Kale, S. (2016), 'Anyone can be a Mermaid. The World of Professional Mermen', *Broadly* [online], ttps://broadly.vice.com/en_us/article/ezjyxe/anyone-can-be-a-mermaid-the-world-of-professional-mermen (accessed 18 July 2017).

Mermaid, R. (2014), *Fishy Business: My Life as a Mermaid*, Raleigh: Lulu.

Petridis, A. (2014), 'Youth Subcultures. Where are they Now?', *The Guardian*, 20 March [online], https://www.theguardian.com/culture/2014/mar/20/youth-subcultures-where-have-they-gone (accessed 27 July 2017).

Spooner, C. & McEvoy, E. (eds) (2007), 'Introduction'. In *The Routledge Companion to Gothic*, London & New York: Routledge.

Thornton, S. (1995), *Club Cultures*, Cambridge: Polity.

Thornton, S. (1997), 'The Social Logic of Subcultural Capital'. In K. Gelder, & S. Thornton (eds), *The Subcultures Reader*, London & New York: Routledge, pp.200–209.

Chapter 9

Adventures in Liquid Space: Representations of the Sea in Disney Theme Parks

Lee Brooks

The Walt Disney Company has long been an almost inexhaustible source of tales and trivia. These have inspired fans, critics and no shortage of academics to study every aspect of its operation and output with a level of detail that is often reserved for global, historical figures or affairs of state. This is hardly surprising when we consider the company's remarkable trajectory from humble beginnings as the Disney Brothers Cartoon Studio in 1923 to its current position as one of the world's largest media companies. *Business Insider* lists Disney second behind Google's parent company, Alphabet, but only consider their media networks and interactive divisions in coming to this judgement (*Business Insider*, 2017). They employ somewhere in the region of 185,000 people worldwide and have a market capitalisation of $169.3 billion (*Forbes*, 2017).

Of all the remarkable facts and statistics about Disney, however, one of the more intriguing and most commonly quoted is that, with 750 floating vessels, the Walt Disney World theme park resort in Orlando, Florida, commands the world's fifth largest navy. While this definition of a navy may be accurate when judged purely in a quantitative sense, the fact that it gives parity between flat bottomed attraction boats, with guide wheels; aircraft carriers; and nuclear submarines; somewhat undermines the veracity of such claims. It does, however, offer a sense of how significant watercraft and waterways are, and have been, in the process of making Disney fantasy a reality in the company's iconic theme parks. Indeed, from the inception of Disneyland, in Anaheim, California, in 1955, representations and the re-imagining of the sea have played a significant role in both the creation and mythology of Disney parks.

This chapter will investigate the evolution of such hydrographic themes within the history of the company's global theme park empire, beginning with the earliest planned ideas for Disneyland in advance of its opening in 1955, and moving through the creation of the second and far more geo-graphically extensive resort, Walt Disney World, in Orlando, Florida, in

1971. It also considers expansion outside the United States with Tokyo Disneyland in 1983; the Euro Disney Resort in Paris (now Disneyland Paris Resort) in 1992; Hong Kong Disneyland in 2005; and the company's latest foreign outpost, Shanghai Disney Resort, which opened in June 2016.

While it is true that the focus of this chapter is primarily concerned with such themes in Disney's parks rather than in its animated and live action cinema releases, it is important to understand that there is little value in isolating a single area of operation of an organisation that, to extend the oceanographic metaphor, is a mass of interconnected tentacles that tie every one of its multiple disciplines together. Indeed, Janet Wasko in her general text on the study of the company's multifaceted operation, *Understanding Disney*, has suggested that 'The Disney company has developed the strategy so well that it represents the quintessential example of synergy in the media/entertainment industry' (Wasko, 2001, 71). It would therefore be impossible and hopelessly unproductive to refrain from reference to Walt Disney's film and television output, but I will do so only where it is repurposed and represented within the parks.

It is also significant to note that, contrary to the way in which they are perceived in the popular imagination, the use of the word resort in many of their titles denotes the fact that an entire ecosystem exists outside the parks themselves. In this context I shall extend the study of these representations beyond the berm of Disneyland, and the areas that are usually understood formally as parks, and into the entire operation of the division of the company designated as Walt Disney Parks and Resorts. This expanded definition will therefore take in not just attractions and shows, but water parks, dining locations, hotels, cruise ships and even the company's private island in the Bahamas.

Perhaps the most famous academic discussion of the nature and significance of Disney theme parks is the contention by Jean Baudrillard in *Simulacra and Simulation* that Disneyland is a 'deterrence machine set up in order to rejuvenate in reverse the fiction of the real' (Baudrillard, 1988: 172). This does not, as some have supposed, suggest a blurring of the lines between the fantastical representations within Disney parks and the reality of that which is being represented. Rather, it indicates a masking of the fact that there is no longer a reality to represent. It is interesting, when considering Baudrillard's celebrated account, that since he expounded this theory in 1981, at a time when only Disneyland and its Florida counterpart the Magic Kingdom existed, there has been exponential growth in Disney theme parks. There are now twelve separate parks that span three continents, two dedicated water parks, more than forty resort hotels, four cruise liners and Castaway Cay, a 1,000 acre private island, some 268 miles from the coast of Florida.

In the context of this discussion, however, the quantitive expansion of Disney themed entertainment experiences is of less concern than the preponderance of oceanographic and nautical themes within them. Throughout the course of this chapter it is my intention to highlight the central role that representations of the sea and marine life, both real and legendary, have played in the creation of Disney's global theme park empire. In addition, I will further investigate Baudrillard's ideas of simulation and hyperreality in the context of these aquatic and maritime representations, and discuss some of the implications that this may have for a populace that have, for the past sixty years, grown up with such images in Disney parks and become increasingly used to the associated narrativisation of public space.

Disneyland Sets Sail

On 31 August 1948 the first recorded internal company memo outlined, to studio artist Dick Kelsey, Walt Disney's thoughts for a new kind of amusement park. Even at this early stage, much of what eventually became the template for Disneyland is clearly laid out in this document. In the context of this chapter, the most interesting observation is that from the very outset, alongside the pen portraits of the encircling railroad and the iconic Main Street, was an insistence upon 'a whole new category of attractions, geared to fantasy and futurism: a canal boat moving past scenes from Disney fairy-tale films…a submarine ride, and a nature preserve on an island circumnavigated by a paddle-wheeler' (Marling, 1997, 54).

The fact that this memo so clearly identifies bodies of water and maritime travel as themes to be developed within the new park is underlined by the existence of boat-based attractions in all of the four lands beyond Main Street USA on opening day in July 1955. The futuristic-looking Phantom Boats in Tomorrowland (actually the shortest lived of any Disneyland attraction in history, due to their chronic mechanical instability); the Canal Boats of the World in Fantasyland; the Jungle Cruise in Adventureland; and the Mark Twain Steamboat in Frontierland, on the expansive 'rivers of America'; all used floating vessels to contribute to the kinetic energy of the park's fantastical narrative architecture. However, as American cultural historian Jackson Lears observed, 'The quintessential product of the [Disney] empire would not be fantasy, but simulated reality; not the cartoon character, but the audio animatronic robot' (Gabler, 2008, 482). Here too, the denizens of the deep would play a crucial, formative role.

Submarines and Cephalopods

Discussing the genesis of their work with three-dimensional animatronic characters on the 17 May 1964 episode of *Walt Disney's Wonderful World of Color*, subtitled: *Disneyland Goes to the World's Fair*, Walt Disney himself identified the need for 'a lifelike monster big enough to destroy a submarine' (Walt Disney's Wonderful World of Color, 1964) in the making of the company's 1954 live action version of Jules Verne's *20,000 Leagues Under the Sea*. The giant animatronic squid that attacked Harper Goff's baroque, steampunk Nautilus submarine in perhaps the movie's most frequently remembered scene, can legitimately lay claim to being the ancestor of those 'quintessential' Disney animatronic robots, and thus an early inspiration for the whole nature of the theme park brand. However, the story of the squid in Disneyland does not end there.

By the time of its opening on 17 July 1955, Tomorrowland was by some margin the least developed area of the park. This was due to a raft of time and budgetary constraints, largely caused by Walt Disney's ever increasing ambition – and thus a spiralling balance sheet for Disneyland. This was underlined by the precarious nature of the company's finances and Walt Disney's signifiant personal financial commitment to the project. One of the first actions that was taken at least partially to rectify this situation was to open an attraction that showcased many of the sets and props from *20,000 Leagues Under the Sea*. This temporary exhibit opened 5 August 1955, less than a month after the park itself, though it ended up running for eleven years. Guests were given the opportunity to see the exterior of the Nautilus and to walk through a series of interior sets of the different sections of the submarine, culminating in a view of the giant squid attacking, out of the salon window.

The continued popularity of this exhibit and the success of another similarly nautical Tomorrowland attraction, the Submarine Voyage, which opened in June 1959, ensured that once planning for Disney's second park, the Magic Kingdom at Florida's Walt Disney World Resort began, the two would be combined into the *20,000 Leagues Under the Sea* Submarine Voyage. This attraction differed little in terms of show scenes from its Disneyland counterpart but used ride vehicles based on Goff's sea monster-inspired Nautilus design, rather than that of contemporary nuclear submarines.

While the Florida version of this attraction eventually closed in 1994, reputedly as a result of the difficulty of maintaining an attraction in which the majority of its moving parts were permanently underwater, the perennial fascination of the subject matter was underlined when in the same year Les Mystères du Nautilus opened at the then Euro Disneyland park in Paris. The European attraction, while appearing from the outside to take place onboard another of Goff's Nautilus submarines (this time partially surfaced in a lagoon surrounding Space Mountain), is actually a walk-through exhibit. It is housed in a completely dry show building, similar in many details to the one originally placed in Disneyland. This time a larger and more technologically advanced audio-animatronic squid attacks the helpless submarine on cue.

An identical tableau of the surfaced submarine is present in the Mysterious Island area of Tokyo DisneySea, looming from the water like a cast-iron Loch Ness monster, though in this instance without the interior walk-through section. The same area of the Japanese park also includes its own *20,000 Leagues Under the Sea* attraction, which uses an equally steampunk inspired Neptune Submarine ride vehicle. It avoids the maintenance issues of its Floridian counterpart by simulating its liquid exterior using lighting and captive bubble effects. Since a brief hiatus between July and August 1955 during the opening of Disneyland, there has been an attraction based on Disney's version of the 1870 Jules Verne tale in continuous operation at a Disney theme park somewhere in the world.

Into the Living Seas

Disney's continuing fascination with Captain Nemo and his cephalopod nemesis were not the company's only seafaring inspiration in the development of its global leisure empire. After the success of Disneyland in 1955 and its east coast counterpart, the Magic Kingdom at Walt Disney World in 1971, the company turned its attention to Epcot. Walt Disney himself described the new park as 'by far the most important part of our Florida project – in fact, the heart of everything we'll be doing in Disney World' (theorigihalepcot.com, 2017). Walt Disney's original vision of Epcot as a prototype city of the future was quickly abandoned by the company after his sudden death from lung cancer in December 1966. By the time of its opening date on 1 October 1982, it had been transformed into a 'world's fair' style theme park, comprising World Showcase and the edutainment based Future World.

Aside from its central lagoon, a handful of boat based attractions and the Fountain of Nations, into which offerings from 25 international waterways were poured, the park, on opening day was largely free from the kind of representations of the sea with which this chapter is primary concerned. In common with a number of the major pavilions in Future World, the Living Seas, while originally slated as an opening day attraction, was slow to progress but did eventually debut on 15 January 1986. With a backstory of aquatic exploration and a journey via 'hydrolators' (simulated undersea elevators) to the mythical Sea Base Alpha, the attraction included a salt water aquarium that was, at 5.7 million gallons, the largest in the world.

While the focus of the Living Seas was very much on educational observation of real marine life exhibits, the plans originally outlined by Disney, and ultimately rejected on cost grounds by the pavilion's sponsor, United Technologies, had a considerably more mythical emphasis. Independent Disney historian Jim Hill points to initial plans in which guests would have encountered 'an oversized Audio Animatronic version of Poseidon, the God of the Sea ... boarded large clear-plastic bubbles and then gone off on this 10-minute long journey through wet-for-dry recreations of some of the wonders of the deep' (Hill, 2006).

A rather more whimsical take on oceanographic research was later adopted when the pavilion was re-themed to become the Seas with Nemo and Friends in 2007 to reflect the success of the Pixar film. This overhaul provided a series of original props and promotional posters for *20,000 Leagues Under the Sea* in its new queuing area, to underscore and broaden the Nemo theme.

Finding Nemo characters were projected via innovative technologies into the main aquarium, alongside the real aquatic species.

West Coast, Far East

The largest and most ambitious representation of the sea in any Disney theme park, however, was eventually unveiled in Tokyo on 4 September 2001 with the opening of Tokyo DisneySea. Adjacent to Tokyo Disneyland, which is based broadly on the company's original theme park, Tokyo DisneySea is in every other respect a departure from this traditional outline.

Based upon the theme of nautical exploration, the entire park is built around a series of waterways, lagoons and man-made oceans with the usual themed lands being replaced in DisneySea's lexicon by seven 'ports of call'. A glance across the park map at the names of these areas, Mediterranean Harbour, Mysterious Island, Mermaid Lagoon, Arabian Coast, Lost River Delta, Port Discovery and American Waterfront, quickly confirms the park's commitment to its overarching theme.

The connection to the sea at Tokyo Disney Resort, however, does not begin and end with its detailed representation within the park. Unlike its American predecessors, which are both based inland, the Japanese park is actually situated in Tokyo Bay, in which the Uraga Channel connects to the Pacific Ocean. It is in this geographical context that we must consider whether DisneySea's hyperreal representations of the sea, within physical view of the sea itself, may constitute a new level of simulation beyond those given voice by Baudrillard some twenty years before its creation. Like many Disney projects, the idea for a park based around and by the sea is one that reaches back over a decade before its grand opening in Tokyo, directly across the Pacific Ocean to Queensway Bay in Long Beach, California.

The DisneySea theme park originally came about, rather improbably, as a consequence of a bid by the company to obtain direct ownership of the Disneyland Hotel. This hotel had been built and operated by the Wrather Corporation at the request of Walt Disney to the company's founder and his close personal friend, Jack Wrather. When Disney acquired the Corporation in September 1987, the company also became lessees of the R.M.S. Queen Mary and rights holders to a significant parcel of land around the ship's dock. At a time when Disney were considering themes and locations for a potential second gate in California, this acquisition led eventually to the concept of Port Disney, an extensive, leisure and retail resort area announced to the public on 31 July 1990, which would encompass the Queen Mary and include an entirely new theme park concept entitled DisneySea.

Just as Epcot is an evolution of the original 'Experimental Prototype Community of Tomorrow' concept, so DisneySea retains elements of Port Disney but is by no means a transplanted clone of the original project. The theme park certainly shares some of the characteristics described in Port Disney News, a one-off publication targeted at Long Beach Residents that welcomed potential visitors to a place where they would 'experience a thrilling journey through the mysteries, challenges and natural wonders of the sea' (Hill, 2005a). In the same publication, David Malmuth, project director and vice president of the Disney Development Company, assured them that they would 'directly experience the sea, to wonder about it, to ask questions and to have a memorable time' (Hill, 2005a).

The project as outlined in Port Disney News and the company's master plan, which was released to the press in July 1990, contains the familiar terminology of ports of call. References to Mysterious Island and a description of a 'boardwalk [that] would recreate the nostalgia of the Long Beach oceanfront in its heyday' (Hill, 2005b) are very reminiscent of the Mysterious Island and American Waterfront areas of the Tokyo park. However, the planned centrepiece, Oceana, which would purportedly have been 'one of the main educational components of the park [in which] guests will experience true-to-life recreations of marine habitats and ecological systems from around the globe' (Hill, 2005a), is far more familiar as a description of the Living Seas pavilion at Epcot than anything that now exists in Tokyo DisneySea. Indeed, the emphasis on education and oceanographic research that seems to have been central to the Long Beach project is entirely absent in the park that now exists in Japan.

Along with a number of other details that mark differences between the Californian and Tokyo projects, perhaps the biggest diversion from the original plan is the direct connection to the sea that existed outside their boundaries. While it is true, as previously noted, that DisneySea is within view of Tokyo Bay, it remains in essence a land-based park, themed after and placed next to the sea.

Port Disney (and its version of DisneySea) on the other hand, was always conceived as an entity that rather than representing the sea, shared a symbiotic link to it. The aforementioned Oceana, for instance, contained an ambitious plan to use 'tidal exchange with the actual ocean, so as the tide changed, the levels of water in the outside display tanks would rise and fall' (Sim, 2014). The published plan for Port Disney included a working ferry boat terminal and multiple cruise ship docks, but perhaps the most visible indication of a link between the Ocean and DisneySea that was clearly drawn in Long Beach but merely simulated in Tokyo, was the icon that sparked the original development of the project, R.M.S. Queen Mary.

Whereas in Port Disney the whole resort was effectively built around this genuine luxury liner that was moored in a dock connected directly to the Pacific Ocean, its Japanese counterpart S.S. Columbia, while visually very similar to the Queen Mary, is an ocean liner, in the same sense that the Nautilus, semi-submerged in the lagoon at the park's Mysterious Island, is a submarine. Both vessels present picture perfect, iconic images that to many guests may even form definitive visions of what a cruise liner or a submarine should be; but neither are authentic, nor could they be functional outside their theme park locales.

As authentic as the Queen Mary may initially have been, the plans that within the Port Disney project would have retrofitted her rendered her no more operational than the S.S. Columbia. These plans included repurposing her as a floating shopping mall, a pleasure palace or even, according Shaun Finnie in his book *The Disneylands that Never Were* 'a haunted hotel…complete with manmade ghosts in some of the rooms' (Finnie, 2006, 164). In this context we can surely look at these two vessels as the embodiment of Baudrillard's contention that 'It is no longer a question of false representation of reality (ideology) but of concealing that the real is no longer real, and thus saving the reality principle' (Baudrillard and Poster, 2007, 172).

Pleasure Cruises and Treasure Islands

It would now seem pertinent to turn our discussion to the entirely operational but no less fantastical vessels that constitute the Disney Cruise Line. The Cruise Line currently consists of four ships, Disney Magic, Disney Wonder, Disney Dream and Disney Fantasy, with another two as yet unnamed craft due to be launched in 2021 and 2023, respectively.

Before the company decided to launch these lavishly themed but relatively conventional cruise ships, it explored the viability of a project bearing the name S.S. Disney that would have constituted a true floating theme park retrofitted into the hull of a supertanker. The project, led by 'imagineer' Mark Hickson, went as far as developing a series of detailed models of the proposed attractions. Hickson recalls that 'Michael Eisner and Frank Wells both loved the project … The strategic planning group at corporate didn't want to do a floating theme park, they wanted to do a cruise ship. Eventually they convinced Michael that a cruise ship was easier to do' (disneyandmore, 2011).

Clearly the corporate desire simply to enter an existing market with a Disney themed offering was a great deal less risky than attempting to create an entirely new one with a floating park. The subsequent global expansion of Disney theme park resorts also made it less pressing to be able to move a park periodically to another continent. Nonetheless, Disney continued to extend Baudrillard's hyperreality and simulacra on to the high seas.

The Pirates of the Caribbean attraction that opened at Disneyland in 1967, and has been regarded by many commentators as the quintessential Disney theme park ride, has in recent years become the inspiration for a phenomenally successful film series that has generated worldwide box offices revenues in excess of $3.7 billion. The success of the films has been reflected in a re-theming of the original attraction to include some of the main characters, while Shanghai Disneyland's version is the first that entirely rejects the

Disneyland template and instead focuses exclusively on the adventures of Captain Jack Sparrow.

It is, however, the use of the franchise on the Disney Cruise Line that is perhaps its most interesting incarnation in the context of the discussion of hyperreality. The Pirates in the Caribbean deck party has become something of a tradition on voyages to a wide range of destinations but began, as its name suggests, on sailings to the Caribbean itself. It is worth noting that even when geographically located within the shipping lanes that may at one time have seen vessels sacked and boarded by their real, historical counterparts, the images conjured up during these entertainments have far more in common with Disney's own romantically imagined versions of Long John Silver and Captain Barbosa than with the murderous criminals who once perpetrated such deeds.

Not only has the cruise line used the distinctly unsavoury theme of a crew of bloodthirsty pirates invading the ship as a source of on-board family entertainment, it has also used the iconic image of a moored version of the legendary ghost ship, the Flying Dutchman from the series, as a piece of elaborate set dressing in the ocean, just off the coast of the company's private island, Castaway Cay. In a parallel to our earlier discussion of the Nautilus and S.S. Columbia, the Flying Dutchman, while giving the visual impression of a bewitched yet ultimately seaworthy vessel, actually only lasted for a short while before the ravages of the real ocean took their toll. What was ultimately an outsized movie prop, and was thus never really designed to withstand such forces, rotted away and was quickly removed.

During a much larger, Disney themed road trip that I took with my family in 2015 I visited both the Walt Disney World Resort in Florida and Castaway Cay in the Bahamas. One of the comparisons that was immediately obvious was the thematic similarity between the Typhoon Lagoon water park in the Florida resort and the real but nonetheless clearly constructed Bahamian island. In terms of attractions, amenities and the general aesthetic of the two areas it would seem apparent that the island in the Bahamas must have served as an inspiration in the development of the Floridian water park. However, since Typhoon Lagoon opened for business in June 1989 and the former Gorda Cay was not leased and rechristened by Disney until 1997, if the two share any visual DNA it was actually the design of the entirely manmade lagoon that shaped the layout of the naturally occurring island, and not vice versa.

Nowhere is this comparison more evident than in Shark Reef at Typhoon Lagoon and the snorkelling area on Castaway Cay. Shark Reef, just like the rest of the water park, was an entirely artificial area in which guests could don flippers and flotation vests and snorkel through a small, salt water lagoon stocked with a multitude of tropical fish and various species of small and decidedly tourist-friendly sharks. The snorkelling lagoon at Castaway Cay, however, offered a similar experience using almost identical equipment, but unlike the tame, Floridian version, the adventure on offer is in a body of water that is actually a netted-off cove of the Atlantic Ocean. While the water park attraction provided a viewing gallery through the portholes of a scuttled and upturned ship, but was otherwise themed to present the visage of an authentic lagoon, the 'real' Bahamian experience offers an array of underwater sights, such as the hull of a wrecked Nautilus submarine, and statues of Mickey and Minnie Mouse.

The quintessential difference between the 'real' and the simulated lagoons, however, is the likelihood and frequency with which the guest will encounter actual beasts of the deep. It is impossible to venture into Shark Reef without immediately coming face to face with the full breadth of aquatic species, and unthinkable that a guest could make it from one side to the other without encountering the creature that gives the attraction its name. However, it is feasible, indeed entirely likely, that a snorkelling adventure at Castaway Cay could be conducted without any such contact. As Umberto Eco has suggested, 'Disneyland tells us that faked nature corresponds much more to our daydream demands' (Eco, 2002, 44). Eco noted his experience of a trip on a riverboat on the 'real' Mississippi in which the captain pointed out the possibility of viewing alligators, only for none to appear. For us, after having seen the Disneyland version of the Atlantic perfectly choreographed to the narrator's script days before, the experience of so much teeming marine life at Typhoon Lagoon left us disappointed and 'feeling homesick for Disneyland' (Eco, 2002, 44) as we emerged from the authentically underwhelming Atlantic at Castaway Cay.

Conclusion

We have seen that from the earliest planning stages, Disney theme parks have relied heavily upon images and representations of the sea, and vessels that travel on or under water, as thematic devices in their construction of hyperreal, kinetic animations in three dimensional space. It has often been a feature of these modes of transportation that while presenting perfect, idealised Kodak moments, that may even seem to guests like the very definition of form and function combined, they are often illusory objects that are something other than that which they purport to be.

From submarines that never submerge; through ocean liners that remain captive within shallow theme park waters; to hydrolators that shake and bubble but never truly ascend or descend; these are simulations of a reality that is itself no longer certain. A reality in which an authentic luxury liner can be docked in the ocean, but remain as stationary as its theme park equivalent; in which it becomes an attraction in which representation and phantasms of its own past become its unique selling point; and in which the very last thing it can be regarded as is ocean-going. A reality in which simulated nature becomes the inspiration and sets the pattern for naturally occurring, geographical spaces; and in which these spaces often fail to live up to the daydream of what nature (in an always 'on' world of instant gratification) should be. A liminal space in which the ocean can at once be wild and under the control of men, but never quite provide the satisfyingly authentic experience that only comes with quintessential audio-animatronic timing.

Architeuthis dux, or the giant squid, is such a rarely seen and elusive creature that for centuries it was believed by many to be the mythical product of the imagination of seafarers, whose minds had been affected by intoxication and the unbearable solitude of their voyages. Even with all of the resources and equipment available to modern oceanographic researchers, it was not until 2006 that a team of Japanese scientists were able finally to capture one on film. Yet as rare and mysterious as this creature is, Disney 'imagineers' were able to give it life and present it on screen long before the advent of computer graphics. Every day since August 1955, somewhere in the world, millions of theme park guests have been able to witness a true-life Kraken that attacks on cue and is in that moment more real than reality.

References

Baudrillard, J. (1988), *Selected Writings*, Stanford: Stanford University Press.

Disney and more (2011), 'The "S.S. Disney" an incredible WDI project – Interview with Mark Hickson', *Disney and more* [online], ttp://disneyandmore.blogspot.co.uk/2011/09/d-archives-ss-disney-incredible-wdi.html (accessed 11 May 2017).

Eco, U. (2002), *Travels In Hyper Reality*, San Diego: Harcourt.

Finnie, S. (2006). *The Disneylands That Never Were*, Raleigh: Lulu.com.

Forbes (2017), 'The World's Biggest Pubic Companies', *Forbes* [online], ttps://www.forbes.com/companies/walt-disney/ (accessed 4 April 2017).

Gabler, N. (2008). *Walt Disney: The Triumph of the American Imagination*, New York: Alfred A. Knopf.

Hill, J. (2005a), 'A watered down version of "Why For"', *Jim Hill Media* [online]. ttp://jimhillmedia.com/editor_in_chief1/b/jim_hill/archive/2005/02/04/538.aspx (accessed 11 May 2017).

Hill, J. (2005b), 'What there would have been to see at Long Beach's DisneySea theme park' *Jim Hill Media* [online], ttp://jimhillmedia.com/editor_in_chief1/b/jim_hill/archive/2005/02/08/540.aspx (accessed 11 May 2017).

Hill, J. (2006), 'Why For: The Seas-and-desist edition', *Jim Hill Media* [online], ttp://jimhillmedia.com/editor_in_chief1/b/jim_hill/archive/2006/06/01/why-for-the-seas-and-desist-edition.aspx?PageIndex=2 (accessed 8 May 2017).

O'Reilly, L. (2016), 'The 30 biggest media companies in the world', *Business Insider* [online], ttp://uk.businessinsider.com/the-30-biggest-media-owners-in-the-world-2016-5/#28-prosiebensat1—291-billion-in-media-revenue-3. (accessed 4 April 2017).

Marling, K. (1997), *Designing Disney's Theme Parks: The Architecture of Reassurance*, Paris: Flammarion.

Sim, S. (2014), 'The Disney Theme Park Where You Are Attacked By Sharks (And 3 Other Crazy Unbuilt Parks)', *Theme Park Tourist* [online], http://www.themeparktourist.com/features/20140331/17223/disney-theme-park-where-you-are-attacked-sharks-and-3-other-crazy-unbuilt-pa (accessed 11 May 2017).

theorigihalepcot.com. (2017) 'Film & Transcript', *the-original-epcot.com* [online], ttps://sites.google.com/site/theoriginalepcot/film-transcript (accessed 8 May 2017).

Walt Disney's Wonderful World of Color: Disneyland Goes to the World's Fair (1964). [TV programme] NBC, 17 May.

Wasko, J. (2001). *Understanding Disney*, New York: John Wiley & Sons.

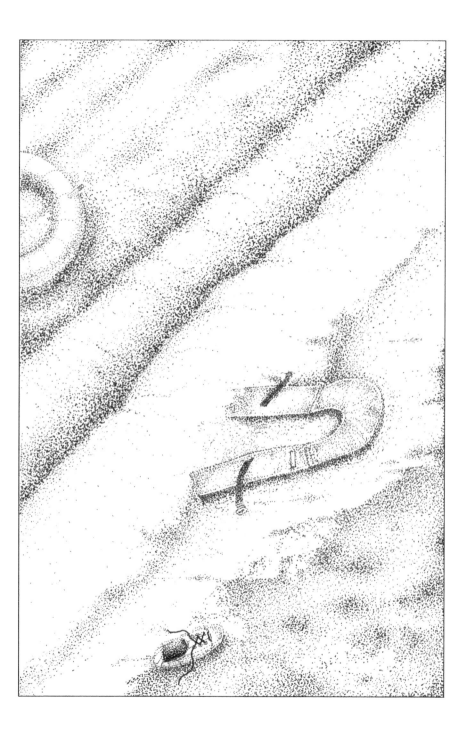

Chapter 10

Rivers of Blood, Sea of Bodies: An Analysis of Media Coverage of Migration and Trafficking on the High Seas

Carole Murphy

Introduction

The source of Enoch Powell's racist and anti-immigration speech can be found in a line from Virgil's *Aeneid* 'I seem to see the River Tiber foaming with much blood'. Known as the 'Rivers of Blood' speech, it foreshadows recent events that transformed the Mediterranean into a 'Sea of Bodies'. The bodies in question, those of refugees, are most often represented in the media as an amorphous mass, a hungry beast, devouring all in its path. This trope draws on both ancient fears of the sea as the repository of unknown monsters and more recent fears of the perceived threat of 'refugee-as-invader' and consumer of homes, jobs and benefits. Occasionally, an individual may be singled out for a more empathetic response, as in the case of 'the boy on the beach', AylanKurdi, but even then, manipulated for political leverage about staunching the flow of immigration.

The Glasgow Media Group conducted an analysis of media coverage of refugees and asylum seekers in the United Kingdom during two key periods, 2006 and 2011. Two main themes were identified in the resulting publication, *Bad News for Refugees* (Philo, Briant & Donald, 2013), highlighting concerns about the language used to describe the refugees and the lack of reporting of political context.

This chapter is based on an analysis of media coverage of the 'refugee crisis' between April and September 2015 in UK print and online news. Themes identified by the Glasgow Media Group are evident, such as the conflation of forced and economic migration, the use of numbers and exaggeration, criminality, threat, deportation and human rights, the need for 'immigration control' and the matter of western responsibility (Philo, Briant & Donald, 2013: 57). Alongside these broad areas, this chapter will also examine the conflation of human trafficking with human smuggling; the purpose this serves in broader political debates; and how these discourses link to representations in the media in which both trafficker and trafficked are characterised as equally culpable in their endeavours to enter Europe illegally.

Such deliberations take place within the context of the 'High Seas' as a site of contestation, particularly around border control (Gammeltoft-Hansen, 2008) Mobile populations invoke anxieties for the keepers of borders who increasingly criminalise unwanted border crossings. European border controls have been introduced in territorial waters, in the territorial waters of third countries and on the High Seas, justified on the basis that the principle of *non-refoulement* does not apply extra-territorially.* In this contested arena, refugees are policed in a paramilitary fashion and human rights are regularly ignored (see Brolan, C. 2003).

The introduction of the Modern Slavery Act into UK law on 25 March 2015, with its commitment to provide enhanced support to victims of modern forms of slavery, including human trafficking,** might have been regarded as a step in the right direction when considering human rights. Expressed in the pledge to improve victim identification and provide enhanced support, there remains, however, much confusion about what constitutes human trafficking and how this differs from human smuggling.

The intersection of human trafficking and discussions about innocence and culpability are evident in the negative discourses that abound in representations in the media. The amorphous mass emerging to the shore embodies cultural anxieties about sea beasts. Media reports utilise these anxieties to dehumanise victims. From this perspective, the Rivers of Blood circa 1968 have, almost 50 years later, been transformed into a Sea of Bodies flooding the shores of Europe. The impact of such reporting on responses from the public and the broader consequences for those communities residing in the UK requires investigation and action to promote a more responsible and ethical reaction to humanitarian crises.

Rivers of Blood, 1968

The Rivers of Blood speech delivered by Enoch Powell in 1968*** represented a dark period in British politics, during which immigrants, especially

---

* A key facet of refugee law that protects refugees from being pushed back to a place where their lives may be threatened.

** The Modern Slavery Act (2015) UK adopted a 4P paradigm as a framework to combat modern slavery and human trafficking. The four points are:
Pursue – Prosecute and disrupt individuals and groups responsible for modern slavery;
Prevent – Prevent people from engaging in modern slavery;
Protect – Strengthen safeguards against modern slavery by protecting vulnerable people from exploitation and increasing awareness and resilience against this crime; and
Prepare – Reduce the harm caused by modern slavery through improved victim identification and enhanced support (Modern Slavery Strategy: 10).

*** Enoch Powell, Address to the Conservative Association Meeting, Birmingham, 20 April 1968.

those from the British Commonwealth, were singled out as a scourge on society. Quoting directly from Virgil's *Aeneid*, a mythological tale about the founding of Rome and the difficulties faced by the Trojan Warrior Aeneas, Powell cited the response of the priestess Sybil to Aeneas to frame what he saw as the challenges facing England in 1968: 'As I look ahead, I am filled with foreboding; like the Roman, I seem to see the River Tiber foaming with much blood.' Metaphors of war and water are often used when speaking of large movements of people. They provoke images of powerlessness in the face of a formidable force that will destroy everything in its path, will cause devastation and despair, and will be unstoppable. References to 'rivers' and 'blood' in Powell's speech insinuate that violence will be inevitable in the battle to retain British identity in the face of a tidal wave of immigrants.

The context for the speech had three key elements. First, amendments to the Race Relations Act (1965), which had made it illegal to discriminate against a person 'in public places and made the promotion of hatred on the grounds of "colour, race, or ethnic or national origins" an offence' (www.parliament.uk), was extended to cover discrimination in housing and employment. Second, the Civil Rights Act was signed into law in April 1968 in the United States. Popularly known as the Fair Housing Act, it 'prohibited discrimination concerning the sale, rental and financing of housing based on race, religion, national origin and sex' (www.civilrights.org). The passing of this Act in the US caused alarm in the UK, indicating as it did the march towards racial equality in the West. Third, this was a period of mass immigration from the Commonwealth into the UK, with estimates of 472,500 persons arriving between 1955 and 1962, and predictions of a further increase rising to three-and-a-half million (www.channel4.com).

In the speech, Powell cited citizens from his constituency of Wolverhampton who had, according to him, expressed fears about the invasion of immigrants in the area. The speech used antagonistic discourse to construct the rising numbers of immigrants to the UK as a direct attack on the status of the existing population. He argued that the benefits to the immigrant upon entry to the UK far outweighed those of the British population, whereupon the immigrant would gain 'admission to privileges and opportunities'. In contrast, 'the impact upon the existing population was very different ... in which they found themselves made strangers in their own country'. The notion of being a stranger at home touches on anxiety about identity and nationhood and produces a 'blockade' mentality. Further, the speech drew upon emotive rhetoric and familiar tropes of the 'other', the interloper whose only interest is to appropriate that which belongs to the indigenous population. Powell said that his constituents:

> found their wives unable to obtain hospital beds in childbirth, their children unable to obtain school places, their homes and neighbourhoods changed beyond recognition, their plans and prospects for the future defeated; at work they found that employers hesitated to apply to the immigrant worker the

standards of discipline and competence required of the native-born worker; they began to hear, as time went by, more and more voices which told them that they were now the unwanted.

Underpinned by divisive and racist rhetoric, the speech effectively ended Powell's political career. However, the underlying discourse persisted and continues to simmer under the surface, with periodic peaks brought about by social and political events.

Globalisation and Mass Migration; 1980s

One of these peaks occurred in the 1980s, during a period of major global transformation, which saw 'the consolidation of globalisation' within the context of 'cultural unrest and political uncertainty', ... and the rise of immigration' (Fojas, 2010: 83). Representations of immigrants in mainstream media during these periods are underpinned by political ideologies that draw on tropes of the invader. In the US, Fojas argues that the fear of being overrun by a 'flood' of immigration led to the belief that this would instigate a process of decline, resulting in the US devolving into an 'underdeveloped and overpopulated third world country' (2008: 88). Within this overarching narrative, the immigrant as the subject is represented as an 'invisible invader, a job and wife taker, and a risk to public health' (Fojas, 2008: 88), reminiscent of the discourse underpinning the Rivers of Blood speech.

Evidently, the media, as a vehicle of communication both locally and globally, plays an important role in identifying, translating and reporting social, cultural and political narratives and disseminating them to a broad audience via a multiplicity of platforms. Modes of communication include screen media, and decoding the underlying discourse is critical to understanding audience reception and how this might impact on everyday actions. Throughout this period, Hollywood films developed a key function in the production and dissemination of media products; they had and continue to have an extensive reach, and the power to communicate specific narratives to a variety of audiences.

For example during this phase of transition in the 1980s, 'border' films, such as *Borderline* (Jerrold Freedman, 1980) *The Border* (Tony Richardson, 1982) and *Flashpoint* (William Tannen, 1984) represent globalization as the main culprit in the opening up of borders to free trade and free movement, allowing entry to a 'flood' of immigrants (Fojas, 2008). Drawing both on the 'invader' trope and on metaphors of a powerful, unstoppable force, the flood summons images of drowning under a tidal wave of aliens. Such representations on screen construct borders and border personnel, at the frontline in stopping this tidal wave of trespassers, as the protector of the nation state, guardians of national identity, and defender against the 'other'.

Both these vignettes of political and media representations at two specific periods in the 20th century set the scene for ongoing negative formulations of people on the move, variously described as 'immigrants', 'refugees', 'migrants' – economic, irregular or other – and 'asylum seekers'. The contested arena of the sea, outside the jurisdiction of the state, complicates the policing of borders. States overcome their obligations to refugees and asylum seekers under international law through interception (or interdiction at sea)

> interception is defined as encompassing all measures applied by a State, outside its national territory, in order to prevent, interrupt or stop the movement of persons without the required documentation crossing international borders by land, air or sea, and making their way to the country of prospective destination.[*]

The prevention or interruption of allowing access of persons 'without the required documentation', together with political rhetoric and racist ideology, combine to incite anxieties about vulnerabilities of borders and consequent loss of identity, position and place. Powell's speech, invoking 'rivers of blood' as the outcome of the perceived invasion, was delivered almost fifty years ago. Writing in 2008, Manzoor argues: '40 years later, it remains a toxic cloud floating above all political debate on race relations' (Manzoor, S. 2008). In the intervening years, Manzoor's words continue to resonate, especially within the context of what has been termed the current Mediterranean Migrant Crisis.

The Mediterranean Migrant Crisis and the Media

Interest in reporting on the crisis increased in April 2015, as hundreds of thousands of migrants and refugees fled war and conflict, mainly from Syria but also Afghanistan, Iraq, Eritrea, and Kosovo (Eurostat, 2017). The situation has since escalated, with 2016 regarded as the 'deadliest year ever' in which 'the death rate has increased threefold' (Spindler, 2016). Through this the transformation of the Mediterranean into a Sea of Bodies is complete.

Reporting in some media tends towards representations of migrants as a mass of invaders, illustrated in headlines such as: 'Draw a Line on Immigration or Else' (The Sun, 18 January 2013), sending a message to David Cameron prior to his trip to meet EU leaders. Dispensing threats to the Prime Minister in this way displays the role played by media as a channel for the communication of powerful vested interests disguised as the voice of the people. Additional headlines during 2015 continue this type of discourse, drawing on the language of invasions and swarms, invoking powerlessness in the face of the invading hordes. Examples include: 'Migrants: How Many More Can We Take?' (*Daily Mail*, 28 August 2015); 'Send in

---

[*]   UNHCR (2000). Interception of Asylum-Seekers and Refugee: The International Framework and Recommendations for a Comprehensive Approach. UN Doc. EC/50/SC/CRP.17. 9 June 2000, p 10.

Army to Halt Migrant Invasion' (*Daily Express*, 30 July 2015) and 'Migrants Swarm to Britain' (*Daily Express*, 29 August 2015).

Clearly, how the media convey information about this crisis, and how these accounts represent immigrants and refugees is crucial for understanding wider responses amongst the European countries most affected. There is some agreement that media coverage has the power to influence public opinion. Bleich, Bloemraad and de Graauw (2015) argue that 'The media inform the public, provide a communicative bridge between political and social actors, influence perceptions of pressing issues, depict topics and people in particular ways and may shape individuals' political views and participation' (2015: 857).

Not previously a major focus for analysis on migration, the role of media in communicating this topic to the public has gained currency in contemporary scholarly literature (see Bleich, Bloemraad & de Graauw, 2015). This is unsurprising given the sharp increase in irregular migrants over recent decades (Donato & Armenta, 2011). In addition, coverage of the most recent situation in the Mediterranean reports not on irregular migration, but on a mass movement of people escaping war, conflict and unstable situations – refugees.

Migrants, asylum seekers and refugees are variously dealt with by politicians and communicated in the media through the rhetoric of boundaries, borders or bombardment, subject to and object of smuggling and trafficking. A selection of the more sympathetic reporting offers a voice to those fleeing crises in foreign lands from which escape is a matter of life and death. These stories appeal to the humanity of the audience in which traumatic former life experiences and eventual escape, involving smuggling, sometimes trafficking and exploitation, and rescue from near death in the sea of bodies, is communicated.

These snapshots fail to influence opinion in Europe to any great degree though, prejudiced as it is by political rhetoric and fuelled by media, much of which supports the closing of borders. Equally, the 'High Seas' as a site of contestation, in which European border controls can be operated in territorial waters and in the territorial waters of third countries, can result in the return of refugees to their country of origin. In this contested arena, refugees are policed in a military fashion, purportedly to attack smugglers, through use of warships and air strikes, and human rights are regularly ignored. Mobile populations, who do not conform to regular entry, because there are no such legal arrangements available to them, invoke anxieties for border control and are increasingly criminalised.

Whilst some of those making this journey may change their status along the way from refugee to asylum seeker, from 'smuggled' to 'trafficked', from gaining official entry to going 'underground', these recent events represent a major humanitarian crisis. The official response, reported most regularly, very successfully conflates the humanitarian issues with crime and border control, reporting on the one hand the numbers of people lost in the seas, side by side with accounts of responses by governments that demand a military reaction.

Another area of contention concerns the conflation of human smuggling with human trafficking, the latter more frequently reported in the media. Interpol defines the differences thus: 'A broad distinction can be made between people smuggling and human trafficking. In general, the individuals who pay a smuggler in order to gain illegal entry to a country do so voluntarily whereas the victims of human trafficking are often duped or forced into entering another country' (www.interpol.int).

In the first case, the 'smuggled' are complicit in their relationship with the smuggler and their objective is to gain illegal entry to a country. In contrast:

> Trafficking in Persons [involves] the recruitment, transportation, transfer, harbouring or receipt of persons, by means of the threat or use of force or other forms of coercion, of abduction, of fraud, of deception, of the abuse of power or of a position of vulnerability or of the giving or receiving of payments or benefits to achieve the consent of a person having control over another person, for the purpose of exploitation. Exploitation shall include, at a minimum, the exploitation of the prostitution of others or other forms of sexual exploitation, forced labour or services, slavery or practices similar to slavery, servitude or the removal of organs. (Article 3, paragraph (a) of the Protocol to Prevent, Suppress and Punish Trafficking in Persons (www.unodc.org)).

In both cases, the smuggler and the trafficker are involved in committing a criminal act. For the 'smuggled', complicity in the criminal act is assumed; they are also regarded as criminals, but with the additional label of potential 'illegal immigrant' and its associated negative connotations. In this instance, the media promote the construction of a powerful 'border mentality' that assumes a purity of nationality and nationhood that must be protected from invaders at all cost, presented as posing serious challenges to 'the sovereignty and jurisdiction of nation states' (Thorbjørnsrud, 2015: 772). For those who are 'trafficked' on the other hand and subjected to 'coercion, fraud or deception', within the law at least, their status is that of a victim of crime. In this case, an empathetic response is validated and encouraged. However, the lack of clarity and consistent conflation of these two terms is problematic and is highlighted in the analysis.

Media Analysis

Because of these recent events in the Mediterranean, there is a growing interest in examining the role of the media in promoting particular discourses about irregular immigration, trafficking and smuggling and migration of refugees, escaping war, conflict and dictatorships. The 'critical role of the media in modern liberal democracies' demands a response that takes account of 'production, text, reception' (Thorbjørnsrud, 2015: 772).

Within this sphere of research, it is important to pay attention to concerns about ownership of newspapers and other forms of media aligned with particular political viewpoints that may influence reporting in print and online news stories. Other issues include agenda setting and framing in different national settings, within which operate varying journalistic practices. Bleich, Bloemraad and de Graauw (2015) also delineate three areas of focus for analysis of media stories on migrants and minorities: information, representations and participation. The role of the media in providing *information* about groups or issues related to migration to the general population is critical in terms of how these groups are constructed and *represented*, and whether they have an opportunity to *participate* in 'a public sphere where they can advance their interests and identities' (2015: 859)

Recent studies have investigated the framing of 'irregular immigration' in the media. One such, a large-scale comparative analysis of mass media reception examined the production of coverage of irregular immigration into the United States, France and Norway, three very different national contexts with varying historical experiences and management of the issue (Thorbjørnsrud (2015). The findings highlighted the 'dominant voices, narratives and arguments in the mainstream media; identified how stakeholders 'work strategically to promote their messages in the media'; and analysed the impact of these media evaluations on the public's attitudes towards immigrants (Thorbjørnsrud, 2017: 771). The analysis that follows will touch on some of these areas, particularly framing, representations and reception.

Media Content: Press Samples between March 2015 and September 2015

During the period of focus, frequent reports and images of migrants and refugees risking their lives to reach Europe were in the news, often on the front pages. The analysis that follows draws on press samples drawn mainly from UK National and London newspapers including the *Daily Mail, The Telegraph, The Guardian, The Independent, The Sun*, the *London Evening Standard* and *The Mail on Sunday*. The focus on this period can be justified for two reasons: it was a period of intensification of migrant flows across the Mediterranean due to the crisis in Syria, as well as ongoing conflict and disruption in African countries; it was also the period directly following the introduction of the Modern Slavery Act into UK law on 25 March 2015, the objective of which was to combat human trafficking and modern day slavery.

A LexisLibrary search was conducted using 'trafficking', 'smuggling', 'migrant' and 'Mediterranean', returning 204 articles. The sample was narrowed further by excluding any references to migrants outside of the EU and by selection of most typical and key stories from that period.

Source

Daily Mail and *Mail on Sunday* (13)
Daily Telegraph (London) (30)
London Evening Standard (London) (6)
Daily Express (5)
The Guardian(London) (36)
The Independent (United Kingdom) (63)
Daily Mirror and *Sunday Mirror* (21)
The Observer (London) (6)
The Sun (England) (23)
The Times (London) (30)

Themes identified in the analysis include:

– Numbers
– Borders: Rescue or Return
– Language of War
– Humanitarian Responses: Sea of Bodies

Numbers

Numbers of lives lost are commonly used in reports on the crisis but often alongside the rising numbers of migrants continuing to risk life and limb on the treacherous journey. 170,000 people reportedly crossed from North Africa the previous year, states Colin Freeman in *The Telegraph* (17 April 2015). Out of these 170,000, only 27,000 had applied for asylum in Italy, with the remainder 'heading north', with the UK as a favoured destination. The tone of this reporting implies an invasion of sorts; a monster that will emerge from the seas in ever growing waves, a threat to the equanimity of European society. Citing the numbers of migrants in this way feeds into the anti-immigrant rhetoric by creating a sense of panic about Europe being swamped by invaders.

Other numbers, such as the proposal by UNHCR that Europe should provide 130,000 places for refugees are equally problematic, notably in the contrasting responses of EU nations in which Germany agreed to take 30,000 and the UK 143 (Townsend, 2015; in *The Guardian*). Four days later, *The Times* reported that despite 1,300 deaths in the previous month and calls to restore search and rescue operations, a poll showed that this may alienate Tory and Ukip voters. Hence, political expediency takes precedence over human life and according to ZeidRa'ad al-Hussein, EU policy consists of 'short-sighted, short-term political reactions pandering to xenophobic populist movements that have poisoned public opinion' (ZeidRa'ad al-Hussein, UN human rights chief, cited in Milmo & Day, 2015a; in *The Independent*)

Often with the intention of eliciting sympathy, numbers illustrating the loss of life represent the huge quantities of refugees risking their survival engaging in the perilous journey across the Mediterranean Sea. Shipwrecks that result in hundreds of lives lost regularly make the headlines. Images show the precarious positions of desperate migrants clinging to whatever will keep them afloat, whilst debates rage about the most effective method of tackling the crisis.

Reports also implicitly link numbers with anti-immigration rhetoric: 'a giant hole has been opened in the Continent's border control policy making a mockery of European leaders' promises to keep tighter curbs on immigration' (Freeman, 2015; in *The Telegraph*). European leaders were and remain

> deeply divided over how to respond, appear impotent in the face of the surge of migrants risking their lives to reach European shores and are reluctant to relax immigration policies for fear of boosting support at home for anti-immigrant parties doing well in many parts of the union (*The Guardian*, 20 April 2015).

The 'giant hole' in border control policy, the failure to keep tighter curbs on immigration and the breaking of promises portray EU leaders as weak and ineffective. Insinuating an inability to protect the borders, and depictions of a bottomless pit through which the trespasser can enter at will, conforms to anti-immigrant rhetoric par excellence. Thus, the monster of the sea has reached the shore and will bring with it a flood of biblical proportions, taking advantage of the unprotected borders, a key theme identified in the analysis.

Borders: Rescue and Return

Unsurprisingly, borders, and linguistic phrases such as 'giant hole[s]' represent a key discourse in the analysis, linked to debates about search and rescue, and the handling of the crisis by European governments. Not only is there a gap in the fence of security surrounding Europe, but rescue operations are taken advantage of by the 'boat people' [who] are primarily economic migrants' according to Graham Leese, a former British Advisor to the EU border force Frontex. Further, the traffickers cut the amount of fuel used in the expectation that the boats will be met halfway, and if they are worried about 'a boat from this miserable armada sinking ... they can always ring the Italian coastguard to pick its benighted passengers up' (Freeman, 2015; in *The Telegraph*).

Underpinning this overarching message, Leese proposes that 'economic migrants are taking advantage of the search and rescue missions and thus the UN's suggestion that Europe is morally obliged to take in 'people coming across in boats' is dangerous and encourages the crossings. The designation as both 'economic migrant' and 'people coming across in boats' implies a lack of legitimacy for taking the journey in the former and a jolly day out in a boat in the latter: an everyday journey dislocated from social, political and cultural context. In this case, the migrants are denied a voice, produced as scavengers and swindlers, complicit with smugglers and therefore deserving their fate, be that death through drowning. Operations to continue search and rescue, such as that undertaken by Médecins Sans Frontières, are equally regarded as complicit in encouraging the smuggling trade.

How these articles are communicated is clearly key to reception by the audience, including issues of space and voice: how much and who gets to speak. Those with power and authority are given legitimacy whilst the refugee is mostly unheard and invisible. A close examination of one article in *The Telegraph*, 'It sounds heartless, but debate rages over whether search and rescue missions just encourage deadly trafficking' (Freeman, 2015) provides context for much of these debates. The phrasing of the title implies that heartlessness can be justified, as search and rescue operations encourage trafficking. These operations, criticised by anti-immigration groups, had been suspended by Italy and the UK on the basis that they encourage migrants to take the journey. Discontinued since October 2014, they were, according to Italian MPs, used as a 'taxi service' for traffickers (Freeman, 2015).

However, considering that Mare Nostrum, an Italian led EU funded search and rescue operation had been set up in response to the drowning of 360 migrants off the coast of the island of Lampedusa in 2013, the discontinuation in response to anti-immigration pressure groups implies that the lives lost in the Lampedusa tragedy had been forgotten. Insinuations that desperate migrants should be left to drown because they are implicit in their own demise, in their desperation to reach the shores, obscures the loss of human life and ignores internationally recognised humanitarian obligations. The termination of search and rescue and the consequent failure to halt the migrant influx demonstrates clearly that whereas Mare Nostrum rescued 100,000 people in the previous year, its cessation has failed to deter others from crossing, and since then, deaths have increased exponentially.

Treatises regarding protecting the borders utilise war rhetoric at the same time as they take on the form of a battle of words between a 'blockade mentality' and the humanitarian stance: politicians who argue for the protection of 'Fortress Europe' (*The Independent*, 21 April 2015), thus appeasing anti-immigration voters in their respective nations, versus those who demand a humanitarian solution to the problem, such as the UN, Médecins Sans Frontières and Save the Children.

At various 'peaks' in the crisis, and often following a large loss of life, politicians, former and current military personnel and anti-immigrant groups such as MigrationWatch UK call for military action to 'Reclaim Europe's borders to stop such tragedies' (*Daily Mail*, 21 April 2015). Contradictory statements such as this, which claim that protecting borders will result in saving lives, are disingenuous and misleading.

The Rhetoric Continues

'EU borders chief says saving migrants' lives "shouldn't be priority" for patrols' (*The Guardian*, 22 April 2015); 'EU draws up plans for military attacks on Libya targets to stop migrant boats' (*The Guardian*, 10 May 2015); 'Britain to confront traffickers in Med' (*The Times*, 18 April 2015). *The Times* reports on the use of warships to attack people smugglers and save lives, the aim of which is to 'capture and destroy' (*The Times*, 24 April 2015). Under the guise of 'stopping tragedies' (*Daily Mail*, 24 April 2015), many of these reports ignore political, economic and humanitarian factors, subscribing instead to inhuman and inhumane interventions.

A good example of this can be found in Burleigh's proposal that the Australian government's refusal to allow migrants to land, sending them to camps with rudimentary facilities, is a solution that may cause hardship, but 'at least they're not drowning in their thousands' (Burleigh, 2015). Once again, stopping migrants is constructed as a humanitarian issue, attempting to obfuscate the underlying crisis. In this way, the public do not have to witness the suffering of refugees because they will be transported elsewhere, out of sight.

Other coverage challenges military style intervention, taking a humanitarian stance, in which reporting suggests that British policy for dealing with the issue through the use of air strikes to 'stem the flow of refugees' is doomed. Other strategies though continue to pander to political aspirations, including the 'rapid returns programme' of the UK (*The Guardian*, 23 April 2015), the return of most of the migrants to their country of origin (*The Telegraph*, 23 April 2015), including 'forced return' (*The Guardian*, 31 July 2015).

The rhetoric of targeting the traffickers to protect the victims from being tricked or forced into making the perilous journey (Philip Hammond, cited in *The Independent*, 21 April 2015) not only ignores the complex factors that push migrants to Europe, including escaping dictatorships and conflict, but also denies the migrants individual agency in their decision to seek a better life away from war, conflict and poverty. Migration experts condemned the 'entirely self-serving' language used by politicians at the time, which conceals the fact that refugees are trying to escape Africa of their own free will (*The Guardian*, 21 May 2015).

As one migrant puts it: 'it is not our choice to penetrate the sea...if no-one can help us, then the only option is to go to the smugglers' (Kingsley, 2015b; in *The Guardian*). The conflation of trafficker and smuggler in these reports serves a particularly insidious purpose according to Aidan McQuade, director of Anti-Slavery International, as it:

> conveniently obfuscates the issues and buys political breathing space. It is a classic public relations move by those faced with evidence of their complicity in human rights abuses – or in this case, arguably, a preventable atrocity.

When faced with such horror, it is easier to make grand statements blaming migrant deaths on evil traffickers than to seek the causes and identify proper responses (McQuade, in *The Guardian*, 22 April 2015)

The Sea of Bodies

The Rivers of Blood speech framed the flood of immigration as a bloodied battle in which the native population must fight to retain their ownership of wives, homes and land. The current migrant crisis has also been constructed as an invasion in which military action, including air strikes, deployment of warships, combat on the ground and use of tear gas and water cannon are all features of control and protectionist measures. Despite the enormous loss of life, the anti-immigration rhetoric continues regardless. Implying a free ride, the headline 'Thanks for the lift Britain' (Brown, 2015; in the *Daily Mail*) represents the migrants as freeloaders. The border mentality, illustrated in the notion that the only way to stop the 'swarms' of migrants, and stem the current 'invasion of Southern Europe and by extension Britain would be to close the EU's borders' (Littlejohn,2015; in the *Daily Mail*).

The ultimate ineffectiveness of these tactics from the perspective of protection of human life is clear. Zoran Milanoviæ, the Croatian Prime Minister at the time, said that 'no country should erect walls and wires in Europe in the 21st century. It sends a terrible message' (*The Guardian*, 19 September 2015). High-level condemnation of the EU response to 'controlling the tide of migrants trying to reach the shore' (*The Independent*, 20 April 2015) followed. Consequently, Europe, accused of 'closing their eyes' to the crisis, will, according to Joseph Muscat, Prime Minister of Malta, be judged in harsh terms. Raising the spectre of previous genocides, comparisons made with the movement of people after the Second World War, coupled with walls and wires, conjures an ugly reality (*The Guardian*, 20 April 2015). The divisive rhetoric of politicians such as David Cameron and other European leaders, and political dialogue that is 'extreme and irresponsible' is equally criticised (Townsend, 2015; in *The Guardian*). Accordingly, UN official Phillipe Douste-Blazy argues that:

> Talk from politicians is of invasion, mass migration. The mood that has been created is one of xenophobia, nationalism, of fear…the wave as the politicians like to call it…in 10 years time will be a tsunami…which needs a long term development plan (cited in Sengupta, 2015; in *The Independent*).

The lack of cohesive planning for a longer-term solution has done little to stem the 'waves of migrants' but much to create a spectre of invasion. When politicians speak out, many do so in their own interests. Matteo Renzi, Italian Prime Minister at the time, declared that the Mediterranean is a sea not a cemetery, all the while promoting military intervention. 'A mass grave is being created in the Mediterranean and European politicians are responsible', stated Loris de Filippi, Italian president of Médecins sans Frontières (*The Guardian*, 20 April 2015). Whilst the 'tide of suffering' is acknowledged, as 'waves of wretched people wash on to the shores' (*The Telegraph*, 20 April 2015) inaction and obfuscation by politicians serves only to shore up their interests, through, in many cases, the introduction of more restrictionist immigration bills (Khan, 2015).

Meanwhile the Mediterranean becomes a Sea of Bodies. A horrible tragedy occurs and a brief interlude transpires. A child's body lies on the shore and the image is shared around the world. The father, Abdullah, who lost his wife Rehan and other son Galip says 'let this be a wake-up call to the world' (Rayner & Squires, 2015; in *The Telegraph*). The death of AylanKurdi provoked a pause, created a silence, a viral reaction, a reality check, a moment to contemplate the value of life. A child, a brief change in reporting; a focus on vulnerable children. A recognition, despite's Littlejohns's claims that most refugees are men (*Daily Mail*, 26 June 2015), that children and families were, are and continue to be caught up in this crisis.

Then, for the politicians, the press and the public, it's back to business as usual. A summit 10 days later in Europe sees the UK commit to a more compassionate policy. On a deeper reading though, and apart from the generous aid package, Britain's policy is regarded as 'deeply cynical' (Moraes, 2015; in *The Independent*) because of the decision to opt out of refugee resettlement. The battle to protect the borders at all costs, even if that means the loss of many lives, continues.

News media ownership, political persuasion and personal experiences are known to shape news stories. Evidence also demonstrates that how stories are framed in the media impacts on public perceptions. This analysis has demonstrated that much of the anti-immigration rhetoric underpinning the Rivers of Blood speech continues to be used as regular currency in the Mediterranean Migrant Crisis.

Media coverage in the main has provided a platform for powerful voices and relies on official sources which 'has helped legitimize the consensus among policymakers while marginalizing alternative views that also might be critical of official policy' (Gulati, 2010: 363). Alternatives to this consensus reporting are required to provide space for different positions and diverse voices. As such 'articles initiated by investigative journalists are more likely to break away from the official frame and report alternative views than articles generated from traditional news beats' (Gulati, 2010: 363). Additionally, through the rise of social media and public reporting of news stories, perhaps a new methodology of creating and disseminating news can be encouraged, as arguments for more responsible, ethical reporting in the traditional press may fall on fallow ground in the midst of a divisive anti-immigration rhetoric fuelled by irresponsible political dialogue. Meanwhile in a migration crisis fuelled by conflict, war and poverty, the Rivers of Blood are long past, whilst the waves of desperate refugees attempting to reach the shores of a better life has turned the Mediterranean into a Sea of Bodies. In the words of one of those who survived:

> they'll risk the journey anyway because they feel it's the least worst option... [In] French we say: 'Cabri mort n'a pas peur du couteau' ... A dead goat doesn't fear the butcher's knife. (Abdo, a Ghanaian interviewee cited in Kingsley, 2015b; in *The Guardian*).

References

Alexander, H. (2015), 'What can be done to end this tide of suffering', *The Telegraph*, 19 April [online].

BBC News (2016), 'Migrant crisis: Mediterranean to have "deadliest year ever"', BBC News, 25 October [online], ttp://www.bbc.co.uk/news/world-europe-37763052 (accessed 19 July 2017).

Bleich, E., Bloemraad, I. & de Graauw, E. (2015), 'Migrants, Minorities and the Media: Information, Representations and Participation in the Public Sphere', *Journal of Ethnic and Migration Studies*, 41 (6), pp.857–73.

Brolan, C. (2002), 'An Analysis of the Human Smuggling Trade and the *Protocol Against the Smuggling of Migrants by Land, Air and Sea* (2000) from a Refugee Protection Perspective', *International Journal of Refugee Law*, 14 (4), pp.561–96.

Brown, L. (2015), 'Thanks for the lift, Britain', *Daily Mail*, 8 June [online].

Burleigh, M. (2015); 'We must reclaim Europe's borders to stop such tragedies repeating themselves', *Daily Mail*, 21 April [online], ttp://www.dailymail.co.uk/news/article-3048032/We-reclaim-Europe-s-borders-stop-tragedies-repeating-MICHAEL-BURLEIGH.html (accessed 19 July 2017).

Chapman, J. (2015), 'Migrants swarm to Britain', *Daily Express*, 19 August [online].

NíChonghaile, C. (2015); 'People smuggling: how it works, who benefits and how it can be stopped', *The Guardian*, 31 July [online], ttps://www.theguardian.com/global-development/2015/jul/31/people-smuggling-how-works-who-benefits-and-how-to-put-stop (accessed 19 July 2017).

Day, M. & Wright, O. (2015); 'Migrant boat disaster: Countries across Europe accused of "closing their eyes" to thousands of deaths in the Mediterranean', *The Independent*, 19 April [online].

Donato, K.M. & Armenta, A. (2011), 'What We Know About Unauthorized Migration', *Annual Review of Sociology*, 37, pp.529–43.

Doughty, S., Drury, I. & Stevens, J. (2015), 'Migrants: How Many More Can We Take?', *Daily Mail*, 28 August [online].

Eurostat (2017), 'Migration and Migrant Population Statistics', *Eurostat* [online], ttp://ec.europa.eu/eurostat/statistics-explained/index.php/Migration_and_migrant_population_statist ics (accessed 19 July 2017).

Fisher, L. & Waterfield, B. (2015), 'EU plan to destroy boats of human traffickers', *The Times*, 21 April [online], ttps://www.thetimes.co.uk/article/eu-plan-to-destroy-boats-of-human-traffickers-zbdfmr5p32l (accessed 19 July 2017).

Fojas, C. (2008), *Border Bandits: Hollywood on the Southern Frontier*, Austin: University of Texas Press.

Freeman, C. (2015); 'The Med is now the most dangerous border in the world', *The Telegraph*, 17 April [online], ttp://www.telegraph.co.uk/news/uknews/immigration/11543336/The-Med-is-now-the-most-dangerous-border-in-the-world.html (accessed 19 July 2017).

Gammeltoft-Hansen, T. (20018), 'The Refugee, the Sovereign and the Sea: EU Interdiction Policies in the Mediterranean', *DIIS Working Paper no 2008/6*, Copenhagen: Danish Institute for International Studies.

Gulati, G.J. (2010), 'News Frames And Story Triggers In The Media's Coverage Of Human Trafficking', *Human Rights Review*, 12 (3), pp.363–79.

Haynes, D. (2015), 'Britain to confront traffickers in Med', *The Times*, [online].

Henderson, B. & Squires, N. (2015), 'Europe ready to declare war on people traffickers', *The Telegraph*, 23 April [online].

Khan, O. (2015), 'How far have we come? Lessons from the 1965 Race Relations Act', Equality and Human Rights Commission [online], ttps://www.equalityhumanrights.com/en/our-work/blogs/how-far-have-we-come-lessons-1965-race-relations-act (accessed 19 July 2017).

Kingsley, P. (2015a), 'Anger over EU's 'slave trade' rhetoric as naval operations begin in Mediterranean', *The Guardian*, 21 May [online], ttps://www.theguardian.com/world/2015/may/21/anger-eu-slave-trade-rhetoric-naval-operations-migration-mediterranean (accessed 19 July 2017).

Kingsley, P. (2015b), 'Risking death in the Mediterranean: the least bad option for so many migrants', *The Guardian*, 17 April [online], ttps://www.theguardian.com/world/2015/apr/17/death-mediterranean-africans-migrant-sea-libya (accessed 19 July 2017).

Kingsley, P., Traynor, I. & Kirchgaessner, S. (2015), 'EU holds migrant boat crisis talks as more deaths reported', *The Guardian*, 20 April [online], ttps://www.theguardian.com/world/2015/apr/20/eu-ministers-meet-migrant-crisis-talks-mediterranean-death-toll-rises (accessed 19 July 2017).

Kingsley, P. & Traynor, I. (2015), 'EU borders chief says saving migrants' lives "shouldn't be priority" for patrols', *The Guardian*, 22 April [online], ttps://www.theguardian.com/world/2015/apr/22/eu-borders-chief-says-saving-migrants-lives-cannot-be-priority-for-patrols (accessed 19 July 2017).

Littlejohn, R. (2015), 'Border controls? Who do you think you are kidding…', *Daily Mail*, 26 June [online].

Manzoor, S. (2008), 'Black Britain's darkest hour', *The Observer*, 28 February [online], ttps://www.theguardian.com/politics/2008/feb/24/race (accessed 19 July 2017).

McQuade, A. (2015),'Migrant crisis: smuggling or trafficking? Politicians don't seem to know', *The Guardian*, 22 April [online], ttps://www.theguardian.com/global-development/2015/apr/22/migrant-crisis-smuggling-trafficking-politicians-dont-seem-to-know (accessed 19 July 2017).

Milmo, C. & Day, M. (2015a), 'UN human rights chief: EU "is turning Mediterranean into a vast cemetery"', *The Independent*, [online].

Milmo, C. & Day, M. (2015b), 'Migrant boat disaster: Leading aid and human rights groups accuse Britain of fuelling refugee crisis', *The Independent*, 20 April [online], ttp://www.independent.co.uk/news/world/migrant-boat-disaster-leading-aid-groups-accuse-britain-of-fuelling-refugee-crisis-10191014.html (accessed 20 July 2017).

Moore, S. (2015), 'On immigration, the language of genocide has entered the mainstream', *The Guardian*, 20 April [online], ttps://www.theguardian.com/commentisfree/2015/apr/20/immigration-language-of-genocide-british-politics (accessed 20 July 2017).

Interpol (2017), 'People smuggling', Interpol [online], ttps://www.interpol.int/en/Crime-areas/Trafficking-in-human-beings/People-smuggling (accessed 20 July 2017).

Moraes, C. 2015), 'EU states are losing sight of our shared values as the world watches us deal with the refugee crisis', *The Independent*, 9 September [online], ttp://www.independent.co.uk/voices/eu-states-are-losing-sight-of-our-shared-values-as-the-world-watches-us-deal-with-the-refugee-crisis-104926 40.html (accessed 20 July 2017).

Philo, G., Briant, E. & Donald, P. (2013), *Bad News For Refugees*, London: Pluto Press.

Powell, E. (1968), Address to the Conservative Association Meeting, Birmingham Conservative Association, 20 April [transcript].

Rayner, G. & Squires, N. (2015), ''My kids have to be the wake-up call to the world', *The Telegraph*, 4 September [online].

Reynolds, M. (2015), 'Send in Army to Halt Migrant Invasion', *Daily Express*, 30 July [online].

Sengupta, K. (2015, 'Migrant crisis: UN official Philippe Douste-Blazy reveals the harrowing sights he encountered among refugees arriving on Lampedusa', *The Independent*, 1 September [online], ttp://www.independent.co.uk/news/people/migrant-crisis-un-official-philippe-douste-blazy-reveals-the-harrowing-sights-he-encountered-among-10481986.html (accessed 20 July 2017).

Siddique, H. & Weaver, M. (2015), 'Refugee crisis: Hungary uses teargas and water cannon at Serbia border – as it happened', *The Guardian*, 16 September [online], ttps://www.theguardian.com/world/live/2015/sep/16/first-refugees-head-for-croatia-after-hungarys-border-crackdown-live-updates (accessed 20 July 2017).

Spindler, W. (2016), UNHCR Press Briefing, Palais Des Nations, Geneva, 20 September [Briefing].

The Sun (2015), 'Brits tell Cameron: Draw a red line on immigration or else', *The Sun*, 5 April [online], ttps://www.thesun.co.uk/archives/politics/433104/brits-tell-cameron-draw-a-red-line-on-immigration-or-else/ (accessed 20 July 2017).

Thorbjørnsrud, K. (2015), 'Framing Irregular Immigration in Western Media', *American Behavioral Scientist*, 59 (7), pp.771–82.

Townsend, M. (2015), 'Migrant boat disaster: "irresponsible" rhetoric blamed for failure to restart rescue', *The Guardian*, 18 April [online], ttps://www.theguardian.com/world/2015/apr/18/mediterranean-migrant-rescue-operation-rhetoric-blamed (accessed 20 July 2017).

Travis, A. (2015), 'EU summit to offer resettlement to only 5,000 refugees', *The Guardian*, 23 April [online], ttps://www.theguardian.com/world/2015/apr/22/most-migrants-crossing-mediterranean-will-be-sent-back-eu-leaders-to-agree (accessed 20 July 2017).

Traynor, I. (2015), 'EU draws up plans for military attacks on Libya targets to stop migrant boats', *The Guardian*, 20 May [online], ttps://www.theguardian.com/world/2015/may/10/eu-considers-military-attacks-on-targets-in-libya-to-stop-migrant-boats (accessed 20 July 2017).

UK Home Office (2015), *Modern Slavery Act 2015*, London: The Stationary Office.

UN General Assembly (200), *Protocol to Prevent, Suppress and Punish Trafficking in Persons, Especially Women and Children, Supplementing the United Nations Convention against Transnational Organized Crime*, United Nations [online], https://www.osce.org/odihr/19223?download=true (accessed 20 July 2017).

UNHCR. *Interception of Asylum-Seekers and Refugees: The International Framework and Recommendations for a Comprehensive Approach*. UN Doc. No. EC/50/SC/CRP.17, United Nations ttp://www.unhcr.org/4aa660c69.pdf (accessed 20 July 2017).

Part 4:

Screening Sea Creatures

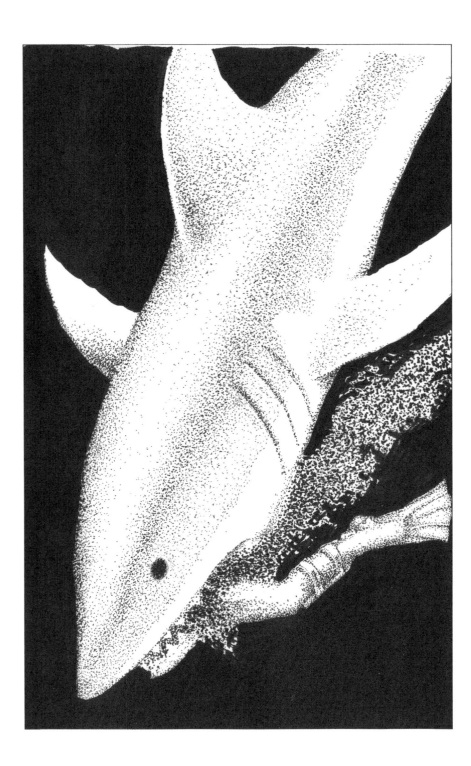

Chapter 11

Becoming-Shark?
Jaws Unleashed, the Animal
Avatar, and Popular Culture's
Eco-Politics

Michael Fuchs

The great white shark starring in *Jaws* (Steven Spielberg, 1975) has generated a host of different interpretations. For example, in one of the earliest scholarly engagements with the movie, Peter Biskind claims that '[t]he shark [...] can only be the young man's sexual passion, a greatly enlarged, marauding penis' (1975: 1). Similarly, Dan Rubey has argued that 'the shark reflects a disguised hatred of women and the preoccupation of our society with sadistic sexuality', which he links to various 'predatory and irresponsible' human actions (1976: 20). While Biskind and Rubey understand the ocean predator as a masculine figure, Jane Caputi has read the movie 'as a full-blown male nightmare', in which the great white shark symbolizes 'not only [...] castration, but also [...] abortion' and embodies a number of feminine figures, including 'the untamed female, the Mother, the *vagina dentata*, the Lesbian, the White Goddess, [...] the wild, the unconscious' (2004: 35–36; italics in original).

Robert Torry has moved away from this primarily gendered thinking and suggested that the shark represents the Vietcong, which is why the movie is an 'obvious wish fulfillment narrative of the annihilation of a murderous, devious and implacable enemy' (1993: 27). More recently, David Ingram has dissected the *Jaws* franchise from a green cultural studies perspective, concluding that the movies reduce the fish to 'a threatening automaton, needing to be controlled and put in its place by human action' (2000: 90). Faced with such an abundance of different interpretations, one may find solace in Fredric Jameson's conclusion that the multiplicity of interpretations 'suggests that the vocation of the symbol – the killer shark – lies less in any single message or meaning than in its very capacity to absorb [...] all of these quite distinct [meanings]' (1979: 142). Nigel Morris has continued this line of thinking, remarking that '[t]he shark' thus 'ceases to be a metaphor' and comes to represent 'nothing other than its terrifying concrete presence' (2007: 53).

The video game *Jaws Unleashed* (Appaloosa, 2006) puts players in control of this body that either symbolizes little more 'than its terrifying concrete presence' or becomes a typical monster, which functions as a 'meaning machine' capable of producing an excess of meaning, as Judith Halberstam has famously explained (1995: 21). To be sure, the animal avatar is 'the user's representative in the virtual universe' (Filiciak, 2003: 89) and defines 'what [...] players are able to do in the game-world' and 'how they do it' (Rouse, 2005: 310). Two questions central to approaching *Jaws Unleashed* from a ludologically oriented green cultural studies perspective emerge from these basic understandings of the player–avatar connection: (a) What can the fact that players control a virtual great white shark tell us about the relationships between the player and the avatar, on the one hand, and the human and the nonhuman, on the other? (b) Since the avatar functions as a tool for the player to act in the gameworld, does this not imply that some sort of agency is bestowed upon the shark-avatar? Does this implication convey any larger messages about shark agency in material reality?

Tellingly, in her BFI companion to *Jaws*, Antonia Quirke maintains that sharks are 'unanthropomorphisable' (2008: 6). However, in this chapter, I would like to suggest that the connection between the player and the digital creature established through the avatar generates a human–avatar–shark–computer hybrid which, as the somewhat cumbersome descriptor implies, indeed features a human component. As such, the virtual shark is, at least to some extent, anthropomorphized, but at the same time, the human player becomes entangled with the nonhuman, de-anthropomorphized, if you will. My exploration of this networked connection, which is full of potentials, will be part of a larger investigation of *Jaws Unleashed*'s green politics. By dissecting its ludic and narrative components, I will demonstrate that the video game finds itself struggling with its ecological message, seemingly unsure what ideas it tries to communicate.

Introducing *Jaws Unleashed*

Jaws Unleashed was released for the PlayStation 2, the original Xbox, and Windows in 2006. The game's story is set in Amity Island, thirty years after the first movie in the *Jaws* franchise. The nearby 'sea island', the opening voiceover explains in marketing-speak, is 'a great attraction' for tourists. Due to the 'recent increase in [the seal] population', Amity Island's governing bodies and the tourism industry expect that the community will experience a great summer (financially, that is). However, when the voiceover mentions the rising number of seals in the area, players can suddenly see a shark appearing and taking down one of the marine mammals. The underlying logic seems apparent enough: great white sharks feed on seals; accordingly, a growing seal population attracts more of these large predators. The voiceover continues, '[N]ew partnerships with corporations such as EnvironPlus will allow us to open our doors to even more visitors'. The visuals do not necessarily support the positive image painted by the voiceover, as first a group of smaller sharks and subsequently a great white attack a submarine sent down to the ocean floor by EnvironPlus. Similar to how the commercial excesses of the Fourth of July weekend brought loads of tasty pieces of human meat to Amity Island in the original movie, Amity's continued development of its tourism industry has attracted an anthropophagic monster in the video game.

The tutorial introduces players to the gameplay mechanics: Basically, the shark can swim, use the tail to stun prey and opponents, bite and eat. In the course of the tutorial, players learn that the shark needs to constantly eat in order to survive and that feeding on jellyfish is not necessarily the best idea, as this diet paralyzes the avatar for a few seconds, turning it into an easy target for attacks. Similarly, when EnvironPlus's research submarines (the so-called 'seaseekers') are nearby, the shark's health meter is drained; accordingly, players and the shark they control are tasked to destroy these research vessels whenever they are in sight. In addition, the video game features a skills tree, which allows players/the shark to develop fancy new abilities, such as spectacular jumps out of the water in order to crash boats, as the game progresses. Overall, the tutorial draws up what Jesper Juul has called the 'general contract' of the game (2013: 29), as it lays out the general parameters of how to survive and how to succeed in *Jaws Unleashed*.

Toward the end of the tutorial, the shark demolishes a few boats, kills a handful of fishermen, divers and swimmers, and eventually destroys a pier, which causes the authorities to step in. A research vessel catches the shark and takes it to a SeaWorld-type theme park reminiscent of the one seen in *Jaws 3-D* (Joe Alves, 1983). Despite public protest to 'free the shark' (as signs in the gameworld suggest), the mayor, true to the franchise, decides to showcase the shark, believing that the animal will 'draw crowds in record numbers'. Michael Brody (older son of Chief Brody and star of the last two movies) warns the mayor, '[W]e are not prepared to display him in the show room tank', only for the mayor to respond, 'Nonsense! The word has already spread. Give the people what they want, Brody'.

Stephen Heath famously wrote that 'the ideology of *Jaws* is clear enough [...]. Mayor Larry Vaughan [...] serves his electors [...] by hushing up a shark attack' (1985: 510). The mayor in *Jaws Unleashed*, likewise, seeks to cover up the fact that the shark killed a couple of people in view of the almighty dollar's seductive powers. As players subsequently guide the animal through the oceanarium, killing human beings, seals, and dolphins on the way, the fish's insatiable appetite outs the predatory excesses characteristic of twenty-first-century capitalism.

When the shark ends up in a killer whale's show tank, the confrontation between these two ocean predators (the first boss fight in the game) becomes a spectacle for the masses gathered in the arena, which concludes with a simultaneously visually excessive and telling brief cinematic moment in which the shark jumps out of the water with the orca in its jaws and tears the aquatic mammal in two in mid-air. With the killer whale out of the way, the great white can return to the freedom of the ocean. Despite the shark's rampage through the aquarium, the mayor stresses that '[t]here is no threat to the safety of vacationers or the citizens of Amity'. Like his father before him, Michael unwillingly becomes complicit in the exploitation of human and nonhuman lives when he announces, 'The threat is minimal, and we'll soon have the shark tracked and captured'.

Once the player has completed the tutorial, *Jaws Unleashed* transforms into a so-called 'sandbox' game, a genre exemplified by popular games such as *Grand Theft Auto III–V* (DMA Design, 2001; Rockstar North, 2008; Rockstar North, 2013), *Red Dead Redemption* (Rockstar San Diego, 2010), and *Mafia III* (2K Games, 2016). This video game genre combines a main plot, played out in successive story missions, and side quests, which are irrelevant to the narrative arch, but allow players and their avatars to refine their skills. In *Jaws Unleashed*'s main story, the shark eventually kills the mayor, a shark hunter tasked to exterminate the beast, and Michael Brody. In clear contrast to the movies, *Jaws Unleashed* 'turn[s] the shark into the outright hero of the narrative', as Ian Hunter has pointed out (2016: 183, no. 37). While a typical animal monster narrative 'tells the story of how a particular animal or an animal species commits a transgression against humanity and then recounts the punishment the animal must suffer as a consequence' (Gregersdotter, Hållén and Höglund, 2015: 3), in *Jaws Unleashed*, the shark evades the human counter-strikes and survives until the end. The side quests, on the other hand, consist of tasks such as killing lifeguards before they can return to the beach, slaughtering seals before an animal lover can rescue them, destroying helicopters, and throwing swimmers at buoys – campy entertainment at its finest.

As my few words on the first boss fight and my brief sketches of the side quests may have already suggested, *Jaws Unleashed* is schlock; the video game equivalent of a low-budget exploitation movie. Indeed, as Mikel Reparaz remarks in an article written for *Games Radar*, '[I]t's possible to enjoy *Jaws Unleashed* on the same level as a bad movie, and it may be the only bad game for which this is true' (2009). While the game's visual excesses will seem rather tame to contemporary players (in part due to its antiquated graphics), it depicts violence in gratuitous detail – you may tear off swimmers' limbs and heads, eat them, let them bleed to death, or wait for smaller sharks to finish up the carnage you started. In addition, the game features explosions galore and its plot (originally advertised as 'realistic' [Dunham, 2004]) defies logic, to put it mildly. For example, the shark not only understands the connection between an ID card and the opening mechanism of a gate, but is, moreover, able to use the ID by way of carrying a researcher to the card reader.

Keza MacDonald's review for *Eurogamer* makes the cognitive disconnect between the tasks players are asked to complete and the avatar they control explicit, writing that when confronted with the problem of retrieving the ID card to open the gate, she wondered, 'I'm a *giant monster shark*, how am I supposed to even use an ID card?' (2006; italics in original). As the game's story unfolds, the shark performs similar tricks on a constant basis, as it, for example, uses explosive barrels to blow up a chemical refinery and destroys control mechanisms to stop EnvironPlus's exploitative practices. Both the game's narrative and its gameplay mechanics are simple, but *Jaws Unleashed* is a rather difficult game, in large part due to the atrocious controls and irritating camera perspective. To quote from MacDonald's review again, the video game is filled with 'broken nonsense' (2006). In particular, the 'awkward control, [...] horrible, horrible camera, completely bizarre mission design and countless smaller, less fundamental annoyances' (MacDonald, 2006) make playing *Jaws Unleashed* an often frustrating experience. However, as someone not immune to the strange attractions of all things trash, causing havoc around Amity Island can also be surprisingly entertaining.

Connecting with the Shark

The first quotation taken from MacDonald's review of *Jaws Unleashed* ('I'm a *giant monster shark*') points at a question game studies scholars have been struggling with for years: the relationship between players and the avatars they play as. This connection is established in the opening moments of any given game, as players are confronted with a new situation which they not only need to make sense of but which also tempts them in a variety of ways.

Jaws Unleashed opens with loading screen, followed by the title menu. This animated title menu does not give away too much information on the game itself, as a great white shark moves through a harbour to the iconic tune of the *Jaws* theme. Launching a new game sets in motion the aforementioned opening cinematic, in which the great white shark players are about to control is a constant presence. While the opening cinematic introduces the world players will explore in, and experience through, the game, the video only provides a tentative clue as to whom players will play as. This implicit hint is established through the intertextual knowledge that a character incarcerated in the opening cinematic will most likely be for the player to free and/or control. As soon as players take control of the virtual shark, they are 'thrown into a new world', as Martin Heidegger might say (1996: 165); introduced to a world 'under the sea'. This new worldview is both confusing and attractive to players. The tutorial then guides them through the controls, helping them to settle into the world, as they begin to inhabit not only the virtual world, but also the avatar's body. As Katie Salen and Eric Zimmerman have suggested, the avatar thus becomes:

a persona through which a player exerts him or herself into an imaginary world; this relationship can be intense and emotionally 'immersive'. However, at the very same time, the character is a tool, a puppet, an object for the player to manipulate according to the rules of the game. In this sense, the player is fully aware of the character as an artificial construct. (2004: 453)

Salen and Zimmerman's explanation highlights the dualism at the heart of the avatar. On the one hand, the avatar allows the player to extend into the game space from the physical space outside it. On the other hand, the avatar allows the player to virtually occupy the game space. As a result, players, the interface, the computer/video gaming console and the virtual worlds become entangled, as players step into a complex relationship with the machine producing the virtual world and the avatar and characters inhabiting it. This connection is characterized by a constant and (potentially) everlasting process of becoming, primarily acted out through the liminal tools of the interface and the avatar.

Video games are 'half-real' (Juul, 2005); similarly, avatars are located in a netherworld between the real and the fictional. As Jesper Juul points out in the opening lines of *Half-Real* (2005): '[V]ideo games are *real* in that they consist of real rules with which players actually interact, and in that winning or losing a game is a real event. However, when winning a game by slaying a dragon, the dragon is not a real dragon but a fictional one'. Accordingly, '[t]o play a video game is [...] to interact with real rules while imagining a fictional world, and a video game is a set of rules as well as a fictional world' (2005: 1; italics in original). The avatar, likewise, simultaneously operates according to the principles of fiction and performs in the real world. The shark in *Jaws Unleashed* follows the (fictive and fictional) protocols of shark behaviour established in the movies. At the same time, however, the virtual shark assumes a presence in the players' world while they are playing the game. As Jonathan Boulter diagnoses, '[W]hen I am alone with my game console, [...] I assume the role, the identity of the avatar', as '[t]he avatar [...] extends my identity and my space' (2015: 8). Colin Cremin, likewise, argues that during gameplay, '[t]he lines separating [...] digital and material worlds dissolve in the space of becoming' (2016: 98). In the words of Donna Haraway, the connection between players and their avatars is defined by 'transgressed boundaries, potent fusions, and dangerous possibilities' (1999: 275).

One of the 'potent fusions' *Jaws Unleashed* opens up is located in the ways in which the video game allows players to imagine another way of being, temporarily inhabiting a space and body the player cannot inhabit outside the virtual realm created by the interaction with the computer/console. The video game promises a momentary bodily extension and 'a certain kind of seamless commingling of subjectivities' (Boulter, 2015: 30). After all, although the virtual great white shark appears to be a 'passive surface [...] on to which [players can] inscribe imagining and ordering of all kinds' (Philo

& Wilbert, 2000: 5), the shark is, in fact, a plurality, created not only out of the collaborative efforts of dozens of programmers and writers, but also out of the dialogic relationship between players and the game, all infusing their identities into the avatar. Accordingly, the processes underlying the player–avatar relationship imply 'the end of the autonomous bourgeois monad or ego or individual' (Jameson, 1991: 15) and replace it with a networked, posthuman self.

In her book *Animalia Americana*, Colleen Glenney Boggs suggests that 'animals function [...] as the ground from which subjectivity becomes possible' (2013: 116). However, in *Jaws Unleashed*, the simulated shark serves a different function. Hans-Georg Gadamer has argued that play only 'fulfills its purpose' when 'the player loses himself' in the activity (2004: 103). While his decision to use the phrase 'loses himself' could be considered metaphoric, Gadamer goes on to stress that 'there are no subjects who are behaving "playfully"' (2004: 103). And herein lies one of the 'dangerous possibilities' *Jaws Unleashed* opens up: During the 'molecular' (Deleuze & Guattari, 1987) experience of becoming-avatar, players leave behind (parts of) their humanity and momentarily become something else, a hybrid creature entangled with human, shark, avatar and computer. Potentially, these becomings, which spread rhizomatically and in unanticipated ways, could upset (or at least challenge) the established anthropocentric world-view, in which humankind sits simultaneously atop and apart from the rest of the world.

The Contradictions of Animal Representations

Indeed, the game text seems to support this message to the point that the video game could be said to flaunt its environmentalist moral. As early as the second main mission, human characters are seen dumping non-descript barrels into the ocean. The facts that the characters perform this action in the vicinity of a refinery and that the barrels explode upon contact suggest that the video game confronts players with a distorted idea of waste man-agement. The next main mission similarly begins with a brief cinematic showing a cargo vessel inadvertently dropping barrels of toxic waste into the ocean. The narrative's ecological subtext is then made explicit when Michael Brody stresses that the machines employed by EnvironPlus 'are having a dramatic effect on the local shark population. It's causing them to approach human settlements and to become increasingly more violent'. Here, the game's narrative highlights how humankind's interventions in natural systems can have negative effects on the ecosystem in question. This mes-sage is supported by a side mission in which the shark destroys the luxurious mansions of EnvironPlus executives and kills the suits. In fact, one may even argue that *Jaws Unleashed* integrates its environmentalist message into the gameplay mechanics, as the negative effects of the presence of EnvironPlus's vessels on the shark's health meter suggests that the company sucks the life blood out of the nonhuman world.

With all of these ideas in mind, the great white shark controlled by players becomes an agent enacting nature's revenge. Here, *Jaws Unleashed* taps into one of the more prominent generic scripts of animal horror:

> An important tradition of animal horror cinema envisages a just and necessary animal revenge. Just as centuries of geographical and epistemic colonisation was disrupted by anticolonial struggle, decolonisation, and postcolonial theory, the exploitation of animals and their habitats is sometimes imagined by animal horror cinema as the real horror that forces animals to respond with disturbing violence. (Gregersdotter, Hållén and Höglund, 2015: 10–11)

Typical of the genre, the narrative thus centres on the conceptual divide between the human and the nonhuman. At the same time, however, the game text opens up spaces in which the spatially and conceptually separated species meet and interact with one another. *Jaws Unleashed* exacerbates this process through the connection between the shark avatar and the human player.

These positive understandings of its eco-politics are what the video game apparently aims for. However, in his assessment of Hollywood movies' green politics, Ingram diagnoses that these texts often exploit their alleged environmentalist concerns. Instead of wholeheartedly committing to their purported 'concern with non-human nature, whether wilderness or wild animals', these movies tend to 'conform to Hollywood's commercial interest in anthropocentric, human interest stories' (Ingram, 2000: 10). Likewise, I would argue, *Jaws Unleashed* fails to convey the ideas it apparently seeks to communicate, as the video game's message relies as much on the conceptual divide between the human and the nonhuman world as it promises to tear the wall separating the two down.

In this context, John Berger has famously pointed out that the relationship between human and nonhuman animals is characterized by 'a narrow abyss of non-comprehension' (1991: 5). Humans cannot really understand animals or perceive the world through their eyes, and neither can animals really understand humans or perceive the world through human eyes. Michael Brody's explanation that some 'machines are causing [the sharks] to approach human settlements and to become more violent' could be said to be such a misunderstanding. While Brody's attempts at intervening in EnvironPlus's practices on behalf of the sharks (and other species living in Amity's waters) most definitely have the creatures' best interests in mind, his statement presents an anthropocentric interpretation of the situation, a seemingly rational explanation, which, however, need not truly capture why the sharks' behaviour has, in fact, changed. Somewhat counter-intuitively, the sharks thus become mere vehicles exploited by Brody in support of his environmentalist agenda, thereby establishing an analogy to the shark avatar which, likewise, could be considered a mere tool the player uses for different purposes.

To be sure, players do enter 'into an affective relation with the molar (representational) [shark] to produce a molecular [shark], through assemblages of different kinds and complexities, [swims, bites, and whips its tail] with various magnitudes of intensity (speed, [force]) that affect every aspect of play' (Cremin, 2016: 98). As Colin Cremin continues, whereas '[t]he human imposes her will on the [...] avatar [...], the avatar indicates ways to proceed' and thus 'to exceed [...] what the [player] was, until then, capable of doing' (2016: 101). However, this notion of what the player is capable of doing is always-already pre-defined by the game's code, written by a human programmer – a human source, no matter how influenced that human might have been by nonhuman forces (such as the nature of the nonhuman code, which, ultimately, a human created). As Boulter concludes, the avatar 'is given to us by the game makers, yet we seem to have some control over the avatar, and the avatar itself seems to have, thus, a strange life of its own, the sense that it comes to us from elsewhere, and responds to our immediate control' (2015: 46). The key word here is 'seems', since Boulter is very much aware of the illusory dimensions of the processes at work while playing video games. Accordingly, instead of celebrating the posthumanist potentials the shark avatar opens up and the utopian promises it makes, the role of the virtual shark in *Jaws Unleashed* may be better understood by turning to an earlier conception of the player–avatar relationship. In 2002, video game scholar James Newman stressed that the avatar first and foremost serves to mediate the player's agency. As Newman put it, avatars 'are embodied as sets of available capabilities and capacities. They are equipment to be utilised in the gameworld by the player. They are vehicles' (2002).

Of course, by conceiving of the shark avatar as a vehicle, the simulated animal is transformed into a tool, a machine even, for the human to control and use. Tellingly, this notion echoes ideas expressed in the movie series. In the original film, for example, marine biologist Matt Hooper announced, 'What we are dealing with here is a perfect engine – an eating machine. [...] All this machine does is swim and eat and make little sharks'. Likewise, in *Jaws: The Revenge* (Sargent, 1987), Michael Brody's fellow marine biology student Jake remarks that sharks 'spend half their lives looking for food, and the other eating it'. Yet even though the shark is conceived as little more than a machine in the movies, the anthropophagic beast evades human control for most of each movie, endowing it with an agency of its own. Of course, this implicit acknowledgement of the animal's agency only lasts for a limited amount of time, as humans kill and thus control it relatively easily. After all, killing animals represents 'human power over animals at its most extreme' (Animal Studies Group, 2006: 4).

The great white shark featured in *Jaws Unleashed* may survive and the video game may not necessarily reduce the shark to an eating machine, but the video game depicts a creature bound to cause chaos and havoc, effectively reducing the shark to its jaws. This process is typical of representations of sharks, as Matthew Lerberg has pointed out: '[C]ontemporary portrayals of sharks are not only reductive in scope, but also in their aesthetic approach. These representations of sharks risk reducing all sharks to "Shark" and then subsequently to fin and jaws, which equals *Jaws*' (2016: 35). Writing about the interconnection between late-nineteenth-century media and animals, Akira Mizuta Lippit has insightfully observed: '[W]hile animals were disappearing from the immediate world, they were reappearing in the mediated world of technological reproduction. [...] Animals had found a proper habitat [...] in the recording devices of the technological media' (2000: 25). However, today the stakes are higher. Through intertextual and intermedial displacements, the shark featured in *Jaws Unleashed* ends up having little to do with any kind of shark inhabiting our planet, substituting the real animals with simulations and consequently effacing material reality as (we think) we know it.

And herein lies probably the gravest problem in *Jaws Unleashed*'s eco-politics: Seemingly unaware, the video game seduces players and draws them into a simulated world, which (at the very least momentarily) not simply replaces but usurps the 'real' world. Likewise, the virtual shark usurps sharks in material reality. As a result, actual sharks disappear from players' experiential realities and, in a next step, disappear from material reality.

References

Animal Studies Group (2006) 'Introduction', in Animal Studies Group (eds.), *Killing Animals*. Urbana: University of Illinois Press, pp.1–9.

Biskind, P. (1975) '*Jaws*: Between the Teeth', *Jump Cut* 9, pp.1, 26.

Berger, J. (1991) 'Why Look at Animals?', in *About Looking*, New York: Vintage International, pp.3–28.

Boggs, C.G. (2013) *Animalia Americana: Animal Representations and Biopolitical Subjectivity*. New York: Columbia University Press.

Boulter, J. (2015) *Parables of the Posthuman: Digital Realities, Gaming, and the Player Experience*. Detroit: Wayne State University Press.

Caputi, J. (2004) *Goddesses and Monsters: Women, Myth, Power, and Popular Culture*. Madison: University of Wisconsin Press.

Cremin, C. (2016) *Exploring Videogames with Deleuze and Guattari: Towards an Affective Theory of Form*. Abingdon: Routledge.

Deleuze, G. & Guattari, F. (1987). *A Thousand Plateaus: Capitalism and Schizophrenia*, trans. Massumi, B. Minneapolis: University of Minnesota Press.

Dunham, J. (2004) 'First Look: *Sole Predator*', *IGN*, 8 March [online], ttp://www.ign.com/articles/2004/03/08/first-look-sole-predator (accessed 12 March 2017).

Filiciak, M. (2003) 'Hyperidentities: Postmodern Identity Patterns in Massively Multiplayers Online Role-Playing Games', in Wolf, M.J.P. & Perron, B. (eds.), *The Video Game Theory Reader*. New York: Routledge, pp.87–102.

Gadamer, H.-G. (2004) *Truth and Method*, 2nd Ed., trans. Weinsheimer, J. & Marshall, D.G., London: Continuum.

Gregersdotter, K., Hållén, N., and Höglund, J. (2015) 'Introduction', in Gregersdotter, K., Höglund, J., and Hållén, N. (eds.), *Animal Horror Cinema: Genre, History and Criticism*, Basingstoke: Palgrave Macmillan, pp.1–18.

Halberstam, J. (1995) *Skin Shows: Gothic Horror and the Technology of Monsters*. Durham: Duke University Press.

Haraway, D.J. (1999) 'A Cyborg Manifesto', in During, S. (ed.), *The Cultural Studies Reader*, 2nd Ed. London: Routledge, pp.271–291.

Heath, S. (1985) '*Jaws*, Ideology, and Film Theory', in Nichols, B. (ed.), *Movies and Methods: Volume II*. Berkeley: University of California Press, pp.509–514.

Heidegger, M. (1996) *Being and Time: A Translation of* Sein und Zeit, trans. Stambaugh, J. Albany: State University of New York Press.

Hunter, I.Q. (2016) *Cult Film as a Guide to Life: Fandom, Adaptation, and Identity*. London: Bloomsbury Academic.

Ingram, D. (2000) *Green Screen: Environmentalism and Hollywood Cinema*. Exeter: University of Exeter Press.

Jameson, F. (1991) *Postmodernism; Or, The Cultural Logic of Late Capitalism*. Durham, NC: Duke University Press.

Jameson, F. (1979) 'Reification and Utopia in Mass Culture', *Social Text*, 1, pp.130–148.

Juul, J. (2013) *The Art of Failure: An Essay on the Pain of Playing Video Games*. Cambridge, MA: MIT Press.

Juul, J. (2005) *Half-Real: Video Games between Real Rules and Fictional Worlds*. Cambridge, MA: MIT Press.

Lerberg, M. (2016) 'Jabbering *Jaws*: Reimagining Representations of Sharks Post-*Jaws*', in George, A.E. and Schatz, J.L. (eds.), *Screening the Nonhuman: Representations of Animal Others in the Media*. Lanham, MD: Lexington Books, pp.33–46.

Lippit, A.M. (2000) *Electric Animal: Toward a Rhetoric of Wildlife*. Minneapolis: University of Minnesota Press.

MacDonald, K. (2006) '*Jaws Unleashed*: Jawful', *Eurogamer*, 9 December [online], ttp://www.eurogamer.net/articles/r_jawsunleashed_x (accessed 15 March 2017).

Morris, N. (2007) *The Cinema of Steven Spielberg: Empire of Light*. London: Wallflower Press.

Newman, J. (2002) 'The Myth of the Ergodic Videogame: Some Thoughts on Player–Character Relationships in Videogames', *Game Studies*, 2 (1) [online], ttp://www.gamestudies.org/0102/newman/ (accessed 15 March 2017).

Philo, C. & Wilbert, C. (2000) 'Animal Spaces, Beastly Places: An Introduction', in Philo, C. & Wilbert, C. (eds.), *Animal Spaces, Beastly Places: New Geographies of Human–Animal Relations*. London: Routledge, pp. 1–34.

Quirke, A. (2008) *Jaws*. London: BFI.

Reparaz, M. (2009) 'The 9 most ridiculous things in *Jaws Unleashed*', *Games Radar*, 6 August [online],ttp://www.gamesradar.com/the-9-most-ridiculous-things-in-jaws-unleashed/ (accessed 15 March 2017).

Rouse III, R. (2005) *Game Design: Theory & Practice*, 2nd Ed. Plano, TX: Wordware.

Rubey, D. (1976) 'The Jaws in the Mirror', *Jump Cut*, 10–11, pp.20–23.

Salen, K., & Zimmerman, E. (2004) *Rules of Play: Game Design Fundamentals*. Cambridge, MA: MIT Press.

Torry, R. (1993) 'Therapeutic Narrative: *The Wild Bunch*, *Jaws*, and Vietnam', *The Velvet Light Trap* 31, pp.27–38.

Verevis, C. (2016) 'Vicious Cycle: *Jaws* and Revenge-of-Nature Films of the 1970s', in Klein, A.A. and Palmer, R.B. (eds.), *Cycles, Sequels, Spin-Offs, Remakes, and Reboots: Multiplicities in Film and Television*. Austin: University of Texas Press, pp. 96–111.

Films and Video Games

Grand Theft Auto III (2001) [Video Game] U.S.A.: DMA Design.

Grand Theft Auto IV (2008) [Video Game] U.S.A.: Rockstar North.

Grand Theft Auto V (2013) [Video Game] U.S.A.: Rockstar North.

Jaws (1975) [Film] U.S.A.: Universal Pictures.

Jaws 3-D (1983) [Film] U.S.A.: Universal Pictures.

Jaws: The Revenge (1987) [Film] U.S.A.: Universal Pictures.

Jaws Unleashed (2006) [Video Game] U.S.A.: Appaloosa Interactive.

Mafia III (2016) [Video Game] U.S.A.: Hangar 13.

Red Dead Redemption (2010) [Video Game] U.S.A.: Rockstar San Diego.

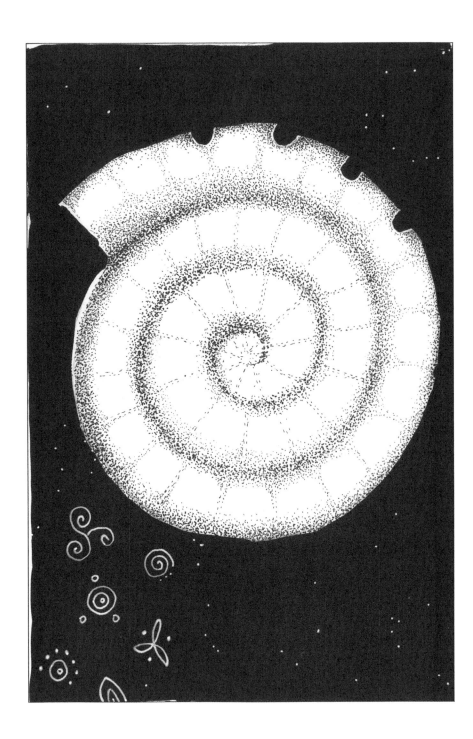

Chapter 12

Songs of the Sea: Sea Beasts and Maritime Folklore in Global Animation

Mark Fryers

Paul Wells provocatively claims that animation is 'arguably the most important creative form of the twenty first century' (2002: 4). Certainly, the study of animation has become more prolific in recent decades, enabled in part by the critical recognition of the Pixar films, the work of Hayao Miyazaki and the continuing wholesale cultural proliferation of the Disney Corporation. In the first two decades of the century, there has been an attendant profusion of animated films featuring the sea and depicting both actual sea creatures and those from mythology and folklore including *Finding Nemo* (Andrew Stanton, 2003), *Legend of the Sea* (Benjamin Toh, 2007) and *Robinson Crusoe* (Vincent Kesteloot & Ben Stassen, 2016).

Technological advances in computer generated imagery, and HD have certainly made the sea a more attractive environment for rendering aquatic imagery, yet the fascination that this unique environment offers surely extends beyond purely technical considerations. Cultural conceptions of the sea suggest a shift in the cultural relationship between humans and the natural environment, one predicated by a heightened sense of human interaction with the sea and marine creatures. In the twenty first century, literal and philosophic representations of this environment have therefore attained a more forceful and immediate significance as the sea has come to represent a space that literally reflects the actions of humankind, from international trade and commerce, military expansion, human movement and displacement, rising sea levels, natural and unnatural catastrophe, and widespread pollution and despoliation. Using the case studies *The Little Mermaid* (Ron Clements & John Musker, 1989), *Ponyo* (Hayao Miyazaki, 2008), *Song of the Sea* (Tomm Moore, 2014) and *Moana* (Ron Clements & John Musker, 2016), this chapter will examine in close textual and contextual detail, how animation as a form often specifically targeted at juvenile audiences and thus performing an educative function, engages with these issues and positions the sea, sea beasts and sea mythology as significant avatars for human morality and behaviour.

Traditionally, the sea and animation have shared a close relationship. One of the earliest experiments in animated film was pioneering animator Winsor McCay's *The Sinking of the Lusitania* (1918), which dramatized the tragic sinking of the passenger ship. By the 1920s and 1930s, the rise of Disney as well as the consolidation of classical Hollywood sound cinema, afforded animation a reputation for escapism and fantasy as well as fun and frivolity aimed primarily at a juvenile and adolescent audience. In the 1930s, Disney's popular *Silly Symphonies* series featured many sea stories such as *Frolicking Fish* (Burt Gillett, 1930), *Water Babies* (Wilfred Jackson, 1935) and *Merbabies* (Rudolf Ising & Vernon Stallings, 1938) whilst Warner Brothers' rival *Looney Tunes* series offered *The Phantom Ship* (Jack King, 1936) and *Shanghaied Shipmates* (Jack King, 1936). In the same decade, the sailor Popeye was also first introduced on film.

Animation is a global phenomenon, however, and in the intervening years, numerous maritime animations have been produced including the Japanese *The Whale* (NoburoOfuji, 1952, a remake of his 1927 film), *The Golden Fish* (Jirí Trnka, 1951, Czechoslovakia), *The Water Babies* (Lionel Jeffries, 1978, UK) & *Benny's Bathtub* (Jannik Hastrup & Flemming Quist Møller, 1971, Denmark).

To return to Disney, the manner in which the sea, sea beasts and folklore are characterised in their 30s shorts is significant. In *Frolicking Fish*, the titular heroes are typified as playful and cute and bullied by a large black octopus, whilst in *Father Noah's Ark* (Wilfred Jackson, 1933), the placid animals assist in the building of the vessel. In the film, two skunks are deliberately left behind, whilst in *Peculiar Penguins* (Wilfred Jackson, 1934) the playful waterfowl are menaced by a baleful shark. Therefore, animals are routinely characterised as good or evil/undesirable. Anthropomorphism and Judeo-Christian myth are therefore important early subjects for Disney, and subjects that would provide a strong foundation for their later films.

Most interestingly for this study is *King Neptune* (Burt Gillett, 1932), which features the Roman god of the sea conjuring up the beasts of the sea and the sea itself when one of his sultry, playful mermaids is kidnapped by fierce pirates. Here, the kingdom of the sea functions as the natural realm and the human interlopers the miscreants. This is indicative of the manner in which the appropriation of different myths of the sea can alter the characterisation of sea beasts. In Greek mythology, the mermaid or siren was dangerous and destructive, deliberately luring ships to their doom, but by selecting Neptune instead of the Greek Poseidon as ruler of the sea, both the mermaids and octopi are shown to be benign in this example As Wells states, the animated film can function to 'challenge' the realities of the world (2002: 5). In the following examples, it is our approach to the natural world that is being challenged.

Disney's Mythical Sea – *The Little Mermaid* (1989) and *Moana* (2016)

Disney historically has been one of the most successful film companies since the 1920s and its global reach is such that their animated films form early memories for generations of filmgoers. As Ward suggests, they provide 'many of the first narratives children use to learn about the world' (2002: 40). Ward also contends that 'Disney helps shape children's views of right and wrong, their morality…[and] are a significant force in children's moral education' (2002: 40). Therefore, the manner in which Disney depicts the natural environment and the beasts that inhabit it is of great cultural significance.

The Little Mermaid (henceforth *TLM*) rejuvenated the finances of the Disney corporation following a fallow period in the 1980s for traditional animation. After a number of years focusing on original screenplays, in *TLM*, Disney returned to traditional fairy tales by loosely adapting the 1837 Hans Christian Andersen fairy tale of the same name. In Andersen's original, the mermaid falls in love with a prince after recuing him from a shipwreck. She longs to be human and have an eternal human soul (mermaids live for 300 years then turn to sea foam) and makes a deal with a sea witch who offers her human legs in exchange for her voice. The caveats are that the prince has to fall in love with her within three days or she will turn to foam. Also, walking on her human legs induces severe pain and suffering. Mistakenly believing another to be the woman who saved him, the prince falls for her instead, dooming the mermaid to her curse. Her sisters offer her a way out of the curse by offering her a dagger, which if she uses to kill the prince will undo the spell. She can't bear to do this but her sacrifice means she is turned into a sea breeze. As this provides comfort for humans she is granted an eternal soul. The tale has been adapted several times in animated form, perhaps most notably in a Japanese co-production in 1975, which featured Fritz, a talking dolphin as the mermaid's (here called Marina) best friend. The film's narrative adheres closely to the original fairy tale.

Disney's version sanitises the darker elements of the story by allowing the Mermaid, called Ariel in the narrative, to find love with the Prince Eric, or as Colless describes, 'myth is translated into the idiom of melodrama' (2007: 235). The storyline involving the dagger is discarded as is both the quest for an eternal soul and the excruciating pain that results from the acquisition of human legs. In the Disney style, diegetic songs punctuate the narrative and the sea is populated by a plethora of anthropomorphised creatures, who share space with the mer-people, led by Ariel's father, King Triton. Ariel's friends include Sebastian the crab and Flounder the fish.

The film creates a dichotomy between the world of the sea and of the land. Ariel longs to be part of the human world but elsewhere, the sea is presented as a beautiful and exotic space, as encapsulated by Sebastian's song 'Under the Sea'. We are first introduced to underwater spaces over the title credits, as we see the bow of the ship from underneath and through sun-dappled water. We then explore the underwater realm through colourful undersea foliage and with equally radiant, tropical fish, soundtracked by ethereal and angelic singing. This is exacerbated by the introduction of the undersea kingdom of Triton and the mer-people, with the central architecture shaped very much like the Disney castle, thus providing a visual shorthand for magic and wonder. There is colour, light and stimulating textures on a grand scale.

The manner in which certain of the sea creatures are anthropomorphised, creates a cultural indicator of the values and associations 'sea beasts' have within a certain context. Here, fish, crustaceans, seabirds, dolphins and whales are all given friendly and placid demeanours (if sometimes comic and inept, as with Sebastian and Flounder) whilst sharks are characterised as dark, predatory and dangerous- evil by comparison (the blockbuster *Jaws*, Steven Speilberg, 1975, is a significant cultural yardstick here). It is the appearance of the evil sea-witch, Ursula, that provides a useful comparative link to traditional western culture's perception of sea beasts. She is drawn in dark tones and colours, typical of Disney's codification for evil (Ward, 2002: 40). Unlike the mer-people, who share a human torso with the tail of a fish, Ursula appears to have a human torso but the tentacled bottom half of an octopus, thus linking her to the nautical demonic.

The Kraken of Nordic lore is often represented as a tentacled squid/octopus creature that ascends from the dark and cavernous fathoms in order to sink ships. Likewise, the 'here be monsters' element of ancient mariners maps, which signified waters to be avoided, was often illustrated as large, tentacled beasts. As Broad posits, the depths of the sea were 'unknown and unknowable, unconnected to anything remotely human' (1998: 21). This was partially linked to actual rare sightings of the giant squid, whose gigantic appearance and abundance of tentacles would have provided a hellish appearance to unwitting mariners. The association with evil and the horrific is compounded by the fact that the octopus is associated with the night and dark spaces, being a nocturnal creature which sutures itself within the cracks of rocks in order to feed on its prey. Its unusual appearance, ability to transform itself into spaces and slimy texture lend itself to associations of the uncanny.

Likewise, Ursula commands dark and slippery eels (Flotsam and Jetsam) to do her bidding, sucking the life out of poor unfortunates, including Triton at the end. This version of the 'horrific' is turned around in the seafood cooking scene, as seen from Sebastian's point of view, with the chef taking on the sinister, shadowy presence of a creature from a horror movie. The practice of eating fish is linked to Ursula as she devours terrified shrimp within another scene. Ursula is also seen as voyeuristic as she watches events through a cauldron, thus linking her with the evil witches of Disney's *Snow White and the Seven Dwarfs* (David Hand (supervising), 1937) and *Sleeping Beauty* (Clyde Geronimi (supervising), 1959).

Following a period in the late 1990s and early 2000s attempting to court a young male audience (including the Indiana Jones style maritime adventure *Atlantis: The Lost Empire*, Gary Trousdale & Kirk Wise, 2001), Disney returned to its successful formula of female princesses in the new century, updating the form to feature a black princess in *The Princess and the Frog* (Ron Clements & John Musker, 2009) and returning to Scandinavian myth with the highly successful *Frozen* (Chris Buck & Jennifer Lee, 2013). *Moana* continued a trend for featuring strong female leads and for offering an ethnically diverse worldview. Here, Disney turned to the mythology of the islands of Polynesia, itself heavily concerned with the sea and seafaring, for the first time and in doing so, offered the reverse dichotomy of Ariel's desire to be part of the landed/human world.

The film opens with the story of TeFiti and Maui, a Polynesian creation myth. It places the sea and femininity as central to the creation of human-kind ('In the beginning, there was only ocean…until the mother island emerged. TeFiti') and male hubris, deception and destruction. TeFiti is the creator whose heart held the power of life. Yet others covet it, including the demigod Maui, capable of shape-shifting into any animal form, who steals it, thus forcing TeFiti to crumble into darkness. He himself loses it to the fire demon Te Ka, as well as losing his enchanted fishhook, the source of his power and potency, and condemning the world to Te Ka's encroaching darkness. The introduction ends with the line: 'Where even now, 1,000 years later, Te Ka and the demons of the deep still hunt for the heart.'

It is then revealed that Moana is the daughter of the chief of a small, self-sufficient island community, to whom she will inherit the title. She is constantly reminded of her duty and discouraged from her yearning desire to explore and adventure on the seas beyond the island. One day, still as a child, the sea presents the heart to her but her father, Chief Tui, snatches her away from the shore and she loses it. As a young adult, she learns that her ancestors were great seafarers, through her sympathetic grandmother, and eventually discovers the fleet of ships on which her ancestors sailed to the island and also that her grandmother retained the heart of the sea the day she found it. As the crops begin to fail and the seas empty of fish due to the encroaching darkness, Moana sets out to find Maui and restore the heart to TeFiti, thus ending the curse of darkness. The reluctant Maui eventually relents, and on retrieving his fishhook, they set out together.

Moana indicates from the outset that the ocean is at the centre of importance, beginning with the line 'In the beginning, there was only ocean' and subsequently linking a move away from marine existence with ignorance and confusion and an unclear sense of identity: 'we have forgotten who we are'. Navigation and seafaring is a constant ancestral refrain in the text. Moana looks to the sea for inspiration and guidance, bemoaning the fact that, 'I wish I could be the perfect daughter, but I come back to the water', and her link to the sea is also a link back to her true identity as part of a seafaring people, 'we know where we are/we know the way'. In return, the sea 'chooses' Moana to restore harmony, acting as her guide and as a sentient being or sea beast in its own right. Every time she falls off her boat, the sea restores her to her rightful position. Even more explicitly, the sea places itself in the command of Moana, twice in the narrative parting for her in the manner of the biblical parting of the Red Sea for Moses. The sea is friendly and idyllic, vibrant, colourful and exotic, appearing even more so in high definition and as CGI. However, it is also a place to be treated with respect and capable of destruction, as in Tui's cautionary tale about heading out of the reef and losing his friend in a storm.

Aside from the sea itself, the beasts of the deep are similarly divided into categories, bound up with Polynesian folklore. Baby Moana is shown to be at one with the benign creatures, helping a baby turtle find safe passage to the sea from its hatch and fending off the attentions of a seagull (thus suggesting the natural predator–prey relationship). Gramma is also positioned as being in tune with the sea and Moana's spiritual mentor. She is often seen on shorelines dancing the traditional Polynesian dance that echoes the undulation of the sea: 'I like to dance with the water, the undertow and the waves'. She also plays with friendly manta rays and after passing away she also visits Moana in the form of a ray.

The opposite of these friendly conceptions is the giant singing, scavenging crab demigod Tamatoa (an original creation and not drawn from mythology). He provides a comic, singing interlude (much like Sebastian in *TLM*) but is also a scary and intimidating presence, particularly in his singing sequence in which a neon-lit series of shots exposes his giant claws. The monstrous claws and shells of horror films such as *Attack of the Crab Monsters* (Roger Corman, 1957), *Mysterious Island* (Cy Endfield, 1961), and *The Lost Continent* (Michael Carreras, 1968) are invoked here. As a mythological creature, it is Maui the demi-God, who is afforded the most attention. He appears in several different Polynesian mythologies and it is the Hawaiian version of his story that closely represents his characterisation here. Rejected by his parents as a baby and thrown into the sea, he liberated by the Gods and made a demigod – his potency deriving from his fishhook (a symbol of human industry) in a manner similar to Triton's in *TLM*. Yet as the opening narrative describes, he is a trickster and over-ambitious, ultimately responsible for bringing darkness to the world. Although he is ultimately offered redemption by helping Moana restore the ocean and taken pity upon by TeFiti (she lets him keep his fishhook, and therefore re-masculates him) he is presented as a vain, ignorant narcissist, who is dismissive of Moana's qualities as a leader.

Therefore, unlike the patriarchal ocean realm of Triton and the mer-people in *TLM*, whereby the female Ursula was the evil witch, *Moana* not only positions the disrupters and deviants as male in the characters of Maui and Tamatoa, and Moana the strong heroic lead, it also gives creative power to

TeFiti, thus making the ocean (and hence centre of the world) a matriarchy. Life and creation is female and the ocean is the benign but powerful symbol of existence, a characterisation echoed in *Ponyo*.

'Humans treat the sea like their empty, black souls', *Ponyo* (2008)

As with Disney's *The Little Mermaid*, the Japanese animation *Ponyo*, from director Hayao Miyazaki, is loosely adapted from Andersen's original story. Miyazaki is a director who is broadly considered as an 'auteur' whose individual style and thematic concerns are imprinted upon his films. Miyazaki and Studio Ghibli films carry a similar cultural cachet to the Disney and Pixar stables. Indeed, Miyazaki is referred to as a moralist in a similar but different manner to Disney. As Ross describes:

> Perhaps the most important realism of all to Miyazaki and Disney, in different ways, might be called moral: that is, showing that human actions have consequences' (2014: 20)

Whereas *TLM* seems to indicate that heteronormative relations have the highest value, *Ponyo* indicates that respect for the natural world, especially the sea, and a stable balance between the human and animal realm are vital to a healthy, functioning world. Although *Ponyo* and *TLM* share much in common, their treatment of the sea, and land and sea creatures, differ in fundamental ways and *Ponyo* has more in common with *Moana*'s treatment of the sea and sea beasts, indicating a broader and literal sea change of marine depictions.

Ponyo concerns the relationship between Sosuke, a gentle boy who lives with his parents on an isolated house by the sea, and Ponyo, a fish who desires to be human after Sosuke frees her from a bottle. Sosuke's father works at sea whilst his mother, Lisa, works at a retirement home. One of the residents of the home warns Sosuke that unless he returns the 'fish with the human face' to the sea, a tsunami will come and reclaim it. Ponyo's father, the sea wizard Fujimoto, commands the sea to reclaim her but she escapes again, with the help of her brothers and sisters and is borne by the sea back to Ponyo's house, by now sporting human limbs. Angered, Fujimoto creates a tsunami in his pursuit of Ponyo which separates Ponyo and Sosuke from his mother at the retirement home. As they set out to be reunited with his mother, they are greeted by the evacuating townspeople. Following a meeting between Ponyo's mother and Grandmamma, it is agreed that Ponyo can stay human as Sosuke promises to love her.

The film introduces the sea in a similar manner to that of *TLM*. From an underwater perspective, we are introduced to fish and jellyfish and a colourful underwater reef full of marine biodiversity, accompanied by serene, romantic and ethereal music. It is full of grand and romantic images of the sea. At one point Ponyo rides on a giant carpet of golden fish. In this conception, all the beasts of the sea are equally respected and there are no evil sharks or sea demons. Indeed, the sea takes on a sentient appearance, able to move, twist and metamorphise at will. The viewer is also reminded that the sea is a complex and multi-faceted environment as evidenced by a sequence featuring marine life from the Devonian era. The conception of the sea is that of a beast itself, a biomass greater than the sum of its parts. It can take on a sinister form, as in the sequences in which it is commanded by Fujimoto to reclaim Ponyo from the land, appearing as a many-headed eel with beady eyes (not unlike the eels in *TLM*).

When the tsunami is created and fulfils the legend of taking back the land, it is not an act of destruction but a temporary act of assimilation: until harmony is restored. The sea and land cohere seamlessly and peacefully (indeed, the gentle undulations of the grasslands echo those of the waves). The retirement home is covered by an underwater biosphere, which acts as a rejuvenating force for the elderly relatives, giving them vigour and vitality. The conception of the sea, and all the beasts within it, is also governed by the gender of its controller – either the male Fujimoto or the female Grandmamma. Fujimoto appears impotent when faced by the greater power that his partner wields, desperately trying to maintain control but realising his limitations: 'I need to ask for her mother's help here'.

The message that *Ponyo* offers is that the sea and the land must be respected and that only when this mutual respect is engendered can harmony be restored. The beasts in this conception are human beings. The beauty of the sea is tempered by the consistent appearance of human-made detritus floating on the waves or half-buried on the seabed. Indeed, it is a discarded bottle that entraps Ponyo before Sosuke rescues her. This is certainly the attitude offered by Fujimoto, who is disgusted by the human race stating that 'humans are disgusting...all this waste...bilge' and that they have 'empty, black souls'. However, unlike the relative Manichaean morality of Disney's fables, Miyazaki is not considered a dogmatist and there is not a clear dichotomy between the sea and the land. The good and bad in both worlds is evidenced by the love between Sosuke and Ponyo and their struggle with Fujimoto, who, in his insistence on division between the two worlds and general ineptitude, represents the weak link between both states. Not being entirely comfortable on sea or on the land, he may represent what Colless describes as the 'violent traffic between two states' (2007: 230–1).

That *Ponyo* depicts the sea as a space of harmony and humans as potentially beastly by comparison is perhaps surprising when we consider the Japanese context. Japanese folklore is rich in sea demons, such as Watatsumi-no-kami the male god of the sea, Umibozu, a sea spirit that capsizes boats and Funayurei, the spirits of people who died at sea. Indeed, one of the most recognisable Japanese images in western culture is artist Hokusai's *The Great Wave off Kanagawa* (1829–32). Japan is also a country geographically and geophysically situated as highly susceptible to natural disasters, especially earthquakes and tsunamis, one of which was to tragically strike in

Fukushima only three years after *Ponyo*'s release, images of which, especially of stranded ships on the seas, are eerily prefigured within the text. It might be expected, therefore, that the sea would represent a folk demon within Japanese culture, which it is, somewhat, within texts such as the disaster movies *Japan Sinks* (Shiro Moritani, 1973) and *The Sinking of Japan* (Shinji Higuchi, 2006), the monster movie *Gojira* (Ishirō Honda, 1954) in which the creature originates from the South China Sea and the original *Ringu* horror films (Hideo Nakata, 1998 and 1999; Norio Tsuruta, 2000) in which the vengeful spirit Sadako is an incarnation of a sea demon. However, as *Ponyo* posits, the relationship between the sea and the land is less equivocal, with the sea also providing sustenance for the marine industries (the sea provides employment for Sosuke's father). Although it is tempting to assume that the treatment of the sea is down to cultural specificity, the transnational nature of culture is far more complex. Indeed, scholars such as Iwabuchi (2002), Napier (2006) and Denison (2015) resist culturally specific interpretations of anime, invoking the notion of *mukokuseki*, or stateless/odourless textuality. The characterisation of the sea and the natural world in *Ponyo* is likely more a product of the imagination of the writer/director Miyazaki himself. Following the tragic events of 2011, Miyazaki took a personal interest in helping the devastated cultural communities to rebuild, including organising free screenings of his film *The Wind Rises* (2013) for schoolchildren. In interviews, he seemed to echo the ethos espoused in *Ponyo*, suggesting that people come back to the sea for business despite the destruction it is capable of: 'just for our desires and our own benefit we build near the sea, so we forget the dangers in Tokyo' (CNN, 2011). As with *Moana*, the message offered is that the sea and the creatures that inhabit it can function as a benign presence, but respect, humility and balance are necessary for this to be the case.

This is similarly the scenario presented in *Song of the Sea*, an animated film steeped in traditional Irish/Celtic folklore, especially of the sea. In common with Japanese and Polynesian culture, sea and water spirits feature heavily in spiritual evocations of the natural realm. As with *Ponyo* and *Moana*, the beasts of the sea are shown as benign and represent, through their anthropomorphic characteristics, a natural order that is capable of great nurturing if properly respected.

The film focuses on Ben and Saoirse who live in a lighthouse on an isolated island with their widower father Conor. Their mother died giving birth to Saoirse and she has never spoken but is constantly drawn to the sea. After a near accident, their grandmother takes the children to live with her on the mainland. They leave for home on the first night and go on an adventure with fairies, battling the evil witch Macha and her dominion of owls. After getting separated, Saoirse eventually uses her singing voice to turn Macha back to good. They are reunited with their mother on the shoreline, who is now a selkie sea spirit, just like her daughter. Conor begs his wife not to take

193

Saoirse with her as 'she's all we've got'. Their mother accedes and tells them to remember her in their stories and in their songs.

As with the previous examples, there is a nexus of importance in this text around the sea, motherhood, the beasts of the sea and mythology. It cleaves closely to the culturally specific mythology of Celtic Ireland, even more pronounced here than in the previous examples (excepting *Moana*) and there are similarities as well as revealing differences. As with *Ponyo* and unlike *TLM*, the creatures of the sea are benign and good; the interfering spirit here is the land witch Macha (as opposed to the sea witch Ursula in *TLM*). Macha is often characterised in Celtic mythology as being the personification of battle and slaughter, taking on traditional male characteristics (Haining, 1994: 61).

Selkies are derived from Scottish folklore and are sea spirits who can take the form of a seal and are able to shed their skin to live on land. In visual depictions, they very much resemble mermaids, taking a female face and form, as is consistent with their categorisation in *Song of the Sea*. Their appearance as seals echo a general global, anthropomorphised image of seals as cute, benign and playful and who represent the need to conserve the probity of nature against the destructive behaviours of man (the fur trade especially). Their importance to the natural world and ethereal nature is underlined in their presentation in the film, appearing as protectors and guides around the human characters, especially Saoirse, guiding Ben to the chest bearing Saoirse's coat and bearing them all safely during the storm. This point is underlined by the ferryman who takes the children over to the mainland. As the seals follow Saoirse on her travels, he remarks 'there haven't been seals around here for years', both highlighting her importance and the need to conserve the species in a wider sense.

A dichotomy is therefore created between the sea and the land in a manner more in common with *TLM*. The opposite of the benign spiritual beasts of the sea is the evil fowl of the land and air in the form of the owl. Here owls have a sinister depiction and motive, at least until the end, reversing their conception as being benign messengers of good (especially in the recent *Harry Potter* films). Likewise the children are drawn to the sea and island spaces as their spiritual home but forcibly taken from it. The further they are taken from that place and towards the city, the less comfortable, happy and aware they are and travel back at the earliest opportunity, helped and guided by the fairies and sprites (although the natural countryside is also a place of magic, emphasising the conservational message of the text). Again, the sea is presented in a romantic and ethereal manner (especially the underwater sequences) and shorelines, islands and other liminal spaces between two worlds, as places of magic and possibility, but like the other texts, a space that also demands human respect and humility, being capable of great power.

As with the previous examples, the lead female's spiritual home is the sea but ultimately she chooses to be on land for her love of human beings (although, unlike the other examples it is hinted that she can/will return there one day). The sea is also a female and feminine space, with the female protagonists wielding great power. The film also engages with the 'mother nature' paradigm in a maritime context, as with *Ponyo*. This is made explicit in flashbacks to Saoirse's traumatic birth. Her mother goes into the sea when she has complications, declaring 'I have to save our baby'. The mother therefore returns to her Selkie form forever and baby Saoirse is borne back to the land and her father's arms by the waves. The space of the sea is therefore linked to motherhood and the amniotic.

Femininity, Mother Nature and Environmentalism

There is a complicated association with gender that exists throughout human history that positions the sea as a site of gender identification and struggle. Foucault (2006) posited that the sea is characterised as feminine in Western culture as it was seen as irrational and untameable. The central irony is that women were kept away from the sea in patriarchal merchant society. As Stark explains:

> The belief was ancient and ubiquitous that women had no place at sea. They not only were weak, hysterical and feckless and distracted the men from their duties, but they also bought bad luck to the ships they travelled in (1996: 1).

Whereas traditional texts like *Treasure Island* (Robert Louis Stevenson, 1883) positioned the oceanic journey as a male rite of passage, these texts offer the sea as a space of female stridency and empowerment. In each of the examples discussed, there is a tension between the female character's freedom of choice and imposed boundaries. King Triton attempts to stop Ariel mixing with the surface people, chief Tui constantly forbids Moana to go out to sea, Fujimoto seeks to thwart Ponyo's progression into a human (physically forcing her limbs back into her body) and in *Song of the Sea*, Ben places his sister on a leash whilst often pulling her back from the sea. Likewise, strong females constantly threaten the potency of the male characters, with Triton and Maui losing their staff of power and Fujimoto overwhelmed by the power of Grandmamma. There is a tendency to present a motherless child or one in which the mother is temporarily absent, whereby the maternal is displaced on to other characters or the sea itself. Central in this rite of passage paradigm is the role of the female voice as site of agency, which is particularly suited to animation in that singing and performing is of central importance.

The most pronounced is that of the sea as female or a feminine space. Again, the final three examples exemplify this explicitly. In doing so, they engage with the trope of 'mother earth' or 'mother nature', with the natural world exemplified as female and nurturing, yet capable of punishment and rebuke for bad behaviour. This personification of nature as of a 'mother' has provenance in many different cultures, through Ishtar in Mesopotamian and Sumerian culture, Mother Gaia in ancient Greek and the fertility goddesses of pagan culture. By personifying the sea as maternal, these films provide a link back to these conceptions. As Wells states, the 'feminine aesthetic' is 'unique to animation' (1998: 9), which reflects both a proliferation of domestic settings and stories and the increasing influence of female film-makers in the field.

It therefore seems that in the twenty first century, the sea is codified as maternal and nurturing. Whilst *TLM* presents a harmonious undersea kingdom full of good and evil beasts, and offers the sea as a site of wonder, the difference and dichotomy between the two kingdoms is pronounced and they can exist only in tandem not in harmony. However, by the time *Moana* is released, the conception of the sea and sea beasts is markedly different. Not only are the creatures of the sea universally good, but the sea itself is a sentient being, demanding of our respect and conservation. It is only the gods and demigods who cause mischief here. However, the message of conservation is made explicit from the beginning, particularly in the island's self-sufficiency, as is made clear in the village song:

> That's all you need...we share everything we make...we use all parts of the coconut...we make our nets from the fibres....we use the leaves to build fires...we cook up the meat inside...the island gives us what we need.

The same sentiments are shared in *Ponyo*, as Sosuke proudly declares that they have their own generator, propane and water tanks, and he pootles along in a small boat powered by a single candle. There is also a harmony between the sea and the land and the sea is sentient, powerful but benign if treated with proper respect. Although the conservation element is less pronounced in *Song of the Sea*, the sea must be respected and is nurturing. The sea is the source of all existence in all these examples and the farther humanity is distanced from it, and thus from its own identity, the more profane and unhappy humans are. Central within this conception, are different folklores, myths and creation stories associated with the sea and its creatures, which although having provenance within different cultural contexts, offer a remarkable consistency of presentation. It should also be noted that anthropomorphism has its disadvantages. Symptomatic of this is the disproportionate desire to own clownfish that followed *Finding Nemo*, which caused a dangerous shortage and unbalance in the ecosystem (Dengate, 2016).

Conclusion

To return to Wells, these films exemplify his adage regarding animation that:

> the body in animation is a form constantly in flux, always subject to re-determination and reconstruction (1998: 215).

The sea represents the perfect material for flux and also a surface upon which to reflect, another common tendency of animated film (Furniss, 2009: 3). As can be seen, the twenty first century has been awash with animated films depicting the sea and conceptions of the beast that dwell within it, embodying the cultural values of the cultures that produced them. These are present here in films such as *Help! I'm a Fish* (Stefan Fjeldmark, Michael Hegner & Greg Manwaring, 2000) and *A Turtle's Tale: Sammy's Adventures* (Ben Stassen, 2010). As the sea has increasingly been the focus of environmental concerns, animation has offered a space to depict the sea as a site of crucial importance in conserving the natural world, often drawing on classical myth and folklore as a reminder of 'who we are', 'where we came from' and 'what's important to us'. In the end, as *Ponyo* concludes, the natural order must be restored.

References

Andersen, H.C. (1836), *The Little Mermaid* [online], ttp://hca.gilead.org.il/li_merma.html (accessed 20 January 2017).

Broad, W.J. (1998), *The Universe Below: Discovering the Secrets of the Deep Sea*, New York: Touchstone.

CNN (2011), *Hayao Miyazaki and Tsunami CNN Interview 2*,[broadcast], ttps://www.youtube.com/watch?v=zRcnp1m3XSk (accessed 14 April 2017).

Colless, E. (2007), 'Between the Legs of the Mermaid'. In A. Cholodenko, (ed.), *The Illusion of Life II: More Essays on Animation*, Sydney: Power Publications, pp.229–242.

Denison, R. (2015), *Anime: A Critical Introduction*, London: Bloomsbury.

Dengate, C. (2016), 'The 'Finding Nemo Effect' Is Plundering Wild Clown Fish Stocks', *Huffpost*, 11 May [online], ttp://www.huffingtonpost.com.au/2016/05/10/the-finding-nemo-effect-is-plundering-wild-clown-fish-stocks/ (accessed 14 May 2017).

Foucault, M. (1996). *Madness and Civilisation*, New York: Vintage Books.

Furniss, M. (2009), *Animation: Art & Industry*, New Barnet: John Libbey Publishing.

Haining, P. (ed.) (1994), *Great Irish tales of the Unimaginable: Stories of Fantasy and Myth*, London: Souvenir Press.

Iwabuchi, K. (2002), *Recentering Globalization: Popular Culture and Japanese Transnationalism*, Durham: Duke University Press.

Napier, S. (2001), *Anime from Akira to Howl's Moving Castle*, New York: Palgrave Macmillan.

Poignant, R. (1975), *Oceanic Mythology: The Myths of Polynesia, Micronesia, Melanesia, Australia*, London: Hamlyn.

Ross, D. (2014), 'Miyazaki's Little Mermaid: A Goldfish Out of Water', *Journal of Film and Video*, 66 (3), pp.18–30.

Stark, S.J. (1996), *Female Tars: Women Aboard Ship in the Age of Sail*, Constable: London.

Stephenson, R.L. (1884), *Treasure Island*, London: Cassell.

Ward, A.L. (2002), *Mouse Morality: The Rhetoric of Disney Animated Film*, Austin: University of Texas Press.

Wells, P. (1998), *Understanding Animation*, New York: Routledge.

Wells, P. (2002), *Animation: Genre and Authorship*, New York: Columbia University Press.

White, S. (1993), 'Split Skins: Female Agency and Bodily Mutilation in The Little Mermaid,' in J. Collins, H. Radner & Preacher Collins, A. (eds), *Film Theory Goes to the Movies*, New York: Routledge.

Yeats, W.B. (ed.) (1973), *Fairy and Folk Tales of Ireland*, Gerrards Cross: Colin Smythe Limited.

Filmography

Atlantis: The Lost Empire (Gary Trousdale & Kirk Wise, 2001)
Attack of the Crab Monsters (Roger Corman, 1957)
Benny's Bathtub (JannikHastrup & Flemming Quist Møller, 1971)
Father Noah's Ark (Wilfred Jackson, 1933)
Finding Nemo (Andrew Stanton, 2003)
Frolicking Fish (Burt Gillett, 1930)
Frozen (Chris Buck & Jennifer Lee, 2013)
Gojira (Ishir? Honda, 1954)
The Golden Fish (JirfTrnka, 1951)
Harry Potter franchise (2001–2011)
Help! I'm a Fish (Stefan Fjeldmark, Michael Hegner & Greg Manwaring, 2000)
Japan Sinks (Shiro Moritani, 1973)
Jaws (Steven Spielberg, 1975)
King Neptune (Burt Gillett, 1932)
Legend of the Sea (Benjamin Toh, 2007)
The Little Mermaid (Karel Kachyòa;1976)
The Little Mermaid (Ron Clements & John Musker, 1989)
The Lost Continent (Michael Carreras, 1968)
Merbabies (Rudolf Ising & Vernon Stallings, 1938)
Moana (Ron Clements & John Musker, 2016)
Mysterious Island (Cy Endfield, 1961)
Peculiar Penguins (Wilfred Jackson, 1934)
The Phantom Ship (Jack King, 1936)
Ponyo (Hayao Miyazaki, 2008)
The Princess and the Frog (Ron Clements & John Musker, 2009)
Ring (Hideo Nakata, 1998)
Ring 2 (Hideo Nakata, 1999)
Ring 0: Birthday (Norio Tsuruta, 20002000)
Robinson Crusoe (Vincent Kesteloot & Ben Stassen, 2016)
Shanghaied Shipmates (Jack King, 1936)
The Sinking of Japan (Shinji Higuchi, 2006)
The Sinking of the Lusitania (Winsor McCay 1918)
Sleeping Beauty (Clyde Geronimi (supervising), 1959)
Snow White and the Seven Dwarfs (David Hand (supervising), 1937)
Song of the Sea (Tomm Moore, 2014)
A Turtles Tale: Sammy's Adventures (Ben Stassen, 2010)
Water Babies (Wilfred Jackson, 1935)
The Water Babies (Lionel Jeffries 1978)
The Whale (NoburoOfuji, 1952)
The Wind Rises (Hayao Miyazaki, 2013)

Chapter 13

The *Mosasaurus* and Immediacy in *Jurassic World*

Damian O'Byrne

Welcome to Jurassic Park

W hen Stephen Spielberg's *Jurassic Park* was released in 1993, it captured the imagination of cinema goers across the world. Spielberg's tale of a millionaire who uses cutting edge technology to bring dinosaurs back from extinction, in the eponymous theme park, made over $900 million and quickly became the highest grossing film of all time (it was finally surpassed by James Cameron's *Titanic* some four years later). Following the phenomenal success of the first film, the series developed, or many would argue declined, through an inevitable slew of diminishing sequels; *The Lost World: Jurassic Park* (1997) and *Jurassic Park III* (2001) emerged every four years with stubborn regularity and an equally unsurprising drop in box office returns. Indeed, upon seeing the dinosaurs for the second time in the sequel, Jeff Goldblum's jaded cynic Dr Ian Malcolm says: "Oh yeah oooh, ahhhh, that's how it always starts", perhaps mirroring the failing interest of the audience. In addition, whilst *The Lost World: Jurassic Park* was once again directed by Steven Spielberg, by the time *Jurassic Park III* arrived he had stepped back to the role of Executive Producer, perhaps suggesting that even he had lost interest in the franchise. At that point, the series seemed to have become extinct with a rumoured fourth film (which supposedly concerned genetically modified human-dinosaur weaponised hybrids) stuck in development hell for over ten years. However, in the summer of 2015 the series was rebooted with the release of Colin Trevorrow's *Jurassic World*. The film offers a new take on the series from an entirely new creative team (although Spielberg served as Executive Producer once again) and one that counted amongst its population the focus of my chapter – the *Mosasaurus*; at 18 metres long, truly a beast of the deep.

In this chapter, I will be examining the role that the *Mosasaurus* plays in *Jurassic World*, not only as another creature to imperil the human cast but also as the embodiment of a broader ideal that Trevorrow is attempting to convey. The *Mosasaurus* appears in three key scenes in the film, one near the beginning, one in the middle and one at the climax. Each time leaping from the depths to devour someone or something. I will explore the effect and impact of each of these 'leaps' in turn, examining how they function as the latest steps in the way that the *Jurassic Park* franchise has continually striven to immerse viewers within the film universe via the technique of immediacy – when 'the user is no longer aware of confronting a medium, but instead stands in an immediate relationship to the contents of that medium' (Bolter and Grusin, 1999, 24). Having situated the cinema audience as visitors to the fictional park, I will then argue that Trevorrow is actually using the *Mosasaurus* as a way of delivering a hidden ideology about the state of a sequel obsessed Hollywood.

The First Leap – The *Mosasaurus* Feeding Show and Immediacy

The earliest signs that *Jurassic World* would be featuring the first aquatic dinosaur* of the franchise emerged whilst the film was still in production with the appearance of a park map that had been given to extras on the film set. It gave fans of the franchise their first glimpse of the new theme park and at the heart of the island was the *Jurassic World Lagoon*, home to the *Mosasaurus Feeding Show*. As further promotional material appeared for the film, the *Mosasaurus* emerged as one of the tentpole additions to *Jurassic World*, and it quickly became the highest profile new dinosaur to be featured in the marketing materials for the new film. Whilst there were several other additions to *Jurassic World*'s menagerie that had not been seen in previous instalments, the *Mosasaurus* was unique amongst the new arrivals in the exposure she received via posters and trailers.

For fans of the *Jurassic Park* franchise, part of the appeal of the inclusion of the *Mosasaurus* was that the franchise had never featured an aquatic dinosaur before. The various promotional trailers and posters implied that she would be playing a key role in the plot of the new film, a concept all the more appealing given that she must surely be constrained to the watery depths. And so, in the first of many examples of life imitating art, the *Mosasaurus* was marketed to cinema-goers as the most exciting new arrival in *Jurassic World*, just as she is marketed to the park visitors as one of the most exciting attractions. The *Mosasaurus* was the new dinosaur that *Universal* believed would draw consumers into the movie, just as she draws *Jurassic World*'s fictional customers into the park.

The real *Mosasaurus* was a whale-like animal, with an elongated snout akin to a crocodile, that lived during the Cretaceous period around 65 to 70 million years ago. It was a marine reptile that, based on the largest known fossilised skeletons, grew to around 15–18 metres and was a contemporary of other *Jurassic Park* alumni like the *T-Rex* and the *Triceratops*. Of course, Hollywood demands that the dinosaurs in these films should be, as the

---

* For the purposes of this chapter we shall join the cinema-going audiences in adopting the Hollywood definition of a dinosaur rather than the scientific one and ignore the fact that the *Mosasaurus* is not technically a dinosaur but rather an aquatic lizard that lived during the time of the dinosaurs.

park's Chief Geneticist Henry Wu (B.D. Wong) states "bigger, scarier, cooler", and so the specimen seen in *Jurassic World* is at the upper end of this size range at 18 metres in length.

We get our first sight of the *Mosasaurus*, 31 minutes into the film, before the dinosaurs have broken loose throughout the park, when brothers Gray Mitchell and Zack Mitchell (Ty Simpkins and Nick Robinson) sit down to watch the *Mosasaurus Feeding Show* that was teased in the leaked production map. By this point in the film Gray, 11, has already been established as a dinosaur fanatic and is hugely excited about the visit to the park. Zack at age 17 however, is entirely unimpressed with the park, seems irritated to have to babysit his younger brother and is far more interested in using his phone and listening to music through his headphones. The brothers are sat in a huge amphitheatre with several thousand* other guests as a *Jurassic World* staff member introduces the show with some familiar tourist spiel. "Okay folks, let's see if she's still hungry after eating today, she's a little shy so be nice and give her a hand when she comes out" announces the compère as a suspended great white shark is winched out across the lagoon. Gray leans forward in excitement whilst his older brother looks at pictures of his girlfriend on his phone. As Gray desperately tries to get Zack's attention, the *Mosasaurus* leaps from the depths of the lagoon and consumes the shark in one bite, revealing to the audience that the snout of the *Mosasaurus* alone is twice the length of the shark. As the *Mosasaurus* falls back into the lagoon, it creates a huge wave that soaks the assembled crowd, many of whom are wearing *Jurassic World* branded ponchos in anticipation, as they scream and cheer. Suddenly, the bleachers begin to sink beneath the amphitheatre to a submerged viewing area where they continue to cheer and clap as the *Mosasaurus* devours the shark. Even the sullen Zack finds himself moved to applause by the wonder of the event and claps along with the rest of the crowd before excitingly asking his brother, "Do you want to do something else cool?" The scene represents the first time that Zach has displayed any affection towards his younger brother and the message is clear, the *Mosasaurus* is so impressive that even social-media obsessed teenagers will drop their omnipresent phones and be taken in by the spectacle.

Not only is the scene visually impressive for both the cinema-goers and the visitors to the park, but it also contains the first knowing wink to the cinema audience from Trevorrow. As soon as we see the great white shark being winched out across the lagoon, we are reminded of Stephen Spielberg's *Jaws* (1975) as the terrifying antagonist of that film is literally and metaphorically hung out to dry. The connective tissue between *Jaws* and *Jurassic World* goes still deeper given that Spielberg claimed that when he directed the original *Jurassic Park* he was "just trying to make a good sequel to Jaws. On land" (McBride, 2011, 418). This will not be the last time in the film that the *Mosasaurus* of *Jurassic World* echoes Spielberg's early thriller and in a 2015

---

* It is suggested that *Jurassic World* is able to accommodate 30,000 guests.

tabloid celebration of the 40th anniversary of *Jaws*, Brian Viner suggested that the *Mosasaurus* actually "owes her very existence to [the] smaller but equally scary beast" (Viner, 2015) that she devours in this scene. In a world where we are used to our cinematic predators feeding on relatively docile and helpless creatures (mice, gazelles, goats etc.), the *Mosasaurus* devouring a great white shark in a single-bite is a clear message to cinema audiences: move over *Jaws*, this is the new king of the deep.

It is no coincidence that the *Mosasaurus Feeding Show* is presented to the cinema audience in a manner that we know and understand, the amphitheatre, the hostess, the concept of a feeding show for a wild animal, all ring true with our own experiences in theme parks, zoos and, until recently at least, *SeaWorld Orlando** reinforcing the idea that "much of *Jurassic Park* is structured like a ride" (Franklin, 2000, 202). The camera is even situated to give the cinema audience a slightly obscured view of the *Mosasaurus* to recreate the familiar frustrations of fellow guests blocking our view. These techniques of framing and production design are not simply part of the mise-en-scène but rather help to present the *Mosasaurus* in a manner that the cinema audience can relate to, developing the *Jurassic Park* series' long quest to draw its audience into its fictional world.

Throughout the *Jurassic Park* franchise, the film-makers have continually attempted to position the cinema going audience as visitors to the park to allow them to share the experiences and emotions of the characters. Of course, this is hardly unique to the *Jurassic Park* films, indeed, the vast majority of film-makers will use various techniques and devices to draw the viewers into their filmic world in an attempt to increase their audience's emotional investment in the film. However, the *Jurassic Park* films have a unique advantage in that the way in which the fictional characters visit the park, sit in amphitheatres and are blown away by the dinosaurs, is directly mirrored by the cinema audiences who sit in very similar seats and marvel at the computer-generated imagery (CGI) and animatronic dinosaurs. This mirrored relationship between the fictional characters and the real-world audience offers the film-makers a unique ability to draw the viewers into the world in a constant quest for immediacy, a situation in which 'the medium itself should disappear and leave us in the presence of the thing represented" (Bolter & Grusin, 1999, 24).

Jurassic Park was certainly not the first film to make major use of CGI, *The Abyss* (1989) and *Terminator 2: Judgement Day* (1991) in particular had both made great strides in the presentation of CGI, but it was the first film to feature fully-realised, photo-realistic animals and "unequivocally demon-

---

★   One wonders what the producers of *Blackfish*, Gabriela Cowperthwaite's 2013 documentary that offered a slamming indictment of *SeaWorld Orlando*'s treatment of its killer whales, would have to say about the treatment of the *Mosasaurus*. According to *Jurassic World*'s fictional website, the 18 metre *Mosasaurus* is kept in an 11 million litre water tank, significantly smaller than the controversial 27 million litre habitat in which *SeaWorld Orlando* houses its far smaller 6–8 metre killer whales. However, perhaps the humane treatment of extinct sea reptiles should be reserved for another publication.

strated for Hollywood the benefits of computer-based imaging in narrative filmmaking" (Prince, 2012, 12). The characters in *Jurassic Park* had never seen real-life dinosaurs just as the cinema audience had never seen such realistic CGI animals and so the stunned reactions of the characters in the film were mirrored by the stunned reactions of the cinema audience. When Alan Grant (Sam Neill) asks, "How'd you do this?" he is articulating the voice of the audience, creating a situation in which the achievements of *Jurassic Park*'s fictional scientists are mirrored by those of the production team and 'the narrative... is reproduced in the visual promise of the cinematic spectacle' (Franklin, 2000, 200). There are numerous examples of this technique at work within *Jurassic Park;* when the characters are taken into a cinema to be shown a film that explains how the dinosaurs were created, they directly mirror the position of the audience in a scene that 'operates within documentary traditions and the conventions of theme-park instructional films to deal with otherwise awkward expositional material' (McClean, 2007, 73). As the lights go down and the film begins, the viewpoint switches to the first-person and the cinema audience learns how the dinosaurs were created, not as CGI creatures but as scientific marvels in a 'twinned moment of spectacularity [that] serves both the narrative and the lived experience of our study of dinosaurs' (ibid, 191).

Sarah Franklin argued that *Jurassic Park* is also notable for 'the commercial infrastructures through which it was marketed, brandnamed, packaged and consumed' (2000, 198) and the effect of immediacy is further developed by a later scene focussing on the merchandise available in the park. Once the dinosaurs have escaped and started to kill the park visitors, a melancholy version of the once triumphant musical score plays as the camera pans over the stocked shelves of the park's gift shop. The audience is shown a selection of *Jurassic Park* branded cuddly toys, T-shirts and lunch boxes whilst the sombre music encourages us to feel despondent that these souvenirs will never be taken home in a 'self-parodying display of merchandizing' (McClean, 2007, 192). However, the scene can be viewed through a more cynical prism with the knowledge that these items would in fact be available to purchase as part of the film's promotional campaign 'which saw the licensing of some fifteen hundred products with the *Jurassic Park* logo' (Friedman, 2006, 133). The fact that the official merchandise from the film was shown on screen gives the impression that it is more authentic and led Lester Friedman to question whether the scene was 'an ironic comment on our commodified culture or a sly advertisement: is it a Marxian critique or a spot on the Home Shopping Network?' (Friedman, 2006, 134).

Perhaps the most multi-faceted item on display is a book upon which the camera lingers to ensure that it registers with the audience. The book is titled *The Making of Jurassic Park* by Don Shay and Jody Duncan and we can safely assume that the book would detail how the park was built and the cutting-edge science that was used to bring the dinosaurs to life. What makes this example unique is that *The Making of Jurassic Park* by Don Shay and Jody Duncan is a real book that was published alongside the theatrical release of the film. Of course, the real version of the book that went on sale detailed the making of the film rather than the fictional park but it further highlights the complicated and interconnected relationship that the *Jurassic Park* franchise has developed with its audience. David Koepp, *Jurassic Park*'s screenwriter, highlighted this complex relationship when he said, 'Here I was writing about these greedy people who are creating a fabulous theme park just so they can exploit all these dinosaurs and make silly little films and sell stupid plastic plates and things. And I'm writing it for a company that's eventually going to put this in their theme parks* and make these silly little films and sell stupid plastic plates' (Shay & Duncan, 1993, 56). And so, as the lines between *Jurassic Park*'s audience and characters become all the more blurred, the film's attempts to achieve immediacy become all the more persuasive.

This quest for immediacy, established in the original *Jurassic Park*, was continued and developed twenty-two years later in *Jurassic World*'s website which, rather than simply being a promotional website for the film, is in fact the website for *Jurassic World* the attraction.

Browsing the website gives the user an incredibly authentic experience analogous with what one might expect from preparing for a holiday to Orlando's *Walt Disney World*. Users can view the latest attendance numbers (the park is at 89% capacity at the time of writing), wait times (currently a 28 minute wait for the Cretaceous Cruise), temperature (26 degrees) and, perhaps most excitingly for this chapter, the time of the next *Mosasaurus Feeding Show* at 2pm! To a fan of the franchise, the website represents an almost irresistible opportunity to explore the park in an unprecedented level of detail. Browsing the interactive map reveals that *Jurassic World*'s Main Street** contains 20 restaurants and 37 shops and that the 16th hole on the golf course is called the *Mosasaurus Mouth* because of its water hazards. Perhaps most convincingly, the *Hilton**** Isla Nublar Resort* section of the website contains reviews of the on-site hotel, several of which are negative:

> "My room felt like an attempt at luxury, not the real thing… it's a stretch to call this a four-star resort. The mattress was too firm… Do NOT get a

---

* Speaking in 1993, Koepp could not have known just how correct he would turn out to be; in 1999, *Universal's Islands of Adventure* theme park was opened with a huge area devoted to an authentic recreation of *Jurassic Park* leading to an interesting situation in which a fictional theme park was directly recreated within a real theme park.

** There can be little doubt that this is a direct reference to the iconic Main Streets found in the various *Disney* theme parks; the use of language that we already associate with existing theme parks furthers the feeling of *Jurassic World*'s verisimilitude.

*** There is a great deal of product placement in *Jurassic World*, as well as the *Hilton* hotel, *Ben and Jerry's*, *American Airlines*, *Starbucks*, *Samsung* and many more are also mentioned. Of course, whilst some critics would dismiss this as a simple attempt to increase profits on the part of the film-makers, these sponsored attractions actually enhance *Jurassic World*'s sense of immediacy as we understand that a modern theme park would genuinely have these kind of corporate sponsors.

west-facing room… you'd think that with all the money they spend on the dinosaurs, they'd figure out how to install towel warmers in the bathrooms." (*Jurassic World International*, 2017)

The website offers such a convincing user experience that it becomes very easy to forget that everything on it is entirely fictional, allowing users to suspend their disbelief and believe that they might actually be planning a trip to the real *Jurassic World*. Of course, it is likely that no-one viewing the website genuinely believed that the resort is real but 'viewers could be sensually persuaded to believe in the fiction and to participate in the pleasures it offered' (Prince, 2012, 33). This sense of immediacy was only increased by the fact that, on the day of the film's release, the website home page was replaced with a pop-up warning that read:

> Excuse our mess, we're experiencing some dino-sized technical issues. Everything is under control. We have experienced a security breach involving several of our attractions. If you are currently at *Jurassic World*, please get indoors immediately and follow all safety instructions. Our trained professionals will have the dinosaurs contained shortly. (*Jurassic World International*, 2017)

Further exploration of the website allows the user to follow a link to the website of the *Masrani Global Corporation*, the fictional owners of *Jurassic World*. This website is far more formal in both its design and content and delivers a wealth of information about *Masrani*'s three key interests *Macom Network*, *Masrani Energy* and *InGen Technologies*. Once again, the experience is entirely authentic and it is very easy to lose yourself in the website which has now been updated with a letter from the CEO that reads:

> Due to the unforeseen circumstances at *Jurassic World* resulting in the worst financial crisis the company has ever seen, the *Masrani Global Corporation* will be holding an emergency board meeting to discuss the future of the company and its various subsidiaries… We encourage our *Jurassic World* employees not to panic, but to have trust in the company's board and financial investors all over the world who will ensure that decisions are made in the best interests of the company and its employees. (*Masrani Global Corporation*, 2017)

It is an astonishingly effective effort from *Jurassic World*'s marketing team that serves to further develop the film's sense of immediacy and, as screenwriter William Goldman claimed, "if the film-maker has done his job and brought you into believability, he can do anything" (Bouzereau, 1995). Trevorrow understands this and, given the extraordinary lengths to which he and the *Jurassic World* production team have gone to achieve immediacy and believability, he is then able to "do anything" by going on to use this technique to manipulate audience expectation on the second occasion that the *Mosasaurus* leaps from the deep.

The Second Leap – Zara's Death and the *Mosasaurus* as Narrative Subversion

After the *Mosasaurus*' spectacular entrance early in the film, it is perhaps surprising that she does not make her next appearance until 50 minutes later. By this point, the serenity of the park has been destroyed and the visitors are being attacked by swarms of flying *Pteranodons* and *Dimorphodons*. As Gray and Zach run for cover from the flying reptiles they are rejoined by Zara Young (Katie McGrath), the park employee who was charged with looking after the boys. At nearly 90 minutes into the film, Zara has only had a handful of short lines and her characterisation essentially amounts to the fact that she is British, fairly mean-spirited and terrible at her job (Gray and Zach easily slip away from her as she snaps down the phone, "No, Alex is not having a bachelor party because all of his friends are animals"); in short, she's a somewhat unlikeable supporting character and it is no surprise to find that she is one of the named characters to be killed by the dinosaurs. As Zara yells at the boys, she is picked up by the shoulders by a *Pteranodon* and dragged screaming into the air where she is tossed to another animal before being dropped into the lagoon. The sight of the lagoon immediately reminds the audience of the *Mosasaurus Feeding Show* and we wait with eager anticipation as Zara plunges into the water. However, Trevorrow then subverts expectations as it is not the *Mosasaurus* that attacks Zara but a *Pteranodon* who swoops down into the lagoon, picking her up in its beak and dragging her screaming back to the surface before dunking her again several times. Eventually, after Zara has been unexpectedly tortured for several seconds, and is being dragged back into the sky, the *Mosasaurus* appears for a second time and leaps from the depths, swallowing the *Pteranodon* and Zara in a single bite.

It is an uncomfortable scene to watch and one which, like the first leap, contains echoes of *Jaws*, in particular the iconic opening scene in which Chrissie Watkins (Susan Backlinie) is dragged through the water to her death. Zara is the first female character to die in any of the *Jurassic Park* films and, whilst the audience may not have expected her to make it to the credits alive, her torture seems unnecessarily graphic. In fact, the violence of Zara's death generated substantial online comment across a range of move websites and blogs: 'It's possible that this is the most horrible death in the entire franchise…It's gruesome and it's painful and it's protracted' (Faraci, 2015), 'I was squirming in my seat because this was no ordinary Jurassic death. This was torture' (Boone, 2015), 'The long, drawn-out death sequence…begins to wander towards the line of torture porn by the end of it' (McConnaughy, 2016). However, rather than being simply a needlessly gruesome death designed to generate internet column inches, Zara's extended demise can be viewed as the next example of Trevorrow using the grammar of film production to further engage the audience. When asked about the reaction to Zara's death scene, Trevorrow said he was:

Trying to find ways to misdirect the audience, but based on the knowledge
that the audience is really savvy and smart. That they're always going to see
something coming...when the girl falls into the water, I know everyone's
going to go, 'I know what's going to happen to her!' but then the *Pteranodons*
come in, and it starts to subvert people's expectations based on assuming their
intelligence. (Lambie, 2015)

Trevorrow is acknowledging that his audience is active and intelligent and
his filmmaking decisions are thus based on an understanding that his
audience understands films. Zara's death is shocking not simply because of
the exaggerated violence but because the narrative turn is unexpected.
Trevorrow uses the second leap of the *Mosasaurus* to make it clear that he
understands how the audience expects the third sequel to *Jurassic Park* to
unfold and that he will not follow a standardised narrative blueprint in the
way the previous sequels have.

It was no surprise to see *Jurassic World* add a new huge beast like the
Mosasaurus to its menagerie given the apparent need for each instalment in
a modern blockbuster franchise to expand, complicate and eclipse previous
franchise entries. This trend is particularly prevalent in superhero films via
the increased number of villains, *Batman* (1989) included the Joker, *Batman
Returns* (1992) included The Penguin and Catwoman and *Batman and Robin*
(1997) featured Mr Freeze, Poison Ivy and Bane. Introducing more villains,
or in this case dinosaurs, is often seen as an easy way to make the sequel
more 'epic' than those that came before in the hope of increasing box office
returns. The *Jurassic Park* series has been guilty of this kind of 'bigger is
better' attitude itself: *Jurassic Park* had the *T-Rex*, *The Lost World: Jurassic
Park* doubled up with two tyrannosaurs and *Jurassic Park III* introduced the
Spinosaurus, a carnivore so large it dwarfed the *T-Rex* and in fact kills a *T-Rex*
on screen as the film-makers attempted 'to achieve greater and greater
breakthroughs in digital computer imagery – both in terms of technological
significance and of spectacle' (McClean, 2007, 43). Therefore, on the surface,
one could simply see *Jurassic World's* fore-grounding of the *Mosasaurus*, a
huge, never before seen dinosaur, as the latest attempt to draw in cinema
goers and achieve the greatest possible box office returns.

However, Trevorrow's understanding of his audience's knowledge and
appreciation of the way films work also allows him to create a second role
for *Jurassic World's Mosasaurus*, that of an opponent to the profit-motivated
sequel strategy described above. When asked about *Jurassic World's* development, Trevorrow said that "there is a magic [in] Steven Spielberg's
original movie" and that "this particular franchise is very difficult to se-
quelize" (Billington, 2015). and it is apparent that he set out to make a
reverential film in the style of the original *Jurassic Park*. Unlike the first two
sequels, *Jurassic World* is set on the same island as the first film and makes
frequent, affectionate references to it – at one point *Jurassic World* employee
Lowery Cruthers (Jake Johnson) specifically states "that first park was

legit", referring to the original *Jurassic Park* resort within the narrative but also reflecting the critical and popular opinion that the first film was the best in the franchise. Johnson's character is also wearing a *Jurassic Park* T-Shirt throughout the film, claiming that he got it on eBay, "For 150 dollars but the mint condition one goes for 300" in another self-referential and world-building nod to the fact that the merchandise from the gift shop in the first film would inevitably now be selling for inflated prices on eBay. These nostalgic callbacks to the original *Jurassic Park* are perhaps most overt in a scene in which Zach and Gray find the abandoned Visitor's Centre and discover a selection of props and vehicles from the first film. Just as it is clear that Trevorrow is affectionately referencing the first film, it is equally clear that he is ignoring the events of the two sequels. *Jurassic World* makes no mention of either *The Lost World: Jurassic Park* or *Jurassic Park III* and the events of these films are entirely omitted from the film's narrative, It would seem that Trevorrow was not impressed by the way the previous sequels expanded the franchise and that he was keen "to build something that can take [kids] to the same place those earlier films took us" (Scirette, 2014). So we can see that Trevorrow is attempting to create the same kind of 'classic' blockbuster as Spielberg did in the late 20th Century as a homage to the original *Jurassic Park;* a blockbuster that avoids the studio-enforced, box office focussed, bloat of the production line sequels of the last twenty years. No-where is this stance against Hollywood's 'bigger is better' attitude more clearly articulated than in the portrayal of the other new dinosaur in *Jurassic World – The Indominus Rex.*

Within the film world, *Jurassic World* has been open for ten years and the park visitors have been growing bored of dinosaurs. Operations Manager Claire Dearing (Bryce Dallas Howard), remarks that, "No-one's impressed by a dinosaur anymore…consumers want them bigger, louder, more teeth", once again reflecting the cinema audience's feelings towards the CGI dinosaurs of the *Jurassic Park* series. Our desire for each instalment of a franchise to be bigger and bolder than the previous ones is reflected by the park's visitors. Both the park's board of directors and the film-makers solve the problem in the same way, by adding another new dinosaur alongside the *Mosasaurus* – The *Indominus Rex,* a genetically engineered hybrid designed to increase the park's profits. Dearing claims that, "The park needs a new attraction every few years in order to reinvigorate the public's interest. Corporate felt genetic modification would up the wow factor…the *Indominus Rex* makes us relevant again" – a quote which mirrors *Universal's* hope that the *Indominus Rex* will make the *Jurassic Park* franchise relevant again.[*]

With the introduction of the *Indominus Rex,* Trevorrow is making a point about the nature of modern Hollywood blockbuster sequels (ironically packaged within the ultimate modern blockbuster sequel). As Trevorrow

[*]   A strategy that worked – *Jurassic World* repeated the success of the original *Jurassic Park* and is currently the 4th highest grossing film of all time.

himself put it in an interview with *Collider*: "The need for profit is dehumanising and can make us forget some of our ethics and our values – we will repeat our mistakes if there's money on the table and we've seen that happen again and again with movies and sequels" (Weintraub, 2015). In one self-aware scene, Cruthers tells Dearing that the original *Jurassic Park*, "Didn't need these genetic hybrids, they just needed dinosaurs" and throughout the film, Trevorrow positions the *Mosasaurus* as the film's new natural dinosaur and the *Indominus Rex* as a monstrous genetic hybrid and the real villain of the film. Given that the *Mosasaurus* and the *Indominus Rex* are shown to respectively represent the original film's simplicity and the sequels' profit-driven mindset, it is perhaps appropriate that they face-off at the film's climax as the *Mosasaurus* makes her final leap from the depths.

The Third Leap – The *Mosasaurus* as Cinematic Saviour

At the climax of *Jurassic World*, the surviving humans have become spectators to a spectacular CGI fight between the villainous *Indominus Rex* and the heroic *T-Rex*. Within the narrative, The *T-Rex* in *Jurassic World* is the same animal seen in the original *Jurassic Park* and so the fight takes on an added symbolic dimension, as the 'real' dinosaur of the first film and the genetically engineered monster of the new film clash – that the audience are supposed to be cheering on the *T-Rex* is clear. As the fight develops, the *Indominus Rex* gets the advantage and is about to kill the *T-Rex* when the park's last surviving *Velociraptor*, another fan favourite from the original film, appears from nowhere, accompanied by a suitably heroic musical cue, and joins the fight against the *Indominus Rex*. Despite the combined efforts of the two dinosaurs, it appears as though the hated *Indominus Rex* will finally get the better of our hero dinosaurs when, at the last minute, the *Mosasaurus* leaps out of the lagoon for the third time in the film, biting the *Indominus Rex* in the neck, dragging her down to the murky depths of her lagoon lair and saving the day. The fact that the *Mosasaurus* attacks the Indominus Rex on the pathway running around the lagoon stretches the limits of believability as presumably she could have used exactly the same technique to devour any of the park guests. However, once again we can perhaps feel the influence of Spielberg who once defended the somewhat outrageous climax of *Jaws* by saying "If I have got them for two hours they will believe whatever I do for the last three minutes" (Bouzereau, 1995). And so, as the *Mosasaurus* saves both the human characters and the other much-loved dinosaurs of the franchise, Trevorrow is positioning his beast of the deep as a 'real' dinosaur that helps to destroy the corporate-sponsored monstrosity that has been created to increase profits.

The *Jurassic Park* franchise, and *Jurassic World* in particular, offers "a movie of a theme park which in turn becomes the main attraction of theme parks... thus redeploying a similar series of dovetailings of rides-within-rides, theme parks-within-theme parks and movies within movies' (Franklin, 2000, 203) which makes it a fascinating target for analysis and discussion. Throughout the film, the *Mosasaurus* is on screen for a total of less than thirty seconds but her presence is felt throughout the film through the omni-present threat of the lagoon and her three great leaps. The first leap uses immediacy to position the cinema audience as park visitors, the second leap demonstrates that Trevorrow respects and understands his audience and will attempt to subvert their expectations and the third shows the *Mosasaurus* killing the dinosaur that represents everything Trevorrow dislikes about the Hollywood production line. Trevorrow is able to successfully convey his meaning and message to the audience because of the extreme lengths to which he has gone to develop *Jurassic World*'s sense of immediacy. The *Mosasaurus* lurks beneath the surface of *Jurassic World*'s lagoon, just as Trevorrow's hidden message about the problems with studio pressure lurks beneath the Hollywood sheen of *Jurassic World*. When the *Mosasaurus* aids the *T-Rex* and *Velociraptor* in defeating the *Indominus Rex*, Trevorrow's underlying message is clear: classic filmmaking will ultimately win out against the profit driven monster of the modern Hollywood blockbuster machine.

References

Billington, A. (2015). *'Jurassic World' Director Colin Trevorrow Talks Dino Love*. Online at http://www.firstshowing.net/2015/interview-jurassic-world-director-colin-trevorrow-talks-dino-love, accessed 23 June 2017.

Bolter, J. D. & Grusin, R. (1999). *Remediation*, Cambridge, MA: MIT Press.

Boone, C. (2015). *Why One Death in Jurassic World is Massively Out of Proportion*. Online at http://nofilm-school.com/2015/06/why-one-death-jurassic-world-massively-out-proportion, accessed 23 June 2017.

Bouzereau, L. (1995). *The Making of Jaws*. USA, Universal Home Video.

Faraci, D. (2015). *The Strangely Cruel And Unusual Death In Jurassic World*. Online at http://birthmovi-esdeath.com/2015/06/15/the-strangely-cruel-and-unusual-death-in-jurassic-world, accessed 23 June 2017.

Franklin, S. (2000). 'Life Itself. Global Nature and the Genetic Imaginary', in Franklin, S. Lury, C. and Stacey J. *Global Nature, Global Culture*, London: Sage.

Friedman, Lester D. (2006). *Citizen Spielberg*, Champaign, IL: University of Illinois Press.

Jurassic World International (2017) [Website] Source: http://uk.jurassicworldintl.com, accessed 23 June 2017].

Lambie, R. (2015). *Jurassic World's Most Horrific Scene and Family Horror*. Online at http://www.denofgeek.com/movies/jurassic-world/35726/jurassic-worlds-most-horrific-scene-and-family-horror, accessed 23 June 2017.

Masrani Global Corporation (2017) [Website] Source: http://www.masraniglobal.com – accessed 23 June 2017.

McBride, Joseph. (2011) *Steven Spielberg: A Biography*, Oxford, MS: University Press of Mississippi.

McConnaughy, J. (2016). *The Death of Zara Young, or: How I Learned to Stop Worrying and Hate Jurassic World*. online at https://www.themarysue.com/jurassic-world-hate, accessed 23 June 2017.

McClean, S. (2007). *Digital Storytelling*, Cambridge, MA: MIT Press.

Prince, S. (2012). *Digital Visual Effects in Cinema*, New Brunswick, NJ: Rutgers University Press.

Scirette, P. (2104). *'Jurassic World' Director Colin Trevorrow Talks Plot Details and Recent Leaks*. Online at http://www.slashfilm.com/jurassic-world-plot-details-colin-treverrow, accessed 23 June 2017.

Shay, D. & Duncan, J. (1993). *The Making of Jurassic Park*, London, England: Boxtree.

Spielberg, S. (1975). *Jaws*. USA, Zanuck/Brown Productions, Universal Pictures.

Spielberg, S. (1993). *Jurassic Park*. USA, Amblin Entertainment, Universal Pictures.

Trevorrow, C. (2015). *Jurassic World*. USA, Amblin Entertainment, Legendary Pictures, Universal Pictures.

Universal Pictures, *Jurassic World* website. Online at http://uk.jurassicworldintl.com, accessed 23 June 2017.

Viner, B. (2015). *How Jaws Nearly Sank Without Trace*. Online at http://www.dailymail.co.uk/tvshow-biz/article-3123999/How-Jaws-nearly-sank-without-trace-stars-hated-fake-shark-went-wonky-wate r-Spielberg-feared-d-monster-flop-40-years-BRIAN-VINER-tells-inside-story.html, accessed 23 June 2017.

Weintraub, S. (2015). *Jurassic World: Colin Trevorrow Talks Building a Foundation for Future Instalments*. Online at http://collider.com/colin-trevorrow-talks-jurassic-world-sequels-blu-ray-and-more, accessed 23 June 2017.

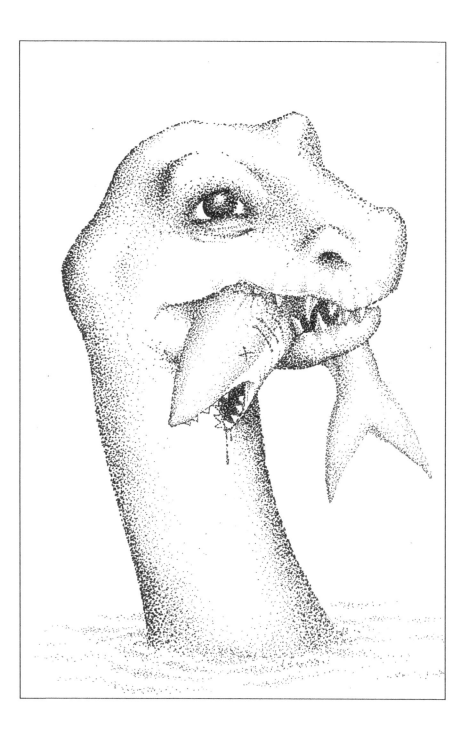

Chapter 14

Nessie Has Risen from the Grave

Kieran Foster and I. Q. Hunter

ammer Films' *Nessie: The Loch Ness Monster* is the great lost British sea beast movie. Developed between 1976 and 1978, *Nessie* was Hammer's most ambitious project, a multimillion dollar co-production with Japan's Toho Studios and Hollywood's Columbia Pictures that would have seen the Loch Ness Monster rampage across the world from Scotland to the Canary Islands and Hong Kong harbour. The global scale of the film's plot was mirrored off screen, with Hammer, desperate for financial backing, entering into a number of ill-fated distribution and finance deals before the production collapsed and Hammer itself went into receivership.

This chapter will track *Nessie*'s failed production and set the unmade film, or rather surviving archival traces of it, in the context of screen representations of the Loch Ness Monster and other sea beasts. Although there is some information on *Nessie* online and in general histories of Hammer (Flint, 1995; Hearn, 2011: 164–65; Meikle, 2008: 219–22), we shall mostly be drawing on the resources of the Hammer Script Archive at De Montfort University. The Archive, which Hammer delivered in 2012, holds over a hundred Hammer screenplays and a wealth of other documentation, such as financial records, correspondence and cast lists. A further donation by Hammer in early 2016 brought us the '*Nessie* File', a ring-binder containing extensive pre-production materials on the project dating from 1976 to 1978. These range from internal office memos and correspondence with potential financiers, to notes on the scripts and letters on the search for a director. Although the Archive already held a 1976 screenplay for *Nessie*, this new delivery also included a shorter, considerably revised draft screenplay dated 1978. Most of the unpublished primary material referenced in this chapter is located in the Hammer Script Archive.

The Loch Ness Monster on Screen

The Loch Ness Monster, or Nessie as she is fondly known, is perhaps the most famous British cryptological aquatic beastie and occupies a prized place in Scottish mythology (Williams, 2015).

Nessie's first screen appearance was in Ealing's *The Secret of the Loch* (Milton Rosmer, 1934), released in May 1934, nine months after 'the single sighting [of the monster crossing the road, by Mr and Mrs Spicer in August 1933] that really got the Loch Ness phenomenon off the ground' (Naish, 2015: Loc 898) and a month after the most famous Loch Ness monster photograph (the so called 'Surgeon's photo', later discovered to be a hoax (Loxton & Prothero, 2013: Loc 3,042; Williams, 2015: 233–7)). A 'quota quickie', inspired by the success of *King Kong* (Merian C. Cooper & Ernest B. Schoedsack, 1933), *The Secret of the Loch* is chiefly notable for being written by Charles Brackett, who worked with Hitchcock, and edited by a young David Lean. The monster, though stated in the film to be a diplodocus, is represented by an rear-projected iguana: 'No one associated with the film seems sure if they are making a comedy or a chiller, least of all the director [Milton Rosmer]', writes Steve Chibnall, who compares it to one of Ed Wood's low-grade Z-movies, such as *Plan Nine from Outer Space* (Edward D. Wood, Jr. 1959) (Chibnall, 2012: 25).

Nessie had few other cameos in films and television till the 1960s and 1970s, when her profile was raised by a flurry of sightings, popular books (Dinsdale, 1961) and the Nessie-hunting that began in earnest with the Loch Ness Phenomena Investigation Bureau, which was set up in 1962. In *What a Whopper* (Gilbert Gunn, 1961), a farce written by Terry Nation, Nessie rears up at the end to announce 'What a whopper' and wink to the camera, while in *The Private Life of Sherlock Holmes* (Billy Wilder, 1969) she is revealed to be a submarine, a model of which was recovered in 2016. 1970 saw the Bureau (renamed the Loch Ness Investigation Bureau) team up with the Academy of Applied Science team to conduct sonar searches for Nessie and the resulting photograph of her supposed flipper (Rines, Wyckoff, Edgerton & Kline, 1976: 27; Williams, 2015: 166–88, 240–43) renewed interest in what had become a 'money-spinner for the Great Glen' (Williams, 2015: 268) and obligatory signifier of Scotland along with Tartan, bagpipes and haggis. In 'Scotland', for example, the first episode of season two of the zany British comedy series, *The Goodies*, which was broadcast in 1971, the Goodies prevent a zookeeper's suicide and travel to Scotland to battle flying bagpipes and capture the Loch Ness Monster for the keeper's new 'monster house' exhibit at the zoo. Rather more notable was Nessie's appearance in the Tom Baker era *Doctor Who* series, 'Terror of the Zygons' (Camfield 1975), written by Robert Banks Stewart and novelised by Terrence Dicks as *Doctor Who and the Loch Ness Monster* (Dicks, 1976). The beast here was a Skarasen, an enhanced cybernetic monster controlled by the alien Zygons, which live off its 'lactic acid' as they wait to emerge from Loch Ness and take over Earth. Sent out to interrupt UNIT's investigation of attacks on North Sea oil rigs, the Skarasen pursues the Doctor to London and ends up in the Thames embankment before returning unharmed to the Loch. More recent Loch Ness films continue to depict Nessie as either a dangerous prehistoric survival or a beloved and benign symbol of Scottish national identity. Aside from *Incident at Loch Ness* (Zak Penn, 2004), a very odd mockumentary with Werner Herzog looking for the creature, they mostly comprise monster-on-the-loose horror movies (*Beyond Loch Ness* (Paul Ziller, 2008)) and British or British co-produced family films like *Loch Ness* (John Henderson, 1996) and *The Water Horse: Legend of the Deep* (Jay Russell, 2007), based on a Dick King-Smith novel (1990), in which Nessie is a friendly 'kelpie' or water spirit, and much like the alien in *E.T.: The Extraterrestrial* (Steven Spielberg, 1982).

The most significant precursor of Hammer's aborted *Nessie*, however, was another unmade venture touted by British independent company Compton in 1964. Michael Klinger and Tony Tenser had risen from local London exhibitors of uncensored or banned films to running their own independent production and distribution company, the Compton Group. In March 1964 the trade magazine *Box Office* reported that Compton had started production on a film called *The Loch Ness Monster*, whose script Tenser heralded as 'one of the most exciting science-fiction screenplays ever written' (Gruner, 1964: 6). Cashing in on the renewed Nessie-fever, Compton's film would have been a late addition to the handful of British outsized monster movies at the turn of the 1960s that included *Gorgo* (Eugène Lourié, 1961) and *Konga* (John Lemont, 1961) and, first and most important, *Behemoth the Sea Monster* (1959), also known tautologically as *The Giant Behemoth* (Conrich, 1999). This British–American coproduction, with stop motion special effects by *King Kong*'s Willis O'Brien, was directed by Douglas Hickox and Eugène Lourié, who made *Beast from 20,000 Fathoms* (1953), which set the template for such defining atomic age sea beast films as *Godzilla* (Ishirō Honda, 1954) and *It Came from Beneath the Sea* (Robert Gordon, 1954). The behemoth itself was a paleosaurus, saturated by the radiation from nuclear tests and electric like an eel, which rises from the sea off Cornwall and attacks London, somehow becoming amphibious in the process. Although Compton's project, which features a radioactive monster like the behemoth (Spicer, 2013: 26), predates Hammer's by over a decade, there are intriguing parallels beyond the general conceit. Like Hammer, Compton recognised that their ambitious project needed international backing. The script, Tenser informed *Box Office* 'demands such a large budget that we thought it was practicable to go to the states to find financial partners' (Gruner, 1964: 6). And like Hammer, Compton struggled to put Nessie on screen. Announced in early 1964, the film 'had started but was postponed' by late 1965 (*Variety*, 13 October 1965) and was still on the production slate in May 1966 (*Variety*, 2 May 1966). Ultimately, the scale of the film and perhaps the quality of the script (Spicer describes it as 'a dull confection…which would have been expensive to make convincingly' (Spicer, 2013: 26)) put paid to the project.

There is no evidence that Hammer's similarly doomed project drew material or inspiration from Compton's. But the continuing interest in Nessie and other cryptids such as the Yeti and Bigfoot made the mid-1970s a perfect time for Hammer to revive the idea (Dinsdale, 1973; Lockton & Prothero, 2013: Loc 1,382–1,840). Crucially, the release of Steven Spielberg's *Jaws* (1975), which became the highest grossing film of all time, had made sea beasts a highly commercial proposition for family-friendly thrillers. Not only a model for future blockbusters, *Jaws* was also the template for numerous '*Jaws*ploitation' movies that reworked its animal attack plot around such predators and sea beasts as bears (*Grizzly* (William Girdler, 1976), *Claws* (Richard Bansbach & Robert E. Pearson, 1977)), piranhas (*Piranha* (Joe Dante, 1976)), killer whales (*Orca* (Michael Anderson, 1977)), and octopi (*Tentacles* (Ovidio G. Assonitis, 1977)) (Hunter, 2016: 77–96). This sub-genre of the 'creature feature' still continues with *Deep Blue Sea* (Renny Harlin, 1999), *Sharknado* (Anthony C. Ferrante, 2013) and many more, most of them mashups, on cable channels like SyFy. Hammer could, in short, be forgiven for thinking that *Nessie* looked set to be both Britain's definitive *Jaws*ploitation film and a serious commercial proposition.*

Pre-production

For Hammer, *Nessie* was an opportunity to revive its fortunes with an unprecedentedly expensive international co-production. Hammer had made its name in the 1950s with period Gothic horror films that updated the genre with lush, colourful but relatively low budget productions such as *The Curse of Frankenstein* (Terence Fisher, 1957) and *Dracula* (Terence Fisher, 1958). In the 1960s the studio successfully diversified its output with black and white thrillers like *Paranoiac* (Freddie Francis, 1963) and prehistoric epics like the international hit *One Million Years B.C.* (Don Chaffey, 1966). By the 1970s, however, Hammer was struggling with the withdrawal of American finance from British film production, as indeed were most British film companies – at the start of 1975 not a single film was in production at any British studio.

In 1972 a loan from Pension Fund Services, a division of the chemicals giant ICI, enabled Michael Carreras to buy the company off his father, James Carreras. The arrangement proved less agreeable than Michael had originally thought, for it transpired that many of Hammer's deals with American studios such as EMI had been developed through personal relationships or friendships with James Carreras. As a result, when James left Hammer, EMI immediately rescinded an agreement to produce another nine films, leaving Hammer with essentially no American backing (Meikle, 2007: 207). Moreover, it was only after Michael Carreras took over the studio that he realised

---

* In the end there were no British *Jaws*ploitation films in the 1970s, though there were British killer beast novels such as *The Surrey Cat* (Andrew Sinclair, 1976) and *Man-Eater* (Ted Willis, 1977). A British *Jaws*ploitation film was, however, nearly made in the 1980s: *The Pike*, produced and written by straight-to-video exploitation king, Cliff Twemlow, and based on his novel of the same name (Twemlow, 1982). Set in Lake Windermere, it was to have starred Joan Collins. Although a robotic giant pike was created, the film collapsed through lack of funding (Lee and Willis, 2009: 212–17). Otherwise the nearest equivalent to a British *Jaws*ploitation film is Ridley Scott's *Alien*, which is Jaws recast as a serial killer in outer space.

that the rights to most of its films were owned not by Hammer but by the companies that had financed them. Carreras quickly grasped that in order to ensure the sustainability of Hammer's financial model, the studio needed to diversify even further away from Gothic, cash in on other generic trends, and begin internationalising.

Whereas Hammer had reaped financial rewards from its Gothic cycle since the late 1950s, it was now reliant on domestic successes like the sitcom spin-off *On the Buses* (Booth 1971), which was the top grossing British film of its year. Aware that Hammer couldn't survive on domestic box office receipts alone, Carreras adopted a strategy that focused on coaxing foreign investment by mounting big budget international productions with A-list actors. This strategy saw Hammer's 'once enviable ratio of produced to unproduced titles' invert by 1975 (Hearn, 2007: 160). In addition to the unmade Dracula-in-India film, *Kali – Devil Bride of Dracula*, 'there were 'four projects [that] dominated Carreras' desk' from 1975 till the studio folded in 1979 (Kinsey, 2007: 412): a Dracula origin story, *Vlad the Impaler*; a comic-book adaptation, *Vampirella*; a remake of Hitchcock's *The Lady Vanishes* (Anthony Page, 1979) (the only one of the four to make it to the screen); and, most ambitious of all, the multi-million dollar *Nessie*.

Of all these enticing projects it is *Nessie* that truly shows Carreras and Hammer out on a limb. To varying degrees *Kali*, *Vlad the Impaler*, and *Vampirella* all fit within Hammer's typical production output. The first two are Dracula films and, though *Vampirella* is as much science fiction as horror, it conforms to Hammer's usual practices of adapting material with a pre-existing fan base and centring a good deal of the marketing on the 'Hammer Glamour' of the prospective female star (in this case, Barbara Leigh). While designed with a bigger budget in mind than Hammer's previous sci-fi/horror films, *Vampirella* clearly complemented the rest of Hammer's filmography. With *Nessie*, however, marketing would have focused on the creature itself and put big-budget special effects front and centre in a way Hammer had never done before. Even the prehistoric films with their stop-motion dinosaurs had given equal billing to the attractions of Raquel Welch and Victoria Vetri.

Nessie started pre-production at the beginning of 1976. At the time Hammer's directors were Michael Carreras and Euan Lloyd, an independent producer who had replaced Roy Skeggs on the board of directors. The storyline for *Nessie* (which is not in the Archive) was by Clarke Reynolds, who had written *The Viking Queen* (Don Chaffey, 1967) for Hammer. At this point the intended film seemed to be called either *Nessie* or *Monster*. When *The Daily Mail* reported on 5 February 1976 that the broadcaster David Frost was planning a rival Loch Ness film, *Carnivore*, Hammer suggested joining forces with Frost's production company, Paradine Films. Hammer and Paradine subsequently struck a deal with Toho Studios in Japan to make a film called *Nessie (The Loch Ness Monster)* with a budget of $3 million. In return for Japanese distribution rights Toho would contribute one-third of the budget in the form of creating the special effects under the supervision of Shokei Nakano, who had taken over as special effects designer on the *Godzilla* films for which Toho had been celebrated since the 1950s. The writer John Starr, who was also working on *Vampirella*, submitted a screen treatment (also not in the Archive) and in April 1976 Chris Wicking produced the first draft screenplay, titled *Nessie*. Wicking was a prominent figure within Hammer as its fortunes became more precarious in the mid-1970s. Originally a script writer for American International Pictures on films such as *The Oblong Box* (Gordon Hessler 1969) and *Scream and Scream Again* (Gordon Hessler, 1970), Wicking was first drafted in by Hammer to write *Blood from the Mummy's Tomb* (Seth Holt, 1971). By 1974, with Hammer in sharp decline, Wicking was promoted as the company's script editor and subsequently contributed to many of Hammer's most notable made and unmade projects. He wrote the second draft of *To the Devil – A Daughter* (Peter Sykes, 1976), Hammer's last horror film till its revival under new ownership in the 2000s, and was involved in writing both *Kali – Devil Bride of Dracula* and *Vampirella*.

With a script for *Nessie* in place, Carreras and Lloyd were tireless in promoting and pursuing finance for Hammer's most expensive film to date. The project gained momentum when Carreras took it to Cannes in May 1976. At the same time he organised an extensive print campaign for *Nessie* in British and American trade papers including *Variety*, which featured a single page black and white advertisement announcing the '$7,000,000 production *Nessie: The Loch Ness Monster*' (*Variety*, 19 May 1976). The print campaign, coupled with Carreras' appearance at Cannes, seemed to have the desired effect. Barry Spikings at the distributors British Lion faxed Carreras to congratulate him on *Nessie*, noting that the 'amount of in-built promotion must be enormous' (Spikings to Carreras, 31 August 1976). Hammer was also approached by the agent of the veteran Canadian director and producer Mark Robson. Robson seemed a wise choice for *Nessie*, having handled a big budget and worked extensively with miniatures on Universal's disaster movie *Earthquake* (1974). However, though Hammer later made enquiries about Robson's interest in the project, June 1976 saw the studio begin to close in on a deal with the British writer/director Bryan Forbes. Linked to Paradine for whom he was making *The Slipper and the Rose* (1976) and fresh from *The Stepford Wives* (1975), Forbes was engaged for four weeks to revise Wicking's script with first option to direct. For $10,000 a week, which was below his market price, and seemingly as a favour, Forbes wrote three drafts, each preceded by extensive discussion in meetings with Carreras and Lloyd. Forbes turned down £200,000 and the chance to direct because he believed that the film was not his style, and indeed the whole project was in many ways beneath such a prominent industry figure, who had been head of production at EMI Films and one of the major creative forces in 1960s British cinema. Forbes' 'final, final version' was delivered on 10 August

1976, but Carreras continued to revise the screenplay behind his back and seems to have reintroduced bits of Wicking's script. In the meantime new drafts and blue pages kept being sent to Toho, whose patience began to wear thin and who also wanted copyright on the *Nessie* character.*

Things turned nasty between Hammer and Forbes. During a social visit to David Frost, Forbes came across a version of his screenplay that was credited solely to Forbes, though he had specifically requested it should not be. This draft was one that Carreras had substantially revised and in Forbes' opinion made considerably worse. In a highly critical letter Forbes presented Carreras with a long list of the failings of the revised screenplay. He was especially scathing about the muddled characterisation and the script's not 'moving away from the conventional formula of these horror-disaster films' (Forbes to Carreras, 28 August 1976). Forbes had been contemptuous of the formula from the start, but as a hired hand he did not have sufficient leeway to alter the plot to make it any more original. It did not help that Hammer wouldn't pay him the extra $10,000 he requested for the additional time he had spent on the screenplay and the issue was resolved only when Carreras finally paid him six months later.

The key problem, however, was not the ever-changing script but the difficulties involved in putting together a large budget from multiple sources, essentially by striking deals with distributors and applying for German tax shelter money. By this point the budget had ballooned, surpassing *Orca*'s $6 million and approaching *Jaws*' $8–9 million. (The average budget for a Hollywood studio film in 1978 was $5 million, rising to $11 million by 1980.) In August 1976, Carreras sent the screenplay for *Nessie* to a Dr Gierse of the Gierse Group in West Germany, in the hope of gaining a loan from his struggling film distribution company Constantin, which had produced genre films in the 1960s and 'was just about kept alive by its sex-film profits' (Bergfelder, 2004: 87). However Carreras' aspirations were seemingly even bigger than the monstrous *Nessie* as he laid out to Gierse an ambitious co-production plan:

> I would like you to consider the possibility of Hammer Films setting up a Production Organization in Germany using the availability of the current Tax Shelter situation and a direct relationship with your Company in terms of investment, to secure the distribution rights of the German, Swiss and Austrian Territories (Carreras to Gierse, 26 August 1976).

*   It is fan lore that Toho 'had done a 'complete story board' for the film, and had reportedly gone so far as to build a one-fourth scale Nessie model' (Berry, 2002: 442) and 'even filmed some sequences before Hammer pulled funding' (Buxton, 2016). Sketches of Nessie do seem to have been produced by Toho's Yasuyuki Inoue, who is reported to have published them in his 2011 book *The World of Special Effects Art Design* (Jarmillo, 2012). As the book is available only in Japanese, the authors have not been able to confirm this, but the purported sketches are available online. There is no evidence at all, and certainly none in the Hammer Script Archive, that any scenes were ever filmed. The Nessie model is rumoured to turn up in the role of a dragon in Toho's *The Princess from the Moon* (Kon Ichikawa, 1987) but, like the claim made on the websites Toho Kingdom and Wikizilla that the *Nessie* screenplay was 250 pages long, this seems to be a myth.

The deal with Gierse was never struck, presumably because Constantin, which the Gierse Group had taken over in 1976, was declared bankrupt a year later (Anon., 1977; Bergfelder, 2004: 87). Undeterred, Carreras and Lloyd sought money from South African investors and from Hemdale and Brent Walker in return for UK distribution rights, but in both cases without success. They also turned to the Hollywood majors, seeking finance from Twentieth Century Fox and Warner Bros in return for distribution rights in the US and a number of foreign territories. Rank did agree to invest £500,000 in return for British distribution rights, but by the end of 1976 the rest of the finance was nowhere near settled, even though principal photography was planned for March 1977. Another Hollywood veteran, Michael Anderson, was pencilled in as director after he finished post-production on *Orca*, but no cast had yet been signed up.

October 1976 saw a more positive development when Hammer approached David Begelman, the head of Columbia, asking for $2.65 million to complete financing. Columbia was interested but did not approve Anderson as director and wanted a special clause inserted into any contract with the producers guaranteeing the quality of Toho's special effects. To ease Columbia's worries, Carreras shipped reels of Toho's *Conflagration* [*High Seas Hijack*] (Katsumune Ishida, 1975), in which Nakano had staged scenes of the destruction of Tokyo harbour, for the sceptical executives to inspect. Columbia was unimpressed by Nakano's efforts, but when Carreras proposed raising the amount allocated to special effects within an increased overall budget of $7.5 million, a negative pick up deal was struck for the $2.65 million and the special quality clause dropped. When Paradine was not able to raise their contribution to the budget, Carreras proposed to ask Columbia for $4.5 million in return for worldwide distribution rights excluding UK and Japan. A new wrinkle appeared around this time: Twentieth Century Fox protested Hammer's use of the title, *The Loch Ness Monster*, on the grounds they also had a Loch Ness film in production.

From this point, the start of 1977, things began to unravel. Hammer approached Iranian bankers with no results and upheavals at Columbia led the studio to pull out entirely (Begelman, who was involved in illegal activity, was suspended in October 1977 and arrested in 1978) (McClintick, 1982)). It remains tantalisingly unclear whether Columbia might have continued their association with Hammer and Toho if what Denis Meikle calls 'musical chairs at Columbia' had not occurred (Meikle, 2008: 221). Toho lost patience entirely and they too vanished from the scene. With a final throw of the dice, Lloyd tried to fund *Nessie* through the same Geneva-based consortium of European banks that had backed his independently produced *The Wild Geese* (Andrew V. McLagen, 1978). In March 1978 a newly revised script was nevertheless produced, presumably by Carreras, which eliminated some of earlier drafts' more expensive special effects and action scenes. By now Richard Harris, Katherine Ross and Richard Widmark were being touted as potential leads. Harris' involvement, in addition to Anderson's, risked making *Nessie* seem even more like a clone of *Orca*. The last we see of the project in the Hammer Script Archive is a letter from Carreras to the independent producer Jack Chartoff in April 1978, in which Carreras presents Chartoff with the new script and a budget breakdown, optimistically suggesting that *Nessie* was still 'viable despite the economic script revisions' (Carreras to Chartoff, 20 June 1978). 'I am personally confident that *Nessie* will hit the silver screen later this year, hopefully Christmas 1978,' Carreras announced in issue 17 of *The House of Hammer* magazine. 'We've got Peter Scott, the naturalist [and Loch Ness Monster enthusiast] involved.... We wanted his approval of the drawings of Nessie and so on' (cited in Berry, 2002: 442). But by then it was all over for Hammer. By the time Hammer's last film, *The Lady Vanishes*, was released in May 1979, the studio's funds had been frozen by PFS. Carreras resigned in April 1979 and Hammer went into receivership. *Nessie* was no more, and Fox's Nessie film didn't materialise either.

Why Did *Nessie* Fail?

How to make sense of this slow motion disaster? Despite the large and obvious problems with analysing unmade films, popular interest (Braun, 2013) and scholarship in the area has grown in recent years, notably around Stanley Kubrick's lost projects such as *Napoleon* and *Aryan Papers* (Phillips, 2005; Castle, 2009). In *Sights Unseen*, the first academic book on unmade films, Dan North remarks of Don Boyd's unfinished *Gossip* that despite never being released 'the film is still textually active as a cultural object, articulating through its own scandalous dissolution something pertinent about its cultural and industrial context' (North, 2008: 170). Exploring the production of unmade films can therefore provide what Peter Krämer refers to as a 'shadow history' of the film industry which integrates its failures into a more comprehensive understanding of the logic and vagaries of film production (Krämer, 2015: 381). Moreover, it enables us to rethink all films in terms of a longitudinal process of repeated acts of adaptation, from screen treatments to draft screenplays and shooting script to revisions made on set, and, as Simone Murray argues, also to foreground the commercial and industrial determinants of textual production. Discussing an unmade adaptation of Murray Bail's 1998 novel *Eucalyptus*, Murray argues that attention to unrealised films frustrates 'adaptation studies' habitual recourse to comparative textual analysis and forces...[it to] engage with potential alternative methodologies for understanding how adaptation functions' (Murray 2008: 6). By focusing on an unmade adaptation, we can shift analysis to the industrial context surrounding the project and 'not just to the what of adaptation but also to the "how" the "why" and the "why not"' (Murray 2008: 16).

Although the chief reason that *Nessie* failed was that Hammer could not raise the budget, the grandiose scheme nonetheless had an undeniable logic. The subject matter, as we've seen, was certainly timely, given that not only Hammer but Paradine and Fox were also preparing Loch Ness films to cash in on the success of *Jaws* and the continuing popularity of the disaster film. The ambitious scale of *Nessie* was designed to rebrand a small British studio as a major international player and the script, with its multiple global locations and elaborate action sequences, could be regarded less as a blueprint than as a calling card to global investors. Indeed, getting both Toho and Columbia interested was something of a coup by the struggling company and on a practical level *Nessie* did keep Hammer afloat in the short term. As Hammer producer Tom Sachs remarked, 'every bit of money that came in – like front monies on *Nessie* at that time – helped not only to launch the picture, but bolster the company's finances as well' (cited in Meikle, 2009: 222). In the end however, *Nessie* was quite simply far too expensive. Compared with *Nessie*'s $7.5 million, *The Lady Vanishes* cost £2.1 million while *To the Devil – A Daughter* had a budget of only £360,000.

The screenplay too was an irresolvable problem. Despite multiple revisions the persistent lack of quality put off possible investors. Martin Wragge of Martin Wragge Productions in South Africa, one of the potential investors that Hammer approached, bluntly itemised the script's problems in a letter to Carreras:

> I think the story is thin, the dialogue functional at best, the characters (with the exception of the girl) unsympathetic, and therefore, it seems to me, the success of the projects turns on the expertise of the spfx people in Japan. IS THAT ENOUGH? (Wragge to Carreras, 31 August 1976)

There are two screenplays in the Hammer Archive. One, 135 pages with 479 scenes and dated August 1976, is clearly the Carreras-amended version of Forbes' third draft screenplay, which so annoyed Forbes. The other, dated 28 March 1978, is only 120 pages long and has fewer and much less ambitious action and special effects sequences. This must be the screenplay that Carreras prepared for a trimmer, post-Columbia version. The authors do not, as we noted previously, have access to the initial screen treatment, Wicking's first draft, or any unamended versions of Forbes' three drafts. This following is therefore a study in 'adaptation' with crucial gaps in evidence of the pre-production process and, of course, with the film itself missing – and the film would undoubtedly have deviated from any of the available screenplays. What we can do, however, is get a sense of the kind of film that was imagined and compare the producers' conception, albeit modified through the various drafts, with other versions of, on the one hand, Nessie films and TV programmes and, on the other, with the late-1970s cycle of *Jaws*ploitation films.

Nessie's basic plot, which is consistent across both screenplays in the Archive, begins with a pre-credit sequence of a truck crashing and spilling gallons of the steroid 'Mutane 4', into Loch Ness. Nessie, a one million year old elasmosaurus, rapidly undergoes steroid-enhanced growth and escapes from the polluted Loch into the North Sea. Nessie then embarks, like Moby Dick, on a world tour to its ancient home in the South China Seas. Meanwhile a somewhat confusing set of characters from around the world attempt to stop her – Mark Stafford, an arrogant television reporter and the film's lead; Susan, a female scientist who wants to study Nessie in a humane environment; Channon, an ill-fated hard-bitten huntsman; and Comfort, a scientist turned company man, who is out to ensure Nessie's demise at the hands of the British and American governments. Both the 1976 and 1978 screenplays are structured around a handful of set piece disaster sequences. As well as an oil rig and hovercraft, Nessie gets entangled with tuna boats and a nuclear submarine before coming to grief some miles from Hong Kong harbour in a sequence which, in the 1976 script, would rival the pyrotechnics of *Earthquake*. In terms of their underlying structure, both screenplays adhere to the sturdy classic linear horror plot employed in animal attack and sea beast films like *It Came from Beneath the Sea* and *Jaws*: the monster is roused from the depths, runs amok, and is finally and spectacularly killed itself. The screenplays' problems lie, first, with the confused characterisation – there are too many protagonists, none of them sympathetic; second, the dreadful dialogue (such as Stafford, the hero of the story, complaining that budget cuts at the network means 'the front office would ask me to fly economy with you peasants' (1976 screenplay)) and, third, the incoherent confluence of influences and generic tropes that both overcomplicate the action and strip it of any real distinctiveness.

Neither screenplay wears its influences lightly. The big game hunter, Channon (presumably the Richard Harris role), is pretty much a substitute for Quint (Robert Shaw), the grizzled shark hunter in *Jaws* (although Channon takes on a more antagonistic role, working against Stafford and Susan to try and kill Nessie instead of capture her). Like Quint, Channon does not make it to the film's conclusion and is beheaded by a tuna fish net at the beginning of the film's third act in a botched attempt to capture Nessie. *Jaws*, which like *Nessie* combined the sea beast and disaster movie, is also referenced directly. The film itself is seen on television on the boat of a couple whom Nessie attacks while they are deep-sea diving and Nessie later encounters a shark described in the script as 'bigger than *Jaws*' (Nessie 1976 screenplay). These connections to *Jaws* were, incidentally, echoed outside of the script itself. After the successful launch of the marketing campaign at Cannes in 1976, Carreras was contacted by Warwick Charlton, a representative of Gateway Projects, the company which 'had been responsible for the merchandising of *Jaws*' (Charlton to Carreras, 24 June 1976). Charlton suggests to Carreras that '*Jaws* will be topped by *Nessie* in the field of character merchandise', and arranges a meeting to discuss merchandising rights. However, the deal was seemingly never formalised and with no sign of the project being produced, discussions came to an end.

One key point of difference between *Jaws* and *Nessie* is that *Nessie*, unlike the shark in *Jaws* but in keeping with many other depictions of the Loch Ness Monster, is essentially a sympathetic creature, a symbol of an ancient natural order abused by modern science. At one point in the South China Seas, for example, Nessie swims past a carving of herself on the wall of an ancient submerged city and 'MUSIC becomes imbued with inevitable tragedy' (*Nessie* 1976 screenplay). As the story goes on, Nessie more closely resembles the tragic anti-hero of *King Kong* than the implacable killer in *Jaws*, and Susan, the scientist, tries, like Fay Wray, to save her from destruction by men.* This sympathy for a sea beast is not a very common twist on *Jaws*ploitation, though it appears in precursors like *Gorgo* and some of the later *Godzilla* movies, and is essayed in *Orca*, in which the killer whale revenges itself on Captain Nolan (Richard Harris), a marine animal hunter, for killing its mate. To complicate matters further, *Nessie* enhances this ecologically sensitive revenge-of-nature scenario with a *Jaws*-derived conspiracy and cover up plot. Nessie becomes not only an over-determined symbol of evil science and the dangers of messing with nature but a victim of governmental and corporate power. Long speeches towards the end belatedly foist on Nessie some of the symbolic meaning that accrued to Godzilla as a product of the modern world (though the likely reference point was the environmental damage of the Torrey Canyon oil spill in 1967 rather than fear of the atomic bomb). When the US air force sets Nessie aflame with oil from a damaged tanker, Stafford begins a live broadcast in which he chastises the American and British governments for their mistreatment of Nessie after the chemical disaster that led to her escape from the Loch. As well as portentous, this seems highly uncharacteristic of the brash and unsympathetic Stafford and we suspect that, as the film builds to its climax, the audience would in any case be more interested in the action and special effects. Martin Wragge in particular did not think much of the ending, wondering 'who would want to watch that asshole being a wiseass for 10 whole bloody minutes' (Wragge to Carreras, 31 August 1976).

The screenplays specify a remarkable number of locations as earnest of the film's international ambitions in worldwide territories. Hence the action skitters from Scotland, Washington, South Africa, and the Canary Islands to Gibraltar, London, and Hong Kong, which seems largely to be a wish list of sites for location shooting. While Carreras clearly wanted to internationalise Nessie herself as a star, the screenplays' global reach is arguably counterproductive as well as ensuring that the budget would be ruinously over-stretched. For one thing, considered as a Nessie film the material is stripped of distinctive local elements of Scottishness (this is no *Wicker Man*

★   It is appropriate that *Nessie* should echo the 1933 *King Kong* as the 'monster fever' that gripped the world after the box office success of '*King Kong* directly inspired the Loch Ness monster. There is no question that the birth of Nessie correlates closely in time with the release of the film' (Loxton and Prothero 2013: Loc 2631 – 2645). It was not so much the film's giant gorilla, though, as the long-necked sauropod depicted in the film that influenced sightings like the Spicers' (Loxton & Prothero, 2013: Loc 2,672–2,725).

(Robin Hardy, 1973) style folk horror fable of the revenge of the Celtic repressed) and indeed of the Britishness long associated with Hammer. Despite the scripts' beginning in Scotland at Loch Ness, Stafford and Susan, the male and female leads, are Americans and only in the area for their respective jobs. It is true that importing American stars into British science fiction films had been standard practice since before *The Quatermass Xperiment* (Val Guest, 1955), but Hammer were perhaps missing a trick by neglecting the local flavour of the material. Compared with the other Nessie movies, from *The Secret of the Loch* to *The Water Horse*, though sharing the latter's ultimately positive view of the monster, the screenplays of Nessie do their best to eliminate the Scottishness of the beast. When disaster first strikes in Scotland and Nessie begins her journey from the Loch to the sea, a Scottish chief constable begins to head up the operation, before being dismissed by a British minister and a member of the US State department. With all local and regional authority of Nessie and the Loch seemingly stripped away, the constable leaves grumpily suggesting that he will 'concentrate on petty vice in Inverness then' (*Nessie* 1976 screenplay). Unlike the other Loch Ness films, *Nessie* promises little of the 'Kailyard' imagery of a touristic version of Scotland, all bagpipes and Tartan, of the sort parodied in *The Goodies* (Martin-Jones, 2009: 89–112). Although the absence of kitschy national stereotypes is welcome, and it is true that Hammer probably wasn't concerned about subtextual niceties, one wonders why the monster is the iconically Scottish Nessie at all, beyond the semi-bankable name recognition. That a British beast in a British location seemed an inadequate scenario speaks too of the waning power and influence of the nation and the diminished kudos of its – and Hammer's – once globally valued contribution to genre filmmaking. As Matthew Jones notes, discussing Hammer's aborted remake of *The Day the Earth Caught Fire* (Val Guest, 1961) in the 1990s, which transferred the setting from London to the United States:

> Once famed for adaptations of British gothic novels and films set against the backdrops of London or the nation's countryside, Hammer seemingly no longer felt this was marketable and had instead turned its attention to settings that would be familiar to US audiences. (Jones, 2015)

As a point of comparison, in terms of using Nessie productively the *Doctor Who* series, 'Terror of the Zygons', is somewhat more successful in mobilising both Scottishness and indeed Britishness. Although the monster is an alien cyborg, hardly a conventional representation of Nessie, the series makes amusingly Gothic play of Highland moors (actually filmed in Sussex) and revels in outrageous Tartan stereotypes, such as the Doctor wearing a tam o'shanter. The series moreover fits neatly into the archetypal scenarios of British science fiction movies. On the one hand, it is about a small scale alien invasion in an unlikely out of the way location, much of the action centres on a pub, and there is a disused quarry (though for once in *Doctor*

Who it is actually a quarry and not a convenient stand in for an alien planet). On the other hand and crucially for our purposes, the Skarasen Nessie, like any properly self-respecting British beast, makes her way to London for the final showdown, as did the monsters in *The Lost World* (Harry O. Hoyt, 1925), *Gorgo*, *Konga*, *Behemoth the Sea Monster* and *Queen Kong* (Frank Agrama, 1976) (Hunter, 1999: 7–11). *Behemoth*, for example, combined the same elements as *Nessie* – a roused and irradiated monster, scenes of destruction – but ended with the plesiosaur rampaging up the Thames and overturning the Woolwich ferry.As in many British science fiction and monster films, the flattening of London carries echoes of the Blitz. In Hammer's somewhat self-defeating attempt at an international epic, *Nessie*'s cruise of holiday locations forgoes such possibilities by having a Scottish monster pitch up in the South Seas.

Of course, from the point of view of textual analysis, it is hard to judge the meanings and resonances that might have emerged from the *Nessie* that got away. We may be short-sighted and parochial in criticising the screenplays for neither exploiting the Scottishness of the legend nor repeating familiar tropes of British science fiction. After all it was in some ways the taint of insular small scale Britishness that Hammer was trying to overcome by promoting Nessie as an international co-production to rival generously budgeted Hollywood hits. Since the 1950s it was not unusual for British films, including many science films, to masquerade as American because the market was dominated by Hollywood (Pirie, 1973: 133; Hunter, 1999: 8). In fact, the *Nessie* screenplays are replete with tantalising possible interpretations. The nostalgic tour of post-imperialism (Gibraltar, South Africa, Hong Kong), the clash of ancient Britain with modernity (Nessie attacking the English Channel hovercraft), the sense of Britain sidelined in an age of American corporate power – these perhaps insinuate an embryonic self-reflexive commentary on British decline along the lines of *Juggernaut* (Richard Lester, 1974) (Sinyard, 2010: 97–110). It is impossible to know whether these emergent themes would have survived translation to the screen.

The final reason for the production's stalling had to do with the uncertain adequacy of the special effects and here *Nessie* was, you might say, a very premature Western Kaijin (sea monster) movie. Columbia was right to be suspicious that Nessie herself was beyond Hammer's and Toho's resources (especially as Columbia was currently engaged in breaking new ground in special effects with Spielberg's $18–$19 million extravaganza *Close Encounters of the Third Kind* (1977)). Since the film's appeal rested on seeing the Monster, Nessie would have been wholly reliant upon the credibility of its special effects. These required not only monster effects but also model sharks and major scenes of oil rigs, hovercraft, oil tankers, and harbours being destroyed. It is unclear how this could this be carried off in those pre-CGI days. Success with studio miniatures was obviously not impossible – *Earthquake*, which abounded in them, had had a similar budget of $7 million – but, so far as creature features went, visions loomed of poor back-projection, men in rubber costumes as in *At the Earth's Core* (Kevin Connor, 1976), and the fiasco of Rick Baker in a gorilla suit in the remake of *King Kong* (John Guillerman, 1976). Even a major Hollywood production like *Jaws* had struggled to get its shark to work, except for the rubbery version at the end, and resorted to keeping the creature mostly offscreen except for point-of-view shots and makeshift synecdoches like barrels and fins. The back-projected glove puppet of *Doctor Who*'s Skarasen was a notorious failure and while staging an oil rig disaster with model work passed muster on children's television, it would hardly do for a major release bidding to compete with *King Kong*. Carreras' promise to Columbia and other investors that the special effects in Nessie would be no worse than those in *Toho's King Kong vs. Godzilla* (Ishirō Honda 1962), in which the creatures were men in costumes, probably did not reassure them. One solution was stop motion animation, as in Behemoth and Hammer's prehistoric films, *One Million Years B.C.* and *When Dinosaurs Ruled the Earth* (Val Guest, 1970), but it was a very slow and expensive process. Before Toho's involvement, Hammer had nevertheless clearly regarded stop motion animation as the only viable way of creating Nessie. There is no evidence that Hammer approached Ray Harryhausen, the leading exponent of the technique, who had contributed stop motion 'Dynamation' creatures to *One Million Years B.C.*, *The Golden Voyage of Sinbad* (Gordon Hessler, 1973) and *Sinbad and the Eye of the Tiger* (Sam Wanamaker, 1977), but, in one of the earliest pieces of correspondence on Nessie held in the Archive, Carreras writes to Euan Lloyd about the possibility of bringing stop motion animator Jim Danforth onto the project (Carreras to Lloyd, 6 January 1976). Danforth had created the impressive prehistoric monsters for *When Dinosaurs Ruled the Earth*, which had earned him an Academy Award nomination. He was unavailable, however, because he was starting work on another unmade monster film, Universal's *The Legend of King Kong*, which was beaten into production by Dino Laurentiis' rival *King Kong*. By March 1976, Hammer had in any case secured a contract with Toho.

As it happens, Hammer were right about Hollywood's shift towards special effects blockbusters, though their decision to make a relatively big-budget film rather than a straightforward *Jaws*ploitation film may seem quixotic in retrospect. They were right too that Hollywood was turning to upscaled exploitation films, like *Jaws*, but *Nessie* was neither a cheap and cheerful horror movie like *Piranha* nor (the option taken by recent Loch Ness films) a kids' movie in the tradition of *King Kong vs. Godzilla* and *Digby – the Biggest Dog in the World* (Joseph McGrath, 1973). Britain would have a role as a player in an industry newly orientated around blockbusters like *Star Wars* (George Lucas, 1977), *Superman* (Richard Donner, 1978), *Close Encounters* (in which EMI had invested money), and *Alien* (Ridley Scott, 1979), but mostly as an investor in an essentially Hollywood product or as a provider of studio space, technicians and other creative talent.

For brave, understandable but misguided reasons, Hammer conceived and promoted *Nessie* as a major special effects driven blockbuster, but, judging by the scripts in the Archive, it lacked any sense of place or grounding in the legend of Nessie, had few prospects of decent special effects, and was lumbered by an incoherent ever-changing screenplay, which Carreras, whose strength lay in idiosyncratic camp like *Prehistoric Women* (Michael Carreras, 1968) and *Moon Zero Two* (Roy Ward Baker, 1969), couldn't stop fiddling with. We suspect that if it had ever made it to the screen, it would have been a British nautical disaster to rival *Raise the Titanic* (Jerry Jameson, 1980).

References

Anon. (1964), 'Young British Producers Expanding In Both Filmaking, Exhibtion', *Boxoffice*, 84 (22), p.7.

_____(1965), 'International: Compton Films Sets 8 New Feature Pix', *Variety* 240 (8), p.30.

_____ (1966), 'Compton', *Variety*, 242 (11), pp.40–41.

_____ (1976), 'Ready For World Release Easter 1977', *Variety*, 283 (2), pp.40.

_____ (1977), 'Certain things settled', *Der Speigel* [online], 21 November,: http://www.spiegel.de/spiegel/print/d-40680598.html (acessed 10 February 2017). [TRANSLATED]

Bergfelder, T (2004), *International Adventures: German Popular Film and European Co-Productions in the 1960s*, New York & Oxford: Berghahn.

Berry, M.F. (2002), *The Dinosaur Filmography*. Jefferson, North Carolina & London:McFarland.

Braun, S. (ed.) (2013), *The Greatest Movies You'll Never See: Unseen Masterpieces by the World's Greatest Directors*, London: Cassell Illustrated.

Buxton, M. (2016), 'The Vaults of Hammer: 14 Unmade Hammer Horror Films', *Den of Geek* [online], ttp://www.denofgeek.com/us/movies/hammer-films/240220/the-vaults-of-hammer-14-unmade-ha mmer-horror-films (accessed 23 October).

Castle, A. (ed.) (2009), *Stanley Kubrick's Napoleon: The Greatest Movie Never Made*, London: Taschen.

Chibnall, S. (2012), 'A Lad, a Lass and the Loch Ness Monster'. In M. Diguid, L. Freeman, K.M. Johnston & M. Williams (eds) (2012), *Ealing Revisited*, London: British Film Institute / Palgrave Macmillan, pp.15–25.

Conrich, I. (1999), 'Trashing London'. In I.Q. Hunter (ed.), *British Science Fiction Cinema*, London & New York: Routledge, pp.88–98.

Dicks, T. (1976), *Doctor Who and the Loch Ness Monster*, London: Target.

Dinsdale, T. (1961), *Loch Ness Monster*, London: Routledge & Kegan Paul.

_____ (1973), *The Story of the Loch Ness Monster*, London: Target.

Flint, D. (1995), 'Hammer: The Ones That Got Away', *The Dark Side* 51 (November), pp.24–8.

Gruner, A. (1964), 'London Report', *BoxOffice* 84 (19), pp.E–6.

Hearn, M. (2011), *The Hammer Vault: Treasures from the Archive of Hammer Films*, London: Titan Books.

Hunter, I.Q. (1999), 'Introduction: The Strange World of the British Science Fiction Film'. In I.Q. Hunter (ed), *British Science Fiction Cinema*, London & New York: Routledge, pp.1–15.

_____ (2016), *Cult Film as a Guide to Life: Fandom, Adaptation and Identity*, London & New York: Bloomsbury Academic.

Jarmillo, M. (2012), 'Toho-Hammer Nessie Movie', *Cryptomundo*, 4 December.[online], ttp://cryptomundo.com/movie-monsters/toho-hammer-nessie-movie/ (accessed 23 July 2017).

Jones, M. (2015), 'Re-igniting the Blaze: Hammer's Unmade Remake of The Day the Earth Caught Fire'. Paper presented to Le studio Hammer: laboratoire de l'horreurmoderne, colloque international, Université Paris 3 Sorbonne Nouvelle, Université Paris Ouest Nanterre La Défense, and Cité international universitaire de Paris, 12 June [Unpublished conference paper.].

King-Smith, D. (1990), *The Water Horse*, London: Random House.

Kinsey, W. (2007), *Hammer Films: The Elstree Studios Years*, Sheffield: Tomahawk Press.

Krämer, P. (2015), 'Adaptation as Exploration: Stanley Kubrick, Literature, and A.I. Artificial Intelligence', *Adaptation* 8 (3), pp.372–82.

Lee, C.P. & Willis, A. (2009), *The Lost World of Cliff Twemlow: The King of Manchester Exploitation Movies*, Manchester: Hotun Press.

Loxton, D. & Prothero, D.R. (2013), *Abominable Science: Origins of the Yeti, Nessie, and Other Famous Cryptids*, New York & Chichester: Columbia University Press.

Martin-Jones, D. (2009), *Scotland: Global Cinema: Genres, Modes and Identities*, Edinburgh: Edinburgh University Press.

McClintick, D. (1984), *Indecent Exposure: A True Story of Hollywood and Wall Street*, London: Corgi.

Meikle, D. (2008), *A History of Horrors: The Rise and Fall of the House of Hammer*, revised edition, Lanham: Scarecrow Press.

Murray, S. (2008), 'Phantom Adaptations: Eucalyptus, the Adaptation Industry and the Film That Never Was', *Adaptation* 1 (1), pp. 5–23.

Naish, D. (2015), *Hunting Monsters: Cryptozoology and the Reality Behind the Myth*, London: Arcturus.

North, D. (2008), *Sights Unseen: Unfinished British Films*, Newcastle: Cambridge Scholars Publishing.

Phillips, G.D. (2005), 'The Epic That Never Was: Stanley Kubrick's 'Napoleon'.', In A. Castle (ed.), *The Stanley Kubrick Archives*, London: Taschen, pp.496–503.

Pirie, D. (1973), *A Heritage of Horror: The English Gothic Cinema, 1946–1973*, London: Gordon Fraser.

Rines, R.H., Wyckoff, C.W., Edgerton, H.E. & Klein,M. (1976), 'Search for The Loch Ness Monster', *Technology Review*, March–April, pp.25–40.

Sinclair, A. (1976), *The Surrey Cat*, London: Michael Joseph.

Sinyard, N. (2010), *Richard Lester*, Manchester: Manchester University Press.

Spicer, A. & McKenna, A.T. (2013), *The Man Who Got Carter*, London. I.B. Tauris.

Twemlow, C. (1982), *The Pike*, Fletham: Hamlyn.

Walker, W. (1998a), 'Nessie: The Loch Ness Monster', *Dark Terrors* 15, pp.26–7.

____ (1998b), 'Nessie: The Loch Ness Monster Part Two', *Dark Terrors* 16, pp.47–8.

Williams, G. (2015), *A Monstrous Commotion: The Mysteries of Loch Ness*, London: Orion.

Willis, Ted (1977) *Man-Eater*. London: Macmillan. Print.

Unpublished Archival Material

Carreras, Michael to Euan Lloyd [correspondence]. 6 January 1976. Hammer Script Archive. Nessie File. Hammer Script Archive. De Montfort University.

Carreras, Michael to Dr. [Helmut] Gierse [correspondence]. 26 August 1976. Hammer Script Archive. Nessie File. Hammer Script Archive. De Montfort University.

Carreras, Michael to Warwick Charlton [correspondence]. Dated 24 June 1976. Nessie File. Hammer Script Archive. De Montfort University.

Carreras, Michael to Jack Chartoff [correspondence]. Dated 20 June 1978. Nessie File. Hammer Script Archive. De Montfort University.

Charlton, Warwick to Michael Carreras [correspondence]. Dated 24 June 1976. Hammer Script Archive. Nessie File. Hammer Script Archive. De Montfort University.

Forbes, Bryan to Michael Carreras [correspondence]. Dated 28 August 1976. Nessie File. Hammer Script Archive. De Montfort University.

Nessie. Unpublished screenplay by Bryan Forbes. Dated August 1976. The Hammer Script Archive. De Montfort University.

Nessie. Unpublished screenplay by Christopher Wicking and John Starr. Shooting script by Bryan Forbes. Dated 28 March 1978. The Hammer Script Archive. De Montfort University.

Spikings, Barry to Michael Carreras [correspondence]. Dated 17 May 1976. Nessie File. The Hammer Script Archive. De Montfort University.

Wragge, Martin to Michael Carreras [correspondence]. Dated 31 August 1976. Nessie File. The Hammer Script Archive. De Montfort University.

The Editors and Contributors

Editors

Dr Jon Hackett is a senior lecturer in film and screen media at St Mary's University. His research interests include film and cultural theory, film history and popular music. He is currently working on a monograph with Dr Mark Duffett of Chester University on popular music and monstrosity, to be entitled, inevitably, *Scary Monsters*.

Dr Seán J. Harrington is an associate lecturer in film and screen media at St Mary's University. His research interests include Lacanian psychoanalysis, animation and popular culture. He has previously published work on animation and psychoanalytic theory and is the author of *The Disney Fetish* (2015).

Contributing Authors

Dr Alexander Hay is an independent researcher and his work combines a wide range of research interests, including strange phenomena and how they are interpreted both by the media and the public at large. He has written on sea life and sea creatures, the history of martial arts, punk rock and the politics of the early 1980s, and digital journalism.

Dr Brigid Cherry has written a film guidebook on horror cinema for Routledge. She has carried out research on a range of fan cultures, including the female horror film audience and science fiction audiences. She has published work in the area of gender, nationality and identity in science fiction fandom, in both online and face-to-face fan communities. She has also written on Jan Švankmajer and *The Wicker Man*, as well as vampire cinema and the Gothic.

Dr Carole Murphy is a Senior Lecturer in the Criminology and Sociology Programmes, and Deputy Director of the Centre for the Study of Modern Slavery at St Mary's University, London. Her main research interests are in the areas of human trafficking and modern slavery; social problems, inequalities and justice; addiction and recovery, social and health/mental health issues. She has recently completed a study exploring long term support for victims of trafficking and modern slavery. Other research interests include examining the response to social problems within the criminal justice system.

Damien O'Byrne is a lecturer in Media Arts at St Mary's University, Twickenham. He teaches across a range of practical modules that focus on magazine design, digital art and photographic manipulation. His research interests concern digital media and specifically the role and impact of live television news from a Baudrillarian perspective. He also edits, designs and publishes an independent magazine about war-gaming in J.R.R. Tolkien's Middle-earth. Damian has recently begun to combine his personal passion for Tolkien with a PhD focusing on the practices of Middle-earth fan communities.

Professor I.Q. Hunter is Professor of Film Studies at De Montfort University. He is the author of *Cult Film as a Guide to Life* (Bloomsbury, 2016) and *British Trash Cinema* (BFI Palgrave, 2013), and editor or co-editor of twelve books, including *The Routledge Companion to British Cinema* (Routledge, 2017), *British Comedy Cinema* (Routledge, 2012) and *British Science Fiction Cinema* (Routledge, 1999).

Kieran Foster is a Midlands3Cities/AHRC funded PhD student at De Montfort University, whose research uses the materials available in the Hammer Script Archive in order to examine the unmade projects of Hammer Films.

Laura Ettenfield is a funded PhD research student and part time lecturer at Leeds Beckett University, having completed both her undergraduate and MA degree at Lancaster University. Her thesis examines submarine space in nineteenth century literature, tracing cultural understandings of the sea through the motifs of the mermaid, the maelstrom, sea beasts, and maternity and sexualisation. Teaching interests include Victorian literature, Gothic short stories, theoretical approaches, and 20th and 21st century dystopian fictions.

Lee Brooks is programme director for film and screen media at St Mary's University. He teaches on and convenes a wide range of practical and theoretical modules that combine his previous professional experience and an academic path that has taken in an HND in Graphic Design and Typography at the London College of Printing, a degree in History at St Mary's University and an Open University Master's in Popular Culture. He has published 'Talent Borrows, Genius Steals: Morrissey and the art of Appropriation' in *Morrissey: Fandom, Representations and Identities* (Intellect Books) and has a second piece on the bequiffed bard of Manchester: 'Ambitious Outsiders: Morrissey, Fandom and Iconography' upcoming in *Subcultures, Popular Music and Social Change* (Cambridge Scholars) and also has research interests in Disney, theme parks and animation.

Marco Benoit Carbone is a PhD Student at UCL, where he is researching media communications, digital cultures and cultural studies.

Dr Maria Mellins teaches on the Film and Screen Media BA (Hons), Media Arts BA (Hons) and MA in Gothic. The modules she delivers include Contemporary Gothic, The Paradox of Horror, Cult Film and TV, and Screenwriting. Maria's research is concerned with exploring how mythical figures, such as the vampire and the mermaid, are reimagined in contemporary popular culture. Having written *Vampire Culture* (Bloomsbury, 2013), a monography that explores vampire fandom in the twenty-first century, Maria's current research interests are now fixed on mermaids and related sea myths. Her novel, *Returning Eden* (Crooked Cat, 2016) is a gothic ocean mystery for young adults.

Dr Mark Fryers has recently completed his Arts and Humanities Research Council funded PhD, *British National Identity and Maritime Film and Television, 1960-2012* at the University of East Anglia where he currently works as an Associate Lecturer and Research Associate. His recent publications include a book chapter on the nautical costume drama *The Onedin Line* and another forthcoming on the naval drama *To the Ends of the Earth* as well as a journal article on the yachting saga *Howards' Way*.

Dr Michael Fuchs is an assistant professor in American Studies at the University of Graz in Austria. He has co-edited three books and authored more than two dozen published and forthcoming journal articles and book chapters on American television, horror and adult cinema, video games, remediation and media convergence, and contemporary American literature. Currently, Michael is working on three monographs and co-editing three books as well as a journal special issue. For further details on these (as well as other past, present, and future) projects, please check out his website at www.fuchsmichael.net.

Dr Richard Mills is a Senior Lecturer in Irish Literature and Popular Culture at St Mary's University, London. Publications include articles on Irish themes for *Irish Studies Review*, *Writing Ulster* and *New Voices in Irish Criticism*. Recent publications are chapters in *Popular Music and Television in Britain* (Ashgate: 2010), *Fifty Years with the Beatles: The Impact of the Beatles on Contemporary Culture (Lodz: 2010)* and *The Playful Air of Lightness in Irish Literature and Culture* (Cambridge: 2011), *Bernard MacLaverty: New Critical Readings*, Richard Russell Rankin (ed.), (Bloomsbury: 2014), *Monty Python in its International Context* (Rowan and Littlefield: 2014) and 'Transformer: David Bowie's rejection of 1960s counter-culture fashion through his 'Glam' re-invention and stylings in the years 1969–1972', *Clothing Cultures*, (Intellect: 2015).

Dr Vivan Joseph is an Associate Fellow of the University of Warwick's Institute of Advanced Teaching and Learning (IATL), and completed his PhD in Philosophy at Warwick in 2015. Long before he started studying philosophy he was gripped by the stories of H. P. Lovecraft, and he remains afflicted by a fascination with deep water that borders on fear.

Printed and bound by CPI Group (UK) Ltd, Croydon, CR0 4YY

13/04/2025